The Power of the Outsider

The Power of the Outsider

A Journey of Discovery

Samuel Kasumu

HODDER &
STOUGHTON

First published in Great Britain in 2023 by Hodder & Stoughton
An Hachette UK company

1

Copyright © Samuel Kasumu 2023

A CIP catalogue record for this title is available from the British Library

Hardback ISBN 978 1 529 39691 1
Trade Paperback ISBN 978 1 529 39692 8
eBook ISBN 978 1 529 39695 9

Typeset in Bembo MT by Hewer Text UK Ltd, Edinburgh
Printed and bound in Great Britain by Clays Ltd, Elcograf S.p.A.

Hodder & Stoughton policy is to use papers that are natural, renewable
and recyclable products and made from wood grown in sustainable forests.
The logging and manufacturing processes are expected to conform
to the environmental regulations of the country of origin.

Hodder & Stoughton Ltd
Carmelite House
50 Victoria Embankment
London EC4Y 0DZ

www.hodder.co.uk

To Barbara, Azariah, and Zoe. I hope this makes you proud.

A special mention for Conor McCrory. One of the most gifted researchers I have come across. Think we make a good team. Thank you.

Dedicated to my Lord and Saviour.

Contents

Prologue

I've always thought I was an outsider, but by early 2021 I was not functioning as well as an outsider could. Choosing to leave any job in any context is a big decision. Choosing to leave Number 10 Downing Street when you are playing a leading role in one of the most important operations since the Second World War (Covid-19 vaccine deployment) was and is difficult to explain. But that is what I did. When the then BBC political editor Laura Kuenssberg broke the news on Radio 4's *Today* programme that I was considering leaving Number 10, a government minister reached out and asked for us to have a Covid-compliant walk through St James's Park. I had known her for many years, and she had played a pivotal role in my political journey. We walked and talked for over an hour. I explained to her that one of my closest colleagues was very upset about the whole situation. He could not quite understand why I had made the decision to leave and why I had been so affected by the events that led to my resignation. The minister turned to me and said, 'He may never understand where you are coming from, Samuel. Because of his class.' That statement made me confused, angry, upset and inquisitive all at the same time. I knew that she was trying to explain that my colleague's inability to empathise with my point of view was because we were from different worlds. The minister, like me, was from a working-class background and no doubt would have had many similar experiences. But what did this say about me and my decision? Was my resignation principled or a sign of me falling short? A display of good character or a lack of it? And what role did my background, good or bad, play in arriving at that moment? Was there knowledge or skills that I was missing that would have allowed me to better manage the situation I was in at the time, or something that I had that my colleague was missing? I suppose my contemplation about this experience is the reason I wanted to write this book. It has made me want to better understand myself as an outsider, and to hopefully help others to understand outsiders too.

I definitely arrived in my role in Downing Street as an outsider. Most of the others had either worked with 'Boris' during his time as Mayor of London or had played a significant role in the Vote Leave campaign that led to Brexit. There were also a few legacy hires from previous administrations, like Sheridan Westlake. Though I had a loose affiliation with some of these tribes, which were themselves intertwined, I was not a member of any of them. I was the only black person in my role for most of my time at Number 10. Not having studied at an Oxbridge college also set me apart. Some people might have thought I would have been delighted to be in such a prestigious position, but being the first or only, or one of few, is not always the source of pride and comfort that people think. Loneliness arising from being different can often accompany the accolades. Being an outsider was an experience I had become quite accustomed to on my journey, initially because of my race but increasingly because of my working-class background, and my politics.

So, who or what is an outsider? The difficulty in defining an outsider is that it has become very much an umbrella term in recent years. The concept crops up in many fields: in literature, to describe the experience of those who do not belong; in sport it is used interchangeably with underdog to describe someone who is not expected to win; in psychology to describe existence on the fringes of a society, environment or group. In ethnography it describes access to community, in broader sociology it is used to examine nonconformity, and in politics it describes a newcomer or surprise entry to the arena. In the world of work, an outsider could be a new chief executive bringing new ways of doing things, or new cultures following a merger or acquisition. Elon Musk entering Twitter HQ following his $44 billion acquisition of the social media firm is one extreme example. So, I am aware that being an outsider takes many forms. In 2019 the boxer Andy Ruiz Jr defeated British heavyweight champion Anthony Joshua in one of the great sporting upsets in modern times. Ruiz Jr was a late challenger to Joshua, and a clear outsider. His victory seemed to have surprised even himself, as he spent the following months embracing his new-found fame and fortune instead of training diligently for the rematch that he was contractually obligated to fight. Ruiz Jr went on to lose to Joshua, and disappeared into the sporting night. As an outsider not expected to win, had he let that belief destroy his chances instead of driving him forward? Was he solely responsible for his swift fall from grace, or did his environment also play a role? This sporting experience can also be applied to other settings. Not expecting to achieve, or not knowing how to handle success, can lead to us being unprepared for what we may face next. It is no accident that many lottery winners go broke within a short space of time. In a host of sectors we see an increase in opportunities for under-represented groups, followed by high attrition rates in those same groups. Studies show that it's because they – for whatever reason – do not feel they fit in. They are classic outsiders. When in government, I could see police forces that were investing significant resources into attracting employees from more diverse backgrounds, only to see high levels of what they call 'wastage', coupled with lower employee satisfaction rates among women and ethnic minority officers. We should also not forget that being an outsider does not necessarily mean that you have characteristics that are visibly distinctive from those of an inside group. You can be the quiet sibling, or the one who appears to be less academic in a large family, or the anti-establishment billionaire who decides to run for president of the United States.

After leaving my role as special advisor, I went on a journey to try to find out what brings all outsider experiences together. What will become clear throughout this book is that outsiders are **individuals or groups set apart for a purpose**. At the intentional risk of sounding religious, I would go further and say they are set apart for a higher purpose. It's as if the differences of being an outsider act as their superpower; they are there to help them to achieve – if only they can grasp the opportunity. I believe defining outsiders in this way creates a number of challenging questions for all of us: firstly, how do we accept that outsiders are set apart, that they are different, in a world where there is so much focus on finding ways for outsiders to fit in? Secondly, how can we identify the purpose of an outsider? What value does their difference add in any given context? Answering these questions will allow us to begin to grasp the power of the outsider. There is now more than ever a need to understand outsiders. I'll tell you why . . .

The Outsider Experience

In the twenty years before the coronavirus pandemic, the UK had experienced an unprecedented level of upward mobility. The number of young people going to university hit record levels. Average earnings in the United Kingdom had grown by over 60 per cent in this period, though the real-terms figure is lower, and inequalities still exist. Technology is increasingly opening up new opportunities, removing geographical and social barriers. Policymakers and corporations are under significant pressure to continue this upward trajectory. Whether it is improving outcomes for the working class, levelling up areas geographically, grappling with racial or gender inequality, or appreciating the value of those who are neurodivergent, most of us are no longer comfortable with the idea of certain spaces remaining the preserve of a privileged few. There has also never been a greater necessity for nations to maximise the productivity of all their citizens. The economic case for creating environments for outsiders to flourish is compelling.

My family and I have benefited from this period of opening up opportunities. Growing up in a single-parent home, living in social housing with five siblings wasn't easy. There were times when we did not know where our next meal would come from. We could not afford to go on holiday, to have the latest clothes, or even to partake in extracurricular activities that in theory would have made us more competitive in the labour market.

Despite this, as you will read about later, my siblings and I have been able to achieve things people would have thought unlikely had they witnessed our upbringing. We are products of Britain's upward-mobility story. Though our journey is not uncommon, we must not forget that being an outsider isn't easy. I have met enough outsiders to know that even those who seem to carry it well often struggle behind closed doors. Even after someone has broken a social barrier there can be a feeling of inadequacy, which is often referred to as impostor syndrome.

Every outsider has had that feeling of inferiority when you cannot fully participate in an activity or a conversation because it was not part of your personal experience growing up. Not knowing how to engage in small talk, the right cutlery to use or even how to dress. I remember once attending a black-tie gala and because I was hot, I took off my jacket. I was then mocked by a 'friend'; I didn't know that in such settings one was supposed to keep one's jacket on until after the 'loyal toast'. Many people will be able to relate to having to remain awkwardly silent as Oxford or Cambridge alumni discuss which college they attended, who they rowed for or their mutual acquaintances. Leadership expert Dr Rose O. Sherman argues that small doses of feeling inadequate might be good as this feeling reminds us to focus on continuously improving our competency levels. It keeps us grounded. However, she also says that too much of this feeling can lead to overthinking or a paralysing fear of failure, to anxiety, perfectionism, burnout and depression. I can now see that this was part of my experience in government, but it wasn't something I thought much about until after that conversation in St James's Park.

There are many ways that we can end up feeling like an outsider. The irony of course is that those who feel isolated as they move up the social strata are part of a much larger cohort of people. Most of the world's citizens are state-educated, do not have wealthy parents relative to their country of origin, and have not benefited from exposure to high society. Ninety-nine per cent of the UK population did not study at Oxford or Cambridge. This is what I have often had to remind myself of during those moments when I could not help noticing that I was one of few or maybe even the only person of a certain background in a certain place. But to be honest, attempts to reassure myself that I am really in the majority have not always helped. Sometimes I feel like removing myself from certain situations altogether, retreating to more familiar surroundings with more familiar people. It's a feeling that many have had and, sadly, many have felt the need to act upon. One very high-profile example is Meghan Markle, an outsider in the royal household, retreating to Los Angeles with her husband and children. But for most of us, taking such an action is much less dramatic and has limited public interest!

It's not all bad news. I want this book to demonstrate that outsiders have a unique value that they bring – if they can seize the opportunity to flourish. This book should be a guide for those who want to further explore what it means to be an outsider, and how they can use it to achieve success. For example, outsiders with dual heritage and strong international ties will play a decisive role in unlocking future opportunities in emerging markets. Outsiders are also uniquely positioned to challenge long-held orthodoxy, including in rural Britain, which has for centuries been the preserve of landowners, with urbanites kept outside.

The idea of owning one's difference, using it as a strength, will be a consistent thread. I believe that outsiders will play a pivotal role in broadening audiences and preserving our arts and culture, as we can already see with the emergence of outsiders disrupting the world of fine art. I meet with one of the UK's foremost psychiatrists, who helps to explain the psychology of outsiders. I look at failure as an outsider and speak about my last conversation in Downing Street with the former prime minister. You will see how successful outsiders give others the freedom to shine.

Who Is This Book For?

This book is not just for those who feel the experience of being an outsider. It is also for leaders and others who are keen to better understand colleagues, friends, associates, and family members who may find themselves in such a position. This is not a book that seeks to further divide, or to condemn individuals for privileges bestowed upon them at birth or from elsewhere. Rather, this should be a guide for those seeking to live in a world where everyone feels a little more comfortable and empathetic regardless of their background. I want this book to make people feel both more in control of their own sense of value and conscious of the impact of their acts or omissions towards others. A missing third way in an age of polarisation driven at least in part by social media algorithms. The world is changing, and opportunities are opening up that have previously been the preserve of elites. This means that there are more people entering spaces for the first time, often with limited guidance about how to navigate them. As one of those people, I want to share how this has been a journey of discovery for me; and I hope it will be for you too.

Chapter 1

A Father's Pain

It's late Friday afternoon in early October 2021 and I'm driving to visit Festus Akinbusoye, Bedfordshire's newly elected police and crime commissioner (PCC). Following my resignation earlier in the year, Festus was one of the people who reached out to check if I was okay. He is an outsider in many ways, having migrated to the United Kingdom from Nigeria, and then from London to this rural part of Bedfordshire. Being a police and crime commissioner means that he is the strategic head of a police force, and like many other elected PCCs Festus does not have a policing background, which makes him an outsider within the organisation that he leads. This is a particularly testing period for police forces across the country, with reports of misogyny and racism constantly making headlines, which further adds to the challenge of being an outsider in his position. Festus is using his difference as a superpower, but that does not mean his journey has been an easy one. I'm meeting him as I think it will help me to further understand how outsiders can use their life experience to do good in public life.

This is the second time I have visited his house. Driving along the country roads, I notice sheep and large, round bales as I wind down my car window so I can breathe the rural air. I turn in to his street and pause for a moment, wondering where this journey I am about to begin will take me. Feeling a little lost and a little insecure. Festus's house is surrounded by extremely tall, wide trees that seem to have hundreds of birds singing simultaneously within them. His house is also large, with light-brown brick and a lot of glass. I feel a sense of pride seeing someone from a similar background to my own who has obviously become so successful.

I press the bell. No one answers. I look for any sign of inhabitants, but I cannot see any lights on. As I walk back to my car to call Festus, I hear the door open, followed by, 'Wasup bro. You good?' The house is quiet, so I ask where his kids are. He shouts each child's name. One after the other they appear from wherever they were hiding. Three teenagers, extremely polite, each saying, 'Good evening' before returning to what they were doing. We head to his office. A square room, large desk with an office chair, and shelves filled with books. Time to start my interview.

Festus was born in Nigeria, where his father, Akinola, was a local government politician. Before Akinola's elevation to political office, he worked as a marketing executive in pharmaceuticals. He went on to become chairman of a local district. Shortly after his appointment, Nigeria came under military rule, led by General Sani Abacha. The general annulled all election results and imposed military rulers at federal, state and local levels. 'So Dad had to leave office literally overnight,' Festus tells me. 'I think after years of, you know, the hustle and bustle of Nigeria, Dad decided he was going to just become an economic migrant to the UK.' Akinola chose to migrate to the United Kingdom because his wife, Taiwo, Festus's mother, ran a business that meant she travelled regularly to London to buy fabrics and textiles, which she imported to Nigeria. She would go to places like Liverpool Street and Shoreditch in east London, where a lot of the African textiles were sold.

'What was really striking for me, though, was the sharp contrast between this and the kind of life that I was used to in Nigeria.' When they arrived in the UK, Festus was thirteen and the family lived in a two-bedroom flat above a textiles factory in Upton Park. 'I still remember the name of the place, the name of the road. There was one bedroom for the four of us. The next bedroom had another family of four in it. Eight of us in a two-bedroom flat.' In Nigeria they had lived in a nine-bedroom house with domestic help and a chauffeur who drove them everywhere. The children went to private schools and were very much part of the upper-middle classes. Festus had never washed a dish before he arrived in England. In many ways they were insiders. 'We had a very, very, very, very good life, very good life, and then came to England and it was all so different. It kind of reminds me of how incredibly resilient the human spirit can be, because the contrast could not be starker.'

Festus's mother Taiwo went back to Nigeria to look after the family business, meaning Festus effectively had a single parent, 'But as an economic migrant, you got to do what you got to do. Right?' I ask him if his dad's lot improved as time went on. 'No, unfortunately until the day he died I always wished it would improve. This guy who was a big man in Nigeria, big man.' He pauses. 'It was very difficult to kind of go around telling people that Dad was a cleaner, you know, when we had his funeral in Nigeria.' Early every day Akinola would go to his morning job at clothing retailer Burton's on Ilford High Street in east London. After finishing there he would travel to Tower Hamlets to work a full day for the council. Then he would come home and have a rest before repeating his routine the next day.

As I listen to Festus speak, I wonder what he is really feeling. I can't quite tell whether this is a story of shame about what his father became, pride in his father's resilience, or appreciation for the sacrifices his father made for him. I listen intently, careful not to interrupt.

'I remember one day Dad came home. I must have been about sixteen at the time. He said, you know the new McDonald's that just opened in Canning Town? I said, oh yeah. So, you're going to be a manager? And he said, no, no, no. I'm going to be the night cleaner. I remember being quite speechless. Like, what's that you're proud of? You got another job as a cleaner. But he was quite proud of that. Just to show how the system grinds people down. I don't think he knew he had any other option.'

Festus reaches for a brown leather folder on the bottom shelf of a white upright book cabinet. 'I've got his payslips in there.' He then reaches below his desk where he is seated and brings out a brown briefcase. 'This is his, too, so these are my two most prized possessions in the world. And some letters that he wrote to me when I was a young man . . . they are in the briefcase. I told the kids if the house ever burned down, these are the only two things that I really care about in the whole building. Apart from the kids, of course.'

The emotions in the room are raw. What we both know about each other is we have similar heritage (although I was born in England), similar politics, and a similar passion for social justice. The common ground coupled with mutual respect and trust is I suppose why Festus has allowed himself to be so vulnerable with me, more than I have ever been with anyone in my whole life. This point of reflection comes to the front of my mind and does not leave me as I listen. I can see that he has decided to trust me with his story. At one point I notice Festus holding back tears, and I wonder if he has noticed the same of me. He continues, 'I remember Dad telling me that he felt belittled because of the colour of his skin. There were some white guys, younger kids, who became his boss . . . his supervisors . . . but they had no qualifications. He decided to go to college, to get qualified, but the promotion still never came.'

I ask him if the way his father was treated affected him. 'Well somehow, I never let that get to me, but I've always been mindful of it. I remember him asking me to help him with his CV when he found a job in the local paper. He called the company. I remember very clearly. I was in the house that day. He rang up the company. They said there was a job available. Bearing in mind Dad would apply for jobs with his British name – Robert. They told him to come straight away to the office. When he got there and they saw him, they told him that he must have come to the wrong place. He replied, I just called you two hours ago. My name is Robert. You spoke with me, right? That's why I'm here. She said, no, I think you must have got to the wrong place. So, he came back home. All of that broke him.'

I begin to understand that this story has nothing to do with shame but is certainly one of pain. Festus's father's story has been permanently written onto the surface of his heart, and to understand Bedfordshire's police and crime commissioner you must first hear about the story that occupies the root of his being.

Festus was twenty-six years old when his father was diagnosed with cancer. 'I remember everything so clearly. Going to St Barts Hospital with him several times. I remember when he was given the catheter. I remember when he had to have chemotherapy. It was difficult when he had to have an operation as well. It was cancer of the colon.' It was 2004 and Festus had just started a security business and had his own young family. 'It was all too much for me. I wanted to give up on everything. I remember Dad saying to me, he said, you know, son, the pain is just temporary. It's hard now. But know that the pain is temporary.' Akinola had always said that his wish was to die in his own home back in Nigeria. Now that he was terminally ill that wish was going to be tested to unimaginable limits.

Though he was of African descent, there are many similarities between Akinola's story and members of the Windrush generation who originate from the Caribbean. Many never planned to be in England forever, the plan for many was to make some money and then go back home. But most never returned from the so-called motherland.

Akinola's health rapidly deteriorated. The time came when he couldn't eat. The pain around his knees was so bad that he was constantly on morphine. There was one occasion in Queen Victoria Hospital as he was lying in his bed when Festus went to sit on the edge. Just the movement on the mattress of someone sitting down left Akinola 'screaming like a baby. He was in so much agony, so much agony, but we tried everything to keep him comfortable.' Festus was determined to make his father's wish to die in his home in Nigeria happen. He booked flights for Akinola and himself, leaving his young family behind. An ambulance had to be arranged to transport Akinola to the airport. Once they arrived at the departure lounge, the pilot came and saw Akinola lying on a stretcher and refused to let them on the flight. Festus recalls, 'I said, why? They said this guy is going to die on the flight. He's too sick. He's too unwell for us to even get him on the plane. I replied, you know this guy is going to die. I don't want him to die here. I need to get him to Nigeria. They said, well, they'll refund my money. I said, I don't want the money back. I want to get on that plane. We need to get to Nigeria.'

The airline refused, leaving no choice but for Akinola to return to hospital. Later the doctors sat down with the family and explained Akinola was so unwell that the cost of continuing to look after him in hospital was simply too high. The hospital wanted to discharge him to a respite home where he would receive palliative care and support until his death. Festus and his siblings refused. 'I said . . . we all said no. I had a one-to-one with the doctors at night. I said, look, guys, you can't do this. Whatever it takes is what we're going to do. They said what do you want us to do? I said I don't know, but he needs to go home alive, even though we knew he could die any time.'

Festus called another airline, Virgin Atlantic. He explained the situation, and they arranged for a form to be faxed over (at the time emails weren't a thing) and asked him to fill it out and fax it back. The airline required Akinola to take several medical tests that he had to pass if they were going to allow him to fly. 'I gave the form to the doctor, and they said to me, look at the facts, all this stuff that they want, he is not going to pass any of them. His blood count level is down. He's extremely diabetic. We don't think this is going to work.'

His voice cracks, the pitch goes higher. Tears roll down his face. 'If I died tomorrow, I would go to my grave, satisfied that I didn't give up for my dad.' Miraculously, Akinola passed all the tests required for clearance to travel. He passed the blood plasma test by just one point. Festus, relieved, headed to the airport with Akinola once again. Just as they were about to board, the flight captain insisted that Akinola take the diabetes test again. They had already taken the same test two days ago but the likelihood of Akinola passing a second time was bleak. Miraculously, he passed again – but only just. The next challenge was to get him onto the plane. Akinola was taken from the ambulance on a stretcher, not in a wheelchair, and was in agony. He was three times his normal size, his body was laced with fluid. The doctors had given Festus some morphine to give to Akinola to manage the pain. They wrapped him in a big blanket to try to minimise the discomfort as he was moved. 'He was just screaming and screaming. But all that was just in my head was one thing. Get this guy to Nigeria. Even if he died on the aeroplane, so long as we are over Nigeria airspace, I would feel like some of this was worth it.'

Before the flight took off the captain went up to Festus and said, 'We are aware of the situation and are very sorry. It's very unusual that we do this, but I must tell you that if your father dies during the flight, we are not going to make an emergency landing.' The realisation of the situation suddenly hit home for Festus. Perhaps until then there had been no time for reflection, just adrenalin to see the mission through, like a soldier in combat. Morphine was administered to Akinola several times throughout the flight, as the high altitude made the pain worse. 'It was bad. It was, it was bad. But all I could just think was, I thank God we're on the plane. That was the longest six hours of my life.'

When the captain announced that they were over Nigerian airspace and would be landing soon, the relief was unspeakable. 'I remember when I heard that. I cannot tell you how I felt. The closest feeling to that was when I was announced as the winner of the police and crime commissioner election. Nothing else has even come close to that feeling.' Then came the landing, which was quite turbulent. When Taiwo first saw her husband at the airport she nearly fainted. This was not the strong man that she had last seen. The patriarch of the household. She had known something was wrong because Akinola had not been able to speak to her for a while as he used to, but her imagination had not taken her anywhere close to the reality of what she met that day. It nearly killed her. Festus says, 'I remember when we finally got him home and placed him on his bed . . .' He pauses. The silence is deafening. I fully expect the next words to be 'he died'. But they aren't. Festus continues, 'It was such a relief. And then the extended family, because we have a big family, were coming in to see him.'

Shortly after their arrival Akinola's already bloated stomach began to expand further. He was no longer able to pass any waste. A nurse had to loosen his bowels. 'When they came to do this, it was such a degrading experience. This is my dad, the guy that was my hero. Having this happen to him.' Festus slept in the room next to his father to be always close. When he was awake, he would sit on the floor of his father's bedroom for the whole day and could see the pain he was in. He would only leave the room for the nurse to clean Akinola. As the pain intensified it became more difficult for everyone to bear. 'I remember getting on my knees and praying. I said, God, I love my dad, but this is too much. I remember saying if there's nothing else for him to learn in life, there's nothing more for us as his children to learn from all this experience, please just take him.' Two days later, Akinola died. That was five days after they had arrived in Nigeria. He died in his own country and his own house the way that he had wanted. Festus was the last person to see him alive. His wife Taiwo was the first to see him dead.

Festus concludes, 'Someone like me doing what I do now. That is what made me.' I ask him to clarify: 'Do you mean the situation leading to your father's death or his story more broadly?' He responds, 'His death! In terms of my resilience and my inner core and my strength and leadership and courage and perseverance. Not taking no for an answer and having that indefatigable spirit. That constant optimism and that constant positivity. That experience I would say is the benchmark for me. It just sweeps all those other little, little things out of the way, just like that. So that is the benchmark for me. I hope I never have to go through that again, but that experience as a twenty-six-year-old man made me who I am today; 100 per cent without any question whatsoever, I believe I can do anything if I want to, because of that. I can't explain enough how much that experience transformed me.'

Akinola's story shows us that being an outsider is not a one-dimensional or static thing or limited to a demographic category. You can be an established insider in one environment, like his family were in Nigeria, and then become an outsider through migration, social mobility or other factors. What we can also learn from Akinola's story is that you can choose how you respond to your outsider status. Even when the environment you are in restricts your ability to flourish, you still have a choice to be your best self in any given circumstance. Martin Luther King Jr famously said, 'If a man is called to be a street sweeper, he should sweep streets even as Michelangelo painted, or Beethoven composed music, or Shakespeare wrote poetry. He should sweep streets so well that all the hosts of heaven and earth will pause to say, here lived a great street sweeper who did his job well.'

We must recognise that the power of choice remains in every situation. It is the foundation for any outsider seeking to realise their full potential. That does not take away, though, from acknowledging that discrimination and prejudice still hold so many people back. Though Akinola's resilience is potent and inspirational, it does not mean that he was not affected by his struggles. Festus shared so many other stories with me about Akinola that I have left out of this chapter because I believe it should be left for Festus to tell them himself. Outsiders can choose how they respond to their situation, but creating an environment for outsiders to flourish is not the responsibility of those outsiders alone.

Akinola's desire was to die in Nigeria, the place he felt was his home, where he had memories of being accepted and respected. That determination to make sure his father had his wish fulfilled perhaps had deeper meaning for Festus. I wonder if part of that desire was because even Festus, despite all his achievements in the United Kingdom, still felt, at the age of twenty-six, like he was not quite at home. I wonder if he even truly feels at home now. I ask if his three children understand what he went through. 'They can never do because no matter how much I explain they can't ever get it, but there are other things that they get. They get the importance of hard work because they see me hustle. They see me put in the grind. They see me obviously, as a single dad, I'm always trying to be in two places at one time. Sometimes I tell them, no, you can't do something because I've got to go to something else, so you have to sacrifice a sleepover with your friends.'

I interrupt him for the first time: 'Do you feel your experience with your father is why you are comfortable being a single—'

Festus corrects me quite sharply. 'I am not comfortable being a single dad. I hate it. You know, it's very lonely. It's not a great place to be, you know. I've been in other relationships since I got divorced. But knowing that I come with . . .' He pauses. 'The reality of having children, potentially needing to blend families together, isn't easy. It's not an easy thing, but I can't say I'm comfortable with it, but I'm confident in my ability to parent.'

I can't help but feel like Festus is trying to avoid being labelled an exception, so I push back. 'That is a useful way to frame your situation. But there are many other guys who could have made the same choice but did not. They left the children with their mother.' He responds, 'Yeah. I think for me growing up, I've always, and I still, love children. Maybe that's the reason.' I'm not entirely convinced by this response, but I do like how he frames his role as a father. 'I love that twinkle in their eyes. Rose-tinted view of the world. But I also feel like, of course, some will lose that innocence. They will lose that dream. They will lose that inspiration at some point. So, I'm going to say that it's my job to try to keep that dream alive for them somewhat. But I look at them now and how great they are doing. I'm very proud of them. There were times when it was very hard. Times when I cried at night, there were times when financially things were very difficult. I remember a time when I was buying three different nappies of different sizes.'

Festus recounts that he has been in relationships with women whose fathers had walked away from them at a young age. He says the lifelong trauma as a result often affects their own subsequent relationships. The impact is also felt by men, though many choose to hide it. He describes a scene in American sitcom *The Fresh Prince of Bel-Air* with Will Smith and Uncle Phil, when Will talks about his biological father who was never a part of his life. And he says to Uncle Phil, 'I don't care about him. He was never there, on my first date, when I scored my first hoop in basketball. When I got my first dog, he was never there. I don't care about hating him. I don't need him.' Will begins to walk away from Uncle Phil. Then he stops and turns round and says, 'Why didn't he want me, Uncle Phil?' And he starts crying on Uncle Phil's shoulder.

As Festus tells this story I feel as though something has pierced through me like nothing ever has before. Festus had just opened a wound in me without knowing it. As I feel tears gather in my eyes, I panic, shake my head and put it down so he doesn't see. I begin to scribble on the paper in my hands with my pen, buying time for me to compose myself. I had come here to learn about the story of the first black police and crime commissioner in the history of the United Kingdom. The son of an immigrant who worked as a cleaner, who was now living in a rural setting and in many respects could be considered the very epitome of an outsider. What I did not expect was that I would realise there were things inside of me that were conveniently buried but equally responsible for shaping my own life. That the same way Festus's father's presence was material to his success is the same way my father's absence was material to both my successes and my failures. I had lived the first thirty-four years of my life not knowing that there was a void. A desire to be comforted by a father figure who would have shown me how to be a man. How to deal with situations. To navigate obstacles. To handle emotions.

That void had perhaps meant that my default at times was to withdraw when things got uncomfortable or unfamiliar. To escape instead of confronting. Like I had done with my role as a special advisor.

Festus was the first person I spoke to as part of my voyage writing this book. I did not know what to expect, or where the conversation would go. I just knew that he was an outsider who in many ways was an ordinary person who had achieved extraordinary things. I wanted to know what we could learn from him. Festus lost his father at the age of twenty-six. I remember, when I was a similar age, I received a call letting me know my father was seriously ill and rushed to hospital. He was a person who at the time I had not known very well. I remember thinking what I should feel if he died and committing to trying to get to know him if he survived, which he did. My father's experiences coming to the United Kingdom were like Akinola's, in so far as he had the potential and intellect to go further than he did. My father had won national awards for his academic achievements, obtaining a distinction for his doctorate. He too was involved in local politics in Nigeria. I am now a father myself and I owe it to my children to try to give them what I did not have as a child. But I also understand that life isn't easy for many first-generation migrants, and that family break-ups are a manifestation of complicated factors.

Festus was much further along than me in his journey of understanding himself, though perhaps it was peculiar that he could not see that the events that led to his father's death were the keys to turbocharging his destiny. I could see that having honoured his father's wish to die in his home is what drives him to never give up on anyone, even young people who have found solace in a gang or county lines drug trafficking. However, I could also see that his father's whole story, not just the latter part, was a lingering shadow over him. That he did not walk away from his children because he saw his father doing everything that he could, often alone, to look after his own children. I could see that his father's commitment to taking pride in his work was key to Festus's world view and politics.

I want to know more about how Festus views himself now and ask if he considers himself to be an outsider. He responds, 'I don't know if I can ever not feel like one. I mean, my accent, you know, it is what it is. Sometimes, I can hear my voice and my accent is kind of fluctuating depending on who I am speaking to [also known as code-switching]. I'm comfortable being around most people, but when I look at pictures sometimes, I'm reminded that I stand out.' He carries on reflectively, 'But I guess what I need to do is to accept that differences are okay. And that being unique is a great thing.' There is no doubt that Festus stands out in many ways. He is a role model. When he was first elected police and crime commissioner, he went through around two months feeling what he recognises as impostor syndrome. He didn't feel as though he belonged, even though he was elected with a larger majority than his predecessor. 'Sometimes I would tell myself that maybe I didn't win. Maybe someone's going to make a complaint to the Electoral Commission and say there was something I forgot to do. I would question myself over and over again.'

Impostor Syndrome, Outsiders and Labels

My conversation with Festus made me think more about the issues around impostor syndrome and outsiders. It's definitely worth diving into some of the academic analysis around the subject – for example, the origins of impostor syndrome are thought to be socialisation, both in the family unit and in broader society. Young people are given labels by their parents that they feel they must live up to.

A study examined two groups within the family unit who were assigned roles by their parents, one the 'sensitive' group and the other the 'intelligent' group. Parents would class one sibling as the intelligent sibling and the other as sensitive or socially adept. The second sibling, who was praised for any skill other than intelligence, began to internalise the narrative that they were not the smart one and therefore needed to work harder to disprove their parents' labelling. That's how the pattern of impostor syndrome begins; no matter how hard the second sibling works, no matter how many accolades they receive, no matter how much academic prowess they attain, the child is still not the intelligent sibling. This leads to a disconnect between external signifiers of intelligence and the internal narrative that the child cannot possibly be the more intelligent one – or even intelligent at all. As for the sibling initially dubbed the intelligent one, they begin experiencing things that do not accord with the parents' narrative that they can accomplish anything. So, they begin to doubt their own ability and gradually internalise that they are not as intelligent as everyone has been led to believe.

The second factor attributed to the formation and maintenance of impostor syndrome is that of societal stereotypes. The narrative that certain groups are less intelligent and competent than others affirms the extant doubts fostered in the family unit; people begin to attribute temporary characteristics such as effort, charm, luck and misjudgement by others to their success. The fear that somehow one's true inferiority will be discovered is constantly present, as we have seen with Festus. It can be debilitating if not dealt with.

Festus confirms that he has had counselling before and was able to draw on useful tools and skills to be able to peel through this period. To understand where the anxiety was coming from. The feeling of not being worthy. Of being undeserving. 'I started to peel it back and I got stuck into myself, telling myself you have done this, you won an election, you fought the campaign, the people gave you a mandate. You have no right to turn that down. And I remember my dad, again, who would always say the head must never become the tail.' He says again, 'I have an undying belief in my calling. I don't know exactly where it's going to end, but I know I am not where I am by accident.' And with that our discussion finishes. The kids have made dinner, including apple pie for dessert. Festus loves food, so there was only going to be one winner for his attention.

That Festus chose to put himself forward to be the police and crime commissioner is a testament to his desire to see outcomes improve for others. I get the feeling that his heart is for young people who are trapped in a cycle of criminality. In his media interviews his tone is very different to other prominent Conservative politicians, who often seem one-dimensional in their analysis of why violent crime continues to engulf certain communities. He has been appointed the national lead for crime prevention by the Association of Police and Crime Commissioners (APCC). Speaking with him leads me to reflect on the events of 6 August 2011, when riots broke out in north London before spreading like wildfire across the UK. Mark Duggan had been shot dead two days earlier by the police, and tensions were running high. Like many of the riots in Britain over the last sixty years, at the heart of those events were tensions between the police and parts of Britain's ethnic minority population. Official data shows that in the years after the 2011 riots most black and Asian Britons had confidence in their local police. However, in the period 2019 to 2021, there has been a reduction in confidence of over 10 per cent. It is almost certain that the trust levels has since diminished across the board since 2021.

If we are keen to avoid riots in the future, more people, particularly those from under-represented backgrounds, will need to be willing to play an active role in public life, like Festus. He is in a unique position to effect change, because of both his role and his story. He sees himself as an outsider, has had challenges that he has overcome; but I reckon his true power will come from using the things that make him stand out. If he was to do this, not only would he be able to achieve even more unique milestones in his life, but he could be the bridge to dealing with historical tensions between the police and the communities that need them most.

I hope you can see from the story of Akinola and Festus that being an outsider comes with challenges, including experiencing different forms of pain, but we must not lose sight of the fact that we can choose how we respond to situations, hard as they may be. We owe it not just to ourselves, but to those who are looking to us, not least our children, to make the most of every day we have on this Earth. The progress we have made as a society is because brave people have challenged the status quo but, as Martin Luther King Jr and many other leaders have made clear, the best way to inspire people is to be an example. To show and not tell. To take pride in your work, to be a role model, to stand out for doing the right thing. That is the lesson I have been reminded of through Akinola and Festus.

Chapter 2

Healing Divisions

It's December 2021 and we are spending the Christmas period at a hotel in Hertfordshire. In the centre of this oasis of calm are my two children, at this point one and six respectively. Both are restless. Keen to find a way to distract at least one of them, I switch on the television in the hotel room and see that they have Disney Plus. A new film has been released. It seems to have captured the children's attention, but my first impression is that it has far too much singing for me. Soon, though, I begin to realise this story is actually quite special. In the Walt Disney animation movie *Encanto*, we see a lively example of how an outsider uses their difference as a superpower to heal divisions.

The Madrigals are a Colombian family within which each descendent is gifted with magical powers to serve the villagers in Encanto. The powers are given to each Madrigal family member via a magical candle. But one person does not have these powers: Mirabel, the youngest daughter of Julieta, who is in turn the daughter of the matriarch of the family, Alma. Mirabel's grandmother, rather than helping her to deal with the insecurities of a fifteen-year-old struggling with her lack of powers – the thing that forms a key part of the family's identity – is hostile towards her. We find out that what Mirabel represents to Alma is her deepest fear, which she is unwilling to confront: that the family will lose their gifts, and subsequently their importance to the community. And while Alma is the only one who actively treats Mirabel as if she is an outcast, the rest of the family are too caught up in their own personal issues to pay any attention to what the one with no (apparent) gift may be going through.

From the beginning of the film Mirabel shows great character, putting on a brave face as she celebrates the gifts of the rest of her family through song. She becomes the backbone of the group, helping others to shine as they serve the village. But she is affected by her difference. She does not feel special like the others. As the movie evolves, we can see that though Mirabel is not gifted in a way that is as obvious as her relatives, she is the one uniquely positioned to save them. She can display empathy in a way that the others cannot, can see things others do not, and ultimately has the courage to confront what others choose to ignore. Eventually, Mirabel's difference helps the family to rebuild their lives and heals divisions, reconciling the family with her exiled uncle Bruno (we don't talk about Bruno). Mirabel's story reminds me of the famous psalm; 'the stone the builders rejected has become the capstone'. The one people least expected something special from became the important one. If you have ever felt rejected, unappreciated or undervalued – trust that the time will come when people need you and what you bring to the table.

Like many of Disney's recent animations, *Encanto* is a movie accessible to children but full of mature themes that can keep an adult just as gripped as a child. We know that in a lot of circumstances people respond to outsiders in a hostile way because they fear what they represent. For a working-class person struggling to get by, a migrant can represent to them competition for housing and jobs. The fear of displacement often drives one's hostility to outsiders, if insiders are unable to see the bigger picture of the value a new entrant can bring to a community. A mother-in-law fearing displacement may be less welcoming to their child's spouse for similar reasons.

Resistance Is Natural

It is important to recognise that it is not unnatural for people to resist change or to seek familiarity. When presented with a psychological threat in the form of difference, people resort to self-affirmation (a positive self-view) as a coping strategy. This can at times explain the lack of nuance in some public debate. The comfort of relative homogeneity draws people to associate with those who are alike, even when those who are different are not deemed a threat. A study by Dr Scott Field on the structural causes of social homogeneity (hanging around people like yourself) concluded that the roots of homophily (shared preferences and attitudes) are systematically derived from what we feel will help us to survive as human beings. He also argues that 'the social structuring of activities tends to bring similar people into frequent contact with one another, and thereby encourages the development of relationships among them'. This is a very important point for policymakers keen to have a society that is better integrated. We must find opportunities for people from different groups to interact intentionally, regularly, and in meaningful ways. Unfortunately, the way that society has evolved does not allow for us to feel safe about admitting we are naturally drawn to people like us and feel safer when we are with the familiar. This inherent feeling is not exclusive to one group, though it is more convenient to imply that only those with power display such behaviours.

Observing the gates of a school while children are being dropped off or picked up will show you just how natural it is for people to gravitate to people like themselves. My son's school is quite mixed in terms of ethnic composition, but I often observe the black parents in one cluster, the white British parents in another, and the Eastern Europeans in a separate group. When the England men's football team were in a camp preparing for the European Championship in 2021, I noticed a photo taken during a lunch period – and again this diverse group of players who play for different clubs had somehow managed to subconsciously divide themselves along racial lines – perhaps because of mutual interests or backgrounds. Such natural behaviours can be overcome if we are conscious of it and make an effort to be welcoming to others who are different. To walk across to the other side of the school gate to speak to another parent. To arrange a social gathering for all parents to meet each other. To invite all the children to a birthday and not just the ones they play with or whose parents you speak with. To sit with a different player at lunch, to connect with an older or younger colleague at work. Some may question whether these natural behaviours need to be overcome at all. We'll deal with this later.

The Power of Agency

Like with Mirabel, feeling like an outsider, impostor, an 'other' or an 'only' can have a significant impact on how we function as individuals. However, it is important to understand the interplay of power and agency in the framing of the experiences of outsiders. Anthony King, in his journal article entitled 'The Outsider as Political Leader: The Case of Margaret Thatcher', states, 'there are many situations in which an individual can choose whether or not he or she wishes to be, or to act as, an outsider. The status of an outsider may be objectively defined, but it may also be subjectively selected.' In other words, your truth or another person's truth, grounded in fact or thought, can be impactful when considering who is an outsider and who is not. For many, being an outsider is an objective fact, a situation that is the consequence of unavoidable circumstance. However, there are those who have used the badge, sometimes disingenuously, for their own advantage. Every successful politician will find a way to define themselves somehow as an outsider, whether through being creative with how they explain their privileged background to show they are different from others or by portraying themselves as the anti-establishment change candidate. In the summer 2022 leadership contest to replace Boris Johnson as the leader of the Conservative Party and prime minister, the last-two candidate Liz Truss conveniently debased Roundhay School in Leeds, the comprehensive she attended, saying it had let down working-class pupils and this motivated her to go into politics. Roundhay has an excellent reputation in the north of England, and the school has produced at least one notable Oxford graduate . . . Liz Truss. This intentional positioning for political gain does not take away from the reality that for many, even tactical outsiders, being an outsider can form a psychological barrier. There are shared experiences for outsiders that have not been fully explored.

What underpins every outsider is a feeling that there is a difference between you or your group and others. How one responds to this or capitalises on one's difference depends on several factors, including the individuals involved and the environment they are functioning in. In the world of sport, a coach could use the label of being the outsider in a cup final to motivate players to prove doubters wrong, or to take more risks. For some players, that could lead to giving the extra effort that will ultimately lead to a better chance of victory, while for others it could result in giving the opposition too much respect and not performing to their highest level. There are other variables that may determine the final outcome but, as we established in the previous chapter, outsiders ultimately have a choice when it comes to how they respond to their difference.

Anthony King in his article goes on to identify three categories of outsider, which I think is helpful when trying to bring a better understanding to the subject: the social or demographic outsider, the psychological outsider and the tactical outsider.

The Social or Demographic Outsider

The social or demographic outsider can take on a plethora of socially defined forms. Examples include a family group, a racial or ethnic group, a social class, a religious community, a circle of friends, an age cohort, the members of a particular political party and the supporters of a particular football club. The criteria for inclusion in these groups are exhaustive, objective facts. One is either a citizen of a particular country or not (although some politicians are beginning to debate this 'fact'). Some of the aforementioned exclusions are fluid, such as in the case of supporting a sports team or player. Others are not. It can be said that social mobility affords fluidity between social classes, but it is very rare that someone consciously accepts and/or announces their upward or downward mobility without making reference to their previous social status. There is also no full clarity around whether someone's profession, income or assets should be the determining factors for confirming a change in socioeconomic category. When can you officially call yourself middle class and why? If you move into an affluent area because of your economic mobility, will the neighbours accept you as one of their own or label you an outsider?

Though individuals may assimilate or become assimilated into a social class or ethnic group through the learning of a language or behaviours, most will never truly overcome the demographic factor linked to their outsiderness. If we cannot alter those circumstances, the question becomes: is difference something that we should seek to overcome? Or is it more important that a society does not make a demographic outsider the subject of prejudice? The social or demographic outsider may or may not feel emotional discomfort if they're categorised as an outsider. In other words, some people are entirely comfortable with their identity, and not fazed by feeling they're an outsider. King provides the example of a Canadian who has lived all his adult life in Great Britain but who has never bothered to apply for United Kingdom citizenship. He may be an outsider in Britain in the sense that he is not a citizen, but he may have no feelings whatsoever of 'outsiderness'.

The Psychological Outsider

The psychological outsider may belong in theory but still feel alienated from what might seem to be their group. Growing up, I was the quiet sibling in my family. The one who wouldn't sing along or dance to music videos. The introvert among a group of very expressive people. The Yoruba tribe in Nigeria is where both my parents originate from. They are a tribe of people known for being colourful, expressive, confrontational, bold and direct. To this day, people who know about the Yoruba tribe tell me that they struggle to believe this is my heritage. I was a psychological outsider growing up.

There are various different things that could make you not feel like you are part of a group. A French national living in the United Kingdom may not feel able to integrate fully due to language or culture. Even if someone does integrate, a change in circumstances that they can't control could make them feel isolated. Many Europeans previously integrated into the United Kingdom will have suddenly felt like outsiders the day after the Brexit referendum.

Some outsiders in this category are 'hidden'. Some people may keep feelings of outsiderness completely to themselves and not be able to share their feelings of alienation. Like Mirabel in *Encanto*, they might feel that it could be seen as a sign of weakness. In an age of culture wars, it could further isolate you from a group that you feel you need to be a part of for you to progress. In my time in Downing Street, I could not have open conversations about how I was feeling, as I was a senior special advisor in a position of power. I felt it would risk me being seen as weak when colleagues seemed so certain of themselves. I feared I would lose my credibility and be unable to drive important policy forward. Being an introvert didn't help with this situation. I wish now I had felt able to be more honest; but being an outsider can be a lonely place.

There is now more data to help us understand this topic, but forming a quantitative grounding is not easy. According to a report published in November 2021, roughly 33 per cent of adults worldwide experience loneliness. The study also found that, of 2,522 young people surveyed, 25 per cent said they often felt left out and 27 per cent felt isolated from others. These statistics, while not produced directly in the line of inquiry into outsiderness, do indicate that feeling left out and isolation are widespread. I believe that understanding the issues that underpin these feelings is crucial to developing remedies. After all, someone may not have chosen to be a psychological outsider. Sometimes individuals exclude themselves out of dysphoria or reject their own group for other reasons. More research would surely be helpful to both individuals and society.

The Tactical Outsider

The tactical outsider is someone who chooses to be an outsider for personal gain, or disdain for the conventions of their circumstances. This is perhaps the type of outsider I've observed most often in politics. For politicians, positioning yourself as an outsider often helps you to appeal to groups less inclined to support 'establishment' figures. You heard earlier about a candidate who was competing to replace Boris Johnson as prime minister. The former leader of the UK Independence Party (UKIP), Nigel Farage, enjoyed arguably unpredicted success for much of the 2010s through his positioning as an anti-establishment outsider, conveniently sidestepping the fact that he attended a prestigious fee-paying school, was a former banker, a friend of media mogul Rupert Murdoch, and altogether extremely well connected. Donald Trump was also able to tap into similar sentiments on his journey to become president of the United States. His appeal was particularly poignant for Americans in the so-called Rust Belt regions that had experienced post-industrial decline. He was a businessman, not an insider politician, who was promising to Make America Great Again. Choosing to be a tactical outsider may have negative consequences, as politicians positioning themselves in this way often forget they will need to work with the same establishment that they use their election campaigns to attack. There is also a risk of overpromising what can be achieved in a relatively short space of time, and a seeming lack of consideration of the impact of external factors out of a leader's control. Despite these risks, this type of outsider has more control over their outsiderness. Instead of attempting to assimilate, tactical outsiders may choose to form their own group for the sake of a set of norms, behaviours and values they feel comfortable with.

Outsiders – Negative or Positive?

While King raises the interesting point that outsiderness is not inherently negative, what is common across all of his demarcations is the potential of outsiderness to negatively impact the individual, whether they feel excluded because of social, psychological or tactical factors. All three types can result in a lack of belonging. On the other hand, all three give us the opportunity to use our difference as a superpower, to be a unique selling point and to open doors. They offer up a strong point of difference in crowded monolithic environments. It is important to mention that you can be all three of King's categories of outsider all at the same time. This chapter has hopefully helped to lay foundations for understanding the outsider phenomenon before I go on to share more of my story and the story of other outsiders. Outsiders can heal divisions between conflicted groups who seem unable to seek out a resolution for themselves. An outsider can bring impartial and fresh perspectives to a situation. It is not unnatural for people to fear change or to gravitate towards the familiar, like parents at a school gate. But we must all find ways to counter conventional behaviour if we are to benefit from the value that outsiders can bring.

Chapter 3

Challenge Orthodoxy

Challenging long-held orthodoxy is not an easy thing to do. In September 2022 the then new Chancellor of the Exchequer Kwasi Kwarteng announced a 'mini budget' that was anything but mini. Tax cuts for the wealthiest, alongside the lifting of the cap on bankers' bonuses, and an untargeted cap on energy prices were among his announcements. As there were no concrete details around how the government would balance the public finances alongside the vast expenditure and tax cuts, the reasonable assumption was that the bulk of these actions would be funded through excessive borrowing. The market's reaction was overwhelmingly negative; gilts (the mechanism of government borrowing) rose sharply, and the country was plunged into crisis. The value of the pound dropped against the dollar and euro. It was a disaster by any stretch of the imagination, and Kwarteng was sacked as a result, becoming the second-shortest-lasting Chancellor of the Exchequer in the history of Britain. Kwarteng had wanted to challenge Treasury orthodoxy, positioning himself as the anti-establishment outsider, but unfortunately was unable to deliver. Cutting taxes for the rich in the middle of a cost-of-living crisis was at the very least immoral. Sacking the permanent secretary of the Treasury department within minutes of taking the job was a display of hubris. The whole episode did not just toxify the very compelling argument that there was a need to think differently in order to transform an economy that had stagnated for over a decade, but it also showed what can happen when orthodoxy is not challenged in a way that works. It's a tricky balancing act that requires recognising the environment you are functioning within.

But this example must not take away from the potential for outsiders with different perspectives to be truly transformative.

Orthodoxy and Royalty

Meghan Markle struggling in the royal household is an intriguing example of what can happen when an outsider can't quite challenge orthodoxy. In her relationship with Prince Harry, Meghan brought with her the opportunity to support the royal family on their journey of modernisation. She was the mixed-race celebrity and gender-equality advocate who was loved by young people, who saw her as a beacon of aspiration and hope. Meghan had the potential to take the royal family into the digital age and to reconnect it with members of the Commonwealth and beyond who could now see themselves within the institution. But it did not work out. She could not adapt to the various protocols associated with the responsibilities of being a royal. In the final analysis it could be said that she was not given enough support, or her expectations were not very well managed by her husband-to-be. In her interview with Oprah Winfrey, she explained that there were many things she was unaware of before her marriage. It was frankly shocking to hear. She confessed to not having bothered to even google the royal family she was about to join. Meghan's experience, while unique in its global exposure, is not exceptional; she is not even the first person to enter the royal family as an outsider that chose to challenge long-held orthodoxy. The late Prince Philip, grandfather to Harry, is one such example.

In an age of movement, he was called a citizen of nowhere. From a very young age Prince Philip was a stateless person, nationally homeless. We know that Meghan's father and siblings were not at the royal wedding; Prince Philip had a similar story to tell. His three surviving sisters and two brothers-in-law were not permitted to attend his wedding in 1947 because they were Britain's enemies, having fought for the Germans. (A third brother-in-law had even been in the SS, working directly for Heinrich Himmler, but had been killed in conflict.) Philip and the then Princess Elizabeth moved into Buckingham Palace upon returning from their honeymoon, only to find that there were courtiers who still treated the prince as an outsider. His life had changed in every way and his independent streak sometimes proved problematic. It is quite striking how history at times repeats itself. Philip's life underwent more seismic changes while on a trip to Kenya with Princess Elizabeth in February 1952, when his twenty-five-year-old wife became queen of England. The prince as husband of the monarch now had to adhere to a different set of royal protocols, including having to walk a few paces behind Her Majesty and refer to her as 'ma'am' when out in public.

Much of the push for transparency regarding the royal family can be traced back to Philip. His unusual upbringing inspired him to modernise the monarchy. When a commission he chaired proposed broadcasting the 1953 investiture ceremony that formally named Elizabeth II as queen on live television, Prime Minister Winston Churchill reacted with outright horror, declaring, 'It would be unfitting that the whole ceremony . . . should be presented as if it were a theatrical performance.' The queen had initially voiced similar concerns, but she eventually came round to the idea, allowing the broadcast of all but one segment of the coronation. More than 20 million people tuned in to the televised ceremony.

Of course, there are differences between the stories of Prince Philip and of Meghan Markle. Though he was stateless, Prince Philip still had royal blood, while Meghan Markle does not. Also, Meghan's relatives were not Nazis. In addition, both Harry and Meghan believe that her race was an additional contributing factor to the outsiderness that other royal spouses have experienced and that Meghan was the victim of racist incidents during her time in England. But I do think there was the same potential for the Duchess of Sussex to do what Prince Philip did for the monarch over fifty years ago. She is an outsider with a different perspective. Patience coupled with understanding of the environment one was operating in were probably amongst the key differences between Philip on one hand and Meghan and Kwasi on the other. It is also worth noting that Meghan and Kwasi were operating during an age of heightened media scrutiny and the influence of social media. However, I believe the principles of how to effectively challenge orthodoxy still stand.

The Black Farmer

It's November 2021 and I'm on my way to meet with Wilfred Emmanuel-Jones, owner of the Black Farmer food and beverage brand. Wilfred was born in Clarendon, Jamaica and grew up in Small Heath, Birmingham, having arrived in Britain as part of the Windrush generation. He is the second of eleven siblings. In the 2010 general election Wilfred stood as a candidate in the Chippenham constituency for the Conservative Party, coming second. He had previously worked in television, as a producer and director, for fifteen years, which gave him the capital to buy Higher West Kitcham Farm, on the border of Devon and Cornwall in St Giles on the Heath near Launceston.

My association with Wilfred goes back over ten years; he spoke at the launch of my first company when I was nineteen years old . . . not that he remembers. We are meeting for dinner at the Royal Automobile Club (RAC) in Pall Mall. It is one of the best-equipped private members' clubs of its kind in London, boasting 108 bedrooms, seven banqueting rooms, three restaurants, a business centre, a full-size marble swimming pool, squash courts, a billiards room and Turkish baths. I forget to pack cufflinks for my shirt and ask if I can quickly purchase a pair from the club store when I arrive. Wilfred replies, 'Oh, come on, you're not meeting with the queen – it's fine.'

Wilfred starts the conversation by speaking about a subject I had yet to consider as part of my reflections on outsiders – land. 'One of the things I feel very, very passionate about is you don't ever feel as though you are part of a country until you own land, and if you are an immigrant all the cards are stacked up against you in that respect.'

Most of the people who own land in the United Kingdom haven't had to go out and buy it. It has been handed down through generations. Even the smallest of farmers, that's how they acquired their land. We also have big institutions that own vast quantities of land, like the National Trust, the Church of England and universities, as well as various landed gentry. Though these landowners often lease out the land, there is no real way in for outsiders. The great irony is that people like Wilfred come from a rural background. His parents were farmers. There are many people who came from rural parts of Jamaica or India who have working with land within their DNA, but there is currently no outlet for them in the United Kingdom.

I ask Wilfred what he would do about this situation. 'What I want to see is a great change and the change is pretty simple. All you have to do is say to the Church of England, who owns a lot of land, you say to them, how much of that land are you asking your land agents to invite people from diverse communities to use? We're not expecting you to give it away for free but let them know there is the opportunity to lease it, to rent it so they could then grow things and then bring about some innovation.'

We have already established that Britain will need to rely on outsiders to look after our elderly, to build relationships with emerging economies, and now Wilfred is highlighting the need for outsiders in agriculture. It is no secret that British farmers rely on labour from abroad, but what Wilfred is talking about is something different. He continues, 'What it means is that you're not bringing in innovative ideas. One of the reasons why the industry has been quite sluggish is because to a certain extent the farming community have not had to innovate because if you are living off subsidies there is less incentive to do so.'

That's been the case for a long time, particularly while we

have been part of the European Union with its Common Agricultural Policy (CAP). Simply put, the goal of CAP is to ensure there is a stable supply of food within the European Union, through the giving of grants to protect the livelihoods of farmers. Other objectives include helping to maintain rural areas. At its peak in 1983, CAP was 73 per cent of the European Economic Community (EEC) budget. It remains a significant 37 per cent of the EU's budget. Those in support of CAP argue that despite the importance of food production, a farmer's income is around 40 per cent lower than non-agricultural income. They also argue that agriculture depends more on external factors like the weather and the climate than many other sectors, and there is therefore a need to ensure consistency for farmers. Part of the counter-argument, which Wilfred is now putting forward, is that large subsidies stifle innovation and do not adequately control for variances across European states.

He opines, 'The irony is that the great landowners are the ones also getting all of these grants. If you're a landowner you go to a bank, you have collateral to access vast amounts of capital too. Everything is all in your favour. And you know, the likes of me, unless you're lucky enough to go out and earn a lot of money to buy just a small piece of land, the odds are absolutely stacked against you. Urban Britain doesn't really understand how rural Britain works. No one has really tapped into one of the greatest injustices and roots of inequality in Britain. The ownership of land is the biggest secret for establishment insiders keen to maintain their power and prestige. I've only got thirty acres; when you think about some of these families, some of them have 5,000, 10,000 acres, and they've had this, not because of their hard work but because of our system where it's been handed down through generations.'

He makes a powerful argument for change. For many people in urban areas there isn't even the possibility of buying a home due to the increase in house prices, let alone the perceived grandiose vision of being a significant landowner. As a farmer who is an immigrant, who grew up in urban Birmingham, and is an entrepreneur, in many respects Wilfred is an outsider within rural Britain. This has given him a unique perspective and the power to challenge long-held traditional views. Someone like Wilfred could be the catalyst for change that could secure a better future for our agricultural sector. That's the power of an outsider. But I'm very sure many farmers would not frame the situation in the way that Wilfred has, so I ask him if he thinks that it would be more difficult to innovate once changes to subsidies for farmers are put in place because of Brexit. He says, 'What would happen is that by getting rid of subsidies, it will then get rid of all those farmers that are not really interested in farming. They've just been living off subsidy, so it will wake them up.' Was he pointing towards some form of market correction? 'Yes. Market correction. One of the things about the farming community is that it is no good us competing with the likes of Poland or Russia, where you have vast swathes of land to grow commodities easily. They can go for miles and miles. We are a small island. Therefore, what we need to do is we need to specialise. We need to do the things that these big companies, these big countries can't do. We as a country should be innovating.'

Adam Smith would be proud of Wilfred's point about free market economics. While I don't think I completely agree with his framing, I can see the logic. We have some of the greatest animal welfare standards in the world, but we do not use this to our benefit. One of the things Wilfred does is produce antibiotic-free pork. And the reason why he has been successful in producing this antibiotic-free pork is that in America there is currently a big demand for it. And the reason why there's a big demand for it is because the Americans for generations have been pumping their animals with growth hormones. Things that are illegal in Britain. Now that American consumers have lost faith in this, they are looking to countries like the UK for a better standard of meat. It has been well documented that the standards in United States farming are below those of the United Kingdom. It's a cause of great tension as we look to secure a trade deal. What most people do not realise is that American citizens themselves are increasingly also concerned by animal welfare and are looking abroad for better standards in the production of meat for them to consume. Such a speciality is what we should be offering to the rest of the world. That would be a long-term benefit for the country. That innovation will improve our competitiveness.

Wilfred continues, 'What outsiders need to do is to start getting into rural Britain. I think it's a very, very important thing because you then really get cemented into the roots of what makes this country tick. Everybody needs to eat food. It's fundamental.' Another salient point. There are a lot of things imported into the United Kingdom that could be grown here that tend to be eaten by people from ethnic minority communities, a growing population. But traditional farmers don't know how to grow them, and they have no interest in doing so. If people from diverse backgrounds had access to land, they could grow and produce those things. It would be good for the economy, potentially boost productivity, and be good for the environment. Wilfred concurs. 'I'm advocating that we need to bring about a lot more awareness that outsiders should be getting our slice of rural Britain. That is what is going to really bring about the change. We could create as much change as we like in urban Britain, but until you really get into the core of where our food comes from, our food security, our land security, until we get into that, we're always still going to be outsiders.'

I ask Wilfred about the journey that he took to acquiring his land. I know his family were farmers in Jamaica, but going from working in the media to farming in the UK must have been an interesting journey for him. 'We were really poor. I can remember my mother having to feed all of us on one chicken. Not one of these large chickens you get in the supermarkets. It was one of these boiler hens you have to cook for three or four days to get anything out of them. I remember going to the Bullring market with my mum to buy the food and, you know, I was always hungry.' His father had an allotment and, as the oldest boy, it was Wilfred's responsibility to look after it. This allotment really became his oasis away from the misery of urban living. He says, 'I can remember as an eleven-year-old boy, I made myself a promise that one day I would own my own farm. Now I didn't know how to do it, but it was a dream that I lodged into the back of my mind. Everything that I subsequently did with my life was to get into a position to have a farm.'

Wilfred wanted to join the BBC because broadcast media was one of his great passions. For two years he struggled to get a job there, but eventually, he got an opportunity helping the security guards to lift the gates to let people in and out of the building. 'They thought, well, this guy is prepared to go out in the cold to open up the gates so we might as well give him a job. I can remember meeting a guy. His name was Jack Gallagher. And I said, look, I want to get a job in television as a producer, director, researcher. And he took me to his office, and he spoke to me for about an hour. And he said, look, you know, you're not supposed to be employed in television because you don't have the academic background. You got a bit of an attitude. And he said, but I'll do this. He said he might come to regret it. He said, I will give you a job as a runner for three months and then let's see what happens. Now that man having the courage to give me that break meant I started a long career in television. What happens with our traditional systems is people like me would have been filtered out. You don't tick that box. You just get filtered out. Change comes about when people make it their personal responsibility to bring about the change. At every single stage of my success, somebody has gone out of their way and said; he doesn't fit the mould, but we'll give him a break. And that is what we need to instil in people. You are not responsible for the outcome, you're only responsible for giving the opportunity. And what tends to happen is people get really caught up about the outcome. Just give the opportunity. A lot of people will fail that opportunity, but it is your responsibility as a human being to give people an opportunity.'

Being the second of eleven siblings is quite something. I want to know what impact that may have had on shaping him. If he thought that it helped him to communicate with different types of people and to learn how to be entrepreneurial and to fight for things. 'Well, no, not really. I mean, I think the thing is that there's no romance about being an immigrant. Living in poverty and misery. My dad was a broken man. He came to this country full of hope and wanted to better his life. Back in Jamaica he was a minister. He was respected. He came to this country and ended up working in a factory on an assembly line and he was . . .' He pauses. 'I just think he was treated appallingly, and it really affected me. Then my mother as well, who in a different age would have been pretty entrepreneurial. There was something about her, perhaps that's why I'm entrepreneurial. They were broken down really by the sort of prejudice that met them. That was just a great source of disappointment. The hope was that us, the second generation, would go on and do better.' Wilfred's mother would tell stories about how she had to walk five miles to collect water before school when she was younger. 'We on the other hand had basics in terms of a national health service, electricity and all that sort of stuff.' All of Wilfred's brothers and sisters went into what he calls traditional Caribbean migrant professions. He has sisters in healthcare, a brother who's an accountant, and says he has another brother who's a crook and ended up in prison. 'I think my siblings all fit into that story and I am the anomaly. Why? I'm still trying to work that out myself.' Did his family feel like he was different growing up? 'How did they feel about me? I just think they noticed my aspiration. Because I always had grand aspirations and they probably thought this guy's nuts. It's just peculiar. So I think again, you see what keeps us prisoners, you know, belonging, you know, I had to leave my background, everything behind in order to achieve my success. If I had stayed, I would have become exactly like my brothers and sisters. Traditional route trapped by culture and a belief system. Whereas everything about me is self-graded.'

He pauses again to reflect, then says, 'I think everybody wants to belong. But you must decide sooner or later in your life whether you want to be or belong. To belong it means you must operate by the rules of the community, by the crowd, you know. If you could accept to be, which means you step out, you don't belong, you're on your own. An outsider. You then actually have a bit more freedom. But you have to make that fundamental decision. Do you want to be, or to belong?' He looks at me: 'You are a great example. You had to make a fundamental decision to belong with the compromises you have to make in a place like Downing Street and how it eats away at your spirit and your soul eventually. But a lot of people, that's their lives, you know, they decided to belong, and they hate it, but they feel that the dangers of stepping out to be is a lot more challenging, but that is a courageous decision. I always felt as though I didn't belong as a child. I knew I didn't belong but did not try to fight it. A lot of people fight tooth and nail to belong. I knew the only way that I would achieve anything is to be. The great irony is that we are here now in the RAC, which is a great temple of belonging, but I am belonging on my own terms and that's a world of a difference. I had to go on a long journey just to be the outsider, not to be accepted, to be seeming a bit peculiar.'

What would his advice be for outsiders navigating the earlier parts of their lives? 'If you're an immigrant, if you're an outsider, the most important thing is to accept that you are different. And never, ever play by the rules. It's a real killer for people who are outsiders because the people who have the courage to go on and do things their own way are initially ostracised. People think you're mad, but eventually people catch up with you. And the biggest theme that I live my life by is make a friend of uncertainty. One of the big dangers about politics is offering people certainty. So why is it some of the greatest leaders are the ones who led on the basis that we are not offering you certainty? You know, we are saying to you, this is going to be a tough journey, whether that's Churchill or whether that is Thatcher, this is a tough journey, but we need to change. I would argue even David Cameron in 2010, you know, economic crisis, he was not promising people that it will be business as usual. And people bought into that and gave him a majority in 2015. It's about not treating people like children. It's better to say to people, we will help you achieve the dreams that you want, but we're not going to say it's an easy road. Life is not easy.'

Wilfred is an example of where a demographic outsider is also a psychological outsider who then uses the art of being different in a tactical way. I explain to him those different types, and what catches his attention the most is the tactical outsider. 'That's me. I knew that I had to change everything about me in order to achieve the things that I wanted to do. So tactical, that's a really good description of me.' He asks me what kind of outsider I would consider myself to be. I respond, 'I think what is most important to me is being myself and being the best me. I have never been interested in just being another number, playing it safe, or following a traditional route. I never got to Number 10 in the same way that others did and to my mind there is no reason for me to start being what I am not. So I suppose I'm consciously tactical in my outlook.' Wilfred agrees.

How would Wilfred respond to someone who says, well, if he hadn't positioned himself as the Black Farmer then maybe he wouldn't have been as successful as he is? 'They'd be correct. But life is about finding out what your most unique selling point is. People look at the farming community then look at me. They think you can't make a living out of thirty acres, you just don't. And so they say well, why is it this guy's managed to do it? And it's not just about how much land you have. It's actually me understanding the people you've got to connect with is the British consumer. The people that buy my brand.

It's not black people. It's white middle England. They're not the cheapest sausages. I might say they are the best sausages, but that's subjective. So why are those people buying into it? It is because of what the brand stands for. What I stand for, that is what people are buying.'

Wilfred continues: 'That's one of the things that I love about politics as well. Politics is about an ideal. It's about a cause. And I think the great politicians are the ones who really understand that. Everybody wants to rally around a cause, an ideal, you know, we live and die based on these causes. Those politicians who are tactical, the ones who become great leaders, are the ones with an ideal. I hope that I do that with my brand. I genuinely believe people are good. If they see authenticity, they will be prepared to give you a break. My sausages came from a manufacturer deciding to help me produce the products. Then I was thinking about what I am going to call this brand. One day it came to me, all of my next-door neighbours down in Devon used to call me the black farmer. And I just thought that's a really good brand because no one else has that idea and it has an edge to it. People aren't too sure about whether it's politically correct or not. The thing about the name, in the society that we live in, where people are really nervous about what is the correct language to use, that is where you have to be courageous. There is a really important lesson in this as well, because even I was a bit worried about using the Black Farmer. All the research came back and said, do not call it the Black Farmer because people will be offended. There would be lots of problems. So this is the lesson. The research would tell you what people were thinking yesterday. Research will tell you what people are thinking today, but research cannot tell you what people will be thinking tomorrow. That's where you need to have your vision. That is where you need to have your purpose.'

The running theme of Wilfred's story is ownership. Whether that be owning land, owning his difference within his family or owning a business. In 2014 Wilfred was diagnosed with myeloid leukaemia. It meant he was in hospital for a year while the doctors worked to save him. He now has something known as graft versus host disease, which means that he has lost pigmentation in his skin.

His reaction to this was in keeping with his character. 'Too much of our lives is consumed by what I call white noise – things that are irrelevant. It's not until you're on death's door that you focus on what is important in life. It gives you a different perspective. I have vitiligo because of the skin transplant. Every day I look in the mirror it is a reminder to make every day count. I can tell you I have been more successful since I have had the cancer.'

There is a lot to admire about Wilfred being bold about telling this part of his story and owning his physical transformation, which makes him look even more distinctive than he previously did. But we must not forget that he is an entrepreneur, a natural disrupter, which means that he has certain character traits, both good and bad, that when blended with his difference have made him truly unique. That does not mean that people less entrepreneurial cannot learn from his experiences. Owning land or property continues to open doors that are often closed to less fortunate people. Assets are a gateway to new opportunities, and the elites continue to benefit from being able to pass their assets through generations. At the core of the art of being an outsider is recognising that difference provides opportunities, and therefore it should be embraced and owned.

If urbanites were to take Wilfred's advice, would they be

welcome? In 1965, researchers Norbert Elias and John L. Scotson investigated how an established settlement reacted to the geographical expansion of their neighbourhood and the impact that this had on community relations. The settlement in question was Wigston Parva in Leicestershire. The inhabitants, at the time, could be divided into two primary communities within the neighbourhood who were dubbed the 'established' and the 'outsiders'. This study examined how the established (indigenous or inside) group were, in terms of social capital, more powerful. Not only did this group hold more power in the community but they translated that power into a feeling of superiority. It is interesting to note here that this feeling of distinction translated into hostility and hostile action against the outsiders by the established, and the results of those actions had real consequences for the feeling of psychological safety among the outsiders.

The established 'refused to have any social contact with [the outsiders]', lumped them all together as people 'less well bred' and 'treated all newcomers as people who did not belong.' This process of profiling and ostracisation meant that the outsiders, after a while, seemed to accept with a kind of puzzled resignation that they belonged to a group of lesser virtue and respectability. This taboo on intercommunity socialisation was kept alive by means of social control such as praise-gossip about those who observed it and the threat of blame-gossip about suspected offenders. The neighbourhood was damaged, both in how the two communities were polarised along power relation lines, and also in how members of the outsiders' community could be criminalised by their compatriots for attempting to integrate. What is also significant is that both the established and the outsiders suffered a loss of psychological safety – the former because of the perceived threat of the outsiders to their established and predictable patterns of behaviour and thought, and the latter because of how the established treated them.

This paradigm is useful in understanding how larger communities such as nations become insular and contemptuous of new arrivals, but also demonstrates that outsiderness can be produced without the presence of social or demographic divisions such as race, class and language. Politicians are constantly looking to exploit actual or perceived divisions to secure or maintain power. It is the main tactic for some of the most successful election gurus of our time, a tactic perfected over centuries. I wonder how outsiders from urban Britain would be received if they began to acquire land to farm. On a recent trip to a rural part of Britain I was given an answer 'they wouldn't be welcome.'

Windrush

Meeting with Wilfred has reminded me of one of the big policy areas I oversaw while at Number 10. He and his family arrived in the United Kingdom as part of the Windrush generation. Back in the summer of 2019, when Boris Johnson and his team arrived in Downing Street, the issue of dealing with the Brexit deadlock was the number one priority for the government. There was a general election in the winter of 2019. This meant that there wasn't much time to really dig into other challenges that were inherited from the previous administration, including the Windrush scandal. Many people who had arrived in Britain legally, including many who had come from the Caribbean to help rebuild post-war Britain, had found themselves in a position where they could not prove their immigration status. This was primarily because the Home

Office had destroyed their records. The total number of those affected may never be known, but some have estimated the figure to be in the tens of thousands. Those who were known to have been affected had experienced some of the most horrific things because of having their status questioned. Some had been deported to countries where they no longer had any meaningful connection. Others died with the uncertainty still lingering over them. Many were unable to work and found themselves in a position of destitution. This was truly a source of national shame. They were made to feel like outsiders, despite many having previously worked in public services including the National Health Service.

As prime minister at the time when the scandal broke, Theresa May had acknowledged that the government was at fault. A compensation scheme was set up for the victims and an independent review to learn lessons was commissioned. The scheme was launched in April 2019 but had been plagued with challenges, which we inherited in the summer. We were continually assured by officials that these issues would be resolved and that the scheme would deliver. By February 2020 the Home Office had had enough time to demonstrate to us that they could make the scheme work, but were not making meaningful progress. Being unconvinced by the second-hand information I was receiving, I decided to convene a meeting of stakeholders in Number 10, including officials, campaigners and others who I felt could offer different perspectives. What I didn't want was a meeting that only involved prominent campaigners, who would inevitably brief the media, both in advance of the meeting and after. I didn't want any pictures of people outside Number 10, and attendees saying that they had gotten into the house and made demands. After all, I was a special advisor, not a minister. My focus was on delivering for the victims and prime minister, not having my name appear in newspapers.

I listened carefully during the meeting. I assured those present that this was now a priority, and that now that they had met me, they could be assured that they would see meaningful action taken. I made a few initial conclusions. The first was that the compensation scheme was not fit for purpose and that major changes would be necessary. The second conclusion was that the Home Office were relying too much on the louder voices within communities for engagement and they needed to hear more from different people if they were going to deliver the cultural change required within the department. People who understood how government worked and could grapple with some of the complicated policy areas to truly hold the Home Office to account.

I asked the civil servants to draw up a number of possible options for what we could do next, and from that advised the prime minister that we needed to dissolve two of the existing Windrush groups in the Home Office and the Ministry of Housing, Communities & Local Government. They would be replaced by a new cross-government working group that would be more effective. We also did something that many people did not think would happen: we accepted every single one of the recommendations from the lessons-learned review into the scandal on the day of publication. We hoped this would send very clear signals that we wanted to make sure that change came about. The former Home Secretary Priti Patel has many critics, but I often found that she was very empathetic on the issue of responding to the scandal. Perhaps this was because she felt that the story of many of the victims could have easily been her parents' story; they were immigrants from Uganda, of Indian heritage, who emigrated to the United Kingdom in the 1960s.

By December 2020 we could see that progress on the

implementation of the lessons-learned review was beginning to happen; but the compensation scheme was still not delivering. To my shock, in a meeting with officials it was revealed that some victims were being offered as little as £250 as an Impact on Life payment. This had never been mentioned to me before. I left my office in Number 10 straight after that meeting and walked over to the head of the Policy Unit, Munira Mirza, who was now based in 70 Whitehall, to discuss this. She asked what I thought we should do. I said for a start the minimum Impact on Life payment should be £10,000. She agreed. I then asked the Windrush Working Group to produce a note that would describe how this uplift could work. Once they had submitted this, I gave it to the Home Office and asked for them to look at how it could be implemented. I made it clear that this was not up for debate and needed to happen in time for a Christmas announcement. Within three weeks the scheme was upgraded, and we managed to even get a positive front page in the *Guardian*. I received a shout-out at the weekly meetings for special advisors (more commonly known among journalists as 'SpAd school').

One of the regrettable parts of politics is that you often have to be cut-throat in order to be able to drive something through. If you are not, officials have ways of resisting and eventually thwarting any desire for change. This is why a lot of good people do not get involved in politics. They don't want to be in such an environment. I would argue that people with the right intentions need to be in those spaces, but one must reconcile good intentions with the need to be as wise as a serpent. An effective special advisor should be respected for being across their brief, known for wanting to do the right thing, but also known for not being a pushover.

A challenge responding to the Windrush scandal was that it was very easy for campaigners to conflate having a Home Office that works better, that was less biased, more transparent, with the challenges of deporting foreign-born individuals who had committed crimes. There was a need to better inform the public around some facts. This included the reality that less than 1 per cent of all individuals who are deported from the United Kingdom following a conviction for a crime and a custodial sentence of twelve months or more are deported to Jamaica. Some headlines would have you think that the proportion was significantly higher.

There were often national security-related criminals who were deported, as well as serious sex offenders, rapists and murderers who had arrived in Britain as adults. We could not and cannot comment on individual cases, but there was definitely a lack of openness around the process for deportations. I began to change that, asking for the drawing up of easy-to-read information sheets and making sure they were being distributed. We sharpened the information that ministers were using in the House of Commons as well. If we were doing the right thing, then there were limited reasons to hide information. My view was that we worked for the public, who were entitled to have the facts before arriving at their conclusions. The Home Office is arguably the most complicated and challenging department; securing borders and protecting citizens are the two most basic responsibilities of any government, but are also the toughest of tasks. The department requires fundamental change, something the former home secretary has admitted on several occasions.

Sadly, I was not able to see through the work around the cultural reforms to the Home Office and getting the compensation scheme to deliver for the victims of the scandal. In time I think I would have been able to see the work through some of the big challenges; however, since I left Downing Street, immigration has once again become a topic of national debate. On the one hand many people understand the need for and benefits of skilled migration, but others see migrants as contributing to the strain on public services. Many agree that both positions have a degree of merit. Small-boat crossings across the English Channel have created a further wedge in the public consciousness, as smuggling gangs profit from this dangerous mode of transport. This context would have made my work more difficult to achieve. In fact, it feels as if we are heading towards a similar situation to that which led to the hostile environment policy, and subsequently the Windrush scandal.

My own views on immigration were influenced by a trip to Angola in Southern Africa with the then Lord Mayor of the City of London. It was during this visit as a young political hopeful that I could see how a developing nation was doing all that it could to protect the livelihoods of its own citizens, whilst trying to benefit from foreign direct investment and skills from abroad. It was then that I realised that it was not racist, but imperative, for every government to control the level of immigration to their country.

My challenge, and an argument that is very difficult to articulate in a short soundbite during a broadcast interview (I have tried), is that the current discourse around this subject pays a disproportionate amount of focus to illegal immigration, when in fact the majority of the people that migrate to Britain arrive on these shores legally.

Between June 2021 and June 2022 net migration to the United Kingdom was over half a million, with roughly 1.1 million long-term arrivals against 560,000 people leaving. Any country in the world (developed or developing) would find such volumes difficult to manage and sustain. It is reasonable to classify the above figures as mass migration. The current focus on illegal immigration (serious as it is) allows politicians to ignore the fact that the vast majority of migrants enter Britain legally. It demonises a group that in many respects are answering a call via our own Shortage Occupation List, which you will read about in the next chapter. Others arrive as high fee-paying international students and we have welcomed many from Hong Kong and Ukraine.

The current immigration levels are largely a matter of policy and not security. The solution to tackling mass migration is maximising the output of existing citizens and fixing structural problems around housing and wage stagnation, in order to reduce the demand for migrant workers. The focus on security when it comes to immigration creates a wedge for political advantage but will never provide significant results. It makes migrants the enemy, which I am uncomfortable with. For context: the migration figure of 1.1 million in the year ending June 2022 does not include those who arrived via small boat crossings.

Whether you agree with her or not, Theresa May was the last leader willing to be honest about the trade-offs required to reduce immigration. We need to have a national conversation about legal immigration rules at least as much as we focus on those arriving illegally. This must be a conversation that has the full context of need, which we will discuss in the next chapter.

Whatever would have happened had I stayed, it is one of my biggest regrets that seventy-five years on from Windrush, we still need to work to create a Home Office able to deal with the immigration question in a pragmatic, informative and compassionate way. We still do not know how to engage with outsiders, despite the value that they bring.

Chapter 4

The Keys to the Future

It can be difficult to imagine that a small island off the coast of continental Europe could have had control over one-quarter of the planet's land. Historians seeking to understand the reason Britain's island story is so unique somehow manage to ignore the one thing that is hidden in plain sight: the fact that Britain is a nation of outsiders, whose strength is based on the contributions of different cultures throughout millennia. The period AD 43 to 410 was one of classical antiquity, as large parts of Great Britain were under the rule of the Roman Empire. The Romans brought with them expertise that helped to develop the nation's agriculture, urban planning, industrial production and architecture. After decades of raiding British villages and sailing back to their homes on the European continent, the Anglo-Saxons put down permanent roots. Following the decay of the Roman Empire, the Anglo-Saxon period in Britain lasted for over six centuries – from AD 410 to AD 1066.

The Anglo-Saxon Outsiders

The period of Anglo-Saxon rule is known as the Dark Ages, mainly because written sources from the early years of Saxon invasion are scarce. Some historians even question whether it was a time of war or simply a period of migration and settling. It saw the breaking up of Roman Britannia into several separate kingdoms, mass religious conversion and, after the 790s, continual battles against a new set of invaders: the Vikings. By AD 650 there were seven separate kingdoms: Kent, Mercia (most of today's Midlands), Northumbria (parts of the north of England), East Anglia, Essex, Sussex and Wessex (most of the south-west). By AD 850 the seven kingdoms had been consolidated into three large Anglo-Saxon kingdoms: Northumbria, Mercia and Wessex. The Anglo-Saxons' contributions to Britain included new religious beliefs, military tactics and literature. Because they had no written language historians do not have a complete picture of their belief system before they converted to Christianity, but we can still see remnants of their religious traditions in the names of the week that we use to this day. Tuesday, for example, has its origin in the old English *Tiwesdæg*, 'day of Tīw', a Germanic god of war and the sky. Thursday originates from the old English *Thu(n)resdæg*, 'day of thunder', and is named after Thunor or Thor, the Germanic god of thunder. Perhaps the Anglo-Saxons' biggest contribution to Britain was their success in merging the different kingdoms into one unified force. For the first time, the people living on British soil viewed themselves as something bigger than their individual kingdoms. They became English.

1066 and On

The Norman Conquest was the eleventh-century invasion and occupation of England by an army made up of thousands of Normans, Bretons, Flemish, and men from other French provinces, all led by the Duke of Normandy, later styled William the Conqueror. On 14 October 1066, William led the famous

Battle of Hastings. Following the decisive victory he distributed land throughout England to his followers, where they built castles commanding military strongpoints. The Normans brought castles to Britain, but the major change from this period was the elimination of slavery in England; by the middle of the twelfth century, it had disappeared. Before this time Britons had enslaved themselves, something that the Normans viewed as barbaric. Five hundred years later (beginning officially in 1663) Britain would become the dominant force in the trans-Atlantic slave trade, enslaving Africans instead of their own citizens. The trans-Atlantic slave trade played an underpinning, if often forgotten, role in producing the raw materials that drove the eighteenth-century Industrial Revolution.

Trans-Atlantic Slave Trade

During the fifteenth century, Portugal became the first European nation to take part in African slave trading. This forced labour was procured initially for use in Atlantic African island plantations and then later for plantations in Brazil and the Caribbean. Enslaved people were sourced first from direct raids on coastal settlements, although this strategy was later revised due to it being costly and largely ineffective against West and Central African military strategies. In 1444, Portuguese marauders arrived in Senegal to assault and capture people using armed soldiers and deep-water vessels but were outmanoeuvred by the Senegalese military who were using shallow-water vessels better suited to the estuaries of the Senegalese coast. Poison arrows which were able to slip between armour were also used against the Portuguese soldiers, decimating their ranks. As a result, Portuguese traders largely abandoned direct assaults and instead concentrated on establishing mercantile relations with West and Central African leaders, who agreed to sell people taken from various wars or domestic trading into slavery. When it was later discovered that comparably peaceful relations with West and Central African leaders did not yield the volume of labour necessary to fuel colonial expansion, the Portuguese and their European competitors began to forge military alliances with certain African groups against their enemies, from which additional people were enslaved.

The Portuguese dominated the early trans-Atlantic slave trade in the sixteenth century, although other states competed to gain their market share. In order of total slaves trafficked after the Portuguese, these were Britain, France, the Netherlands, Spain, the United States (once formed), and Denmark. Access to the slave trade by such countries was initially acquired through privateering (attacking and looting enemy ships under the auspices of one's own government) during wars with the Portuguese rather than through direct trade. After the temporary alliance of Portugal and Spain in 1580, the Spanish disrupted the extant monopoly held by Portugal by offering direct slave trading contracts to other European merchants; this was known as the asiento system. The Dutch initially took advantage of this system to compete with Portugal and were eventually followed by the British and the French.

By the eighteenth century, at which point the trans-Atlantic slave trade was at its peak, Britain, followed by France and then Portugal, was the largest carrier of enslaved Africans. The overwhelming majority of forced labourers went to Brazil and the Caribbean, although a small proportion went to North America as well as parts of Central and South America. According to the database project slavevoyages.com, almost 11 million Africans were enslaved between 1514–1866. The slave trade was outlawed first by Denmark in 1792, then France in 1794 (on a temporary basis, to be reinstated in 1802), and then England in 1807. This was mainly due to large-scale slave rebellions, such as the Haitian revolution and the Jamaican Baptist War, which disrupted the revenue generated by plantations and incurred enormous military and logistical costs to the trading nations. Other significant events, such as the publication of Olaudah Equiano's autobiography in 1789, drew attention to the harm inflicted upon real, living, breathing people and attracted outcry from people of the trading states. This was complemented, although not instigated by, prominent political figures such as William Wilberforce and Abraham Lincoln. Slavery was outlawed much later than the slave trade (1833 in Britain, 1863 in the USA, 1888 in Brazil). The slave trade benefited many parts of British life and its economy, from the businessmen, financiers and landowners who ran and profited from the trade, to domestic businesses, workers and consumers. The trade involved thousands of slave ships, tens of thousands of sailors, and armies of British workers. The rewards of the trans–Atlantic slave system were everywhere. From the urban fabric of slave ports, to the grand homes of those made wealthy, to the jobs created in industrial cities, to the coffee and tobacco shops dotting British towns.

British Empire

The British Empire was the most extensive the world had ever seen and lasted for over 300 years, from the seventeenth century until the twentieth century. Neither its emergence nor its demise happened overnight. The empire grew with maritime capability, which saw the establishment of overseas colonies in the seventeenth century, whereas repeated rebellion and political pressure formed the antecedent to its decline. At its height in 1922, the British Empire covered roughly a quarter of the Earth's land surface and ruled over 458 million people, including large swathes of North America, Africa, Asia, and Australasia. The British Empire is often described using two terms to denote distinct historical periods. The 'First' British Empire refers to the seventeenth and eighteenth centuries, a period which is broadly accepted to be concluded by the American War of Independence, which saw Britain lose control of a huge part of its empire. The 'second' British Empire refers to events thereafter and prior to its decline, during which Britain established colonies in Australia, Trinidad, Ceylon, Singapore, and Hong Kong. In some senses, the British Empire never truly vanished, but morphed into the less imperial British Commonwealth which later became the Commonwealth of Nations. There are, however, certain events such as India securing its independence (1947) and the Malayan Emergency (1948–60) to which the decline of Britain's dominion is attributed. It is argued by some that the rise of the United States of America following World War Two and its opposition to imperialism influenced the transformation of the British state and its approach to negotiating geopolitics.

Commonwealth

The early Commonwealth, otherwise known as the British Commonwealth, was formed in 1926 at the Imperial Conference. This conference was attended by the leaders of semi-independent dominions under the British Empire, including Australia, Canada, India, the Irish Free State, New Zealand, and South Africa. At this conference, Britain and the Dominions agreed that each were equal members of a community within the British Empire, all of which owed allegiance to the British monarch. This was enshrined in the Balfour Declaration. Following the Imperial Conference, the Balfour Declaration was formalised officially in section 4 of the 1931 Westminster Statute. The modern Commonwealth, formed in 1949 through the London Declaration, was born out of a desire held by former Dominions of the British Empire to achieve independence whilst retaining certain commonalities in the approach and goals of economic and political systems. The Commonwealth is unlike other global organisations such as the United Nations or the World Trade Organization in the sense that it has no formal constitution nor any bylaws. Member countries do not have any legal or formal obligations to one another. Rather, they are bound by voluntary shared traditions, institutions, and experiences as well as mutual economic interest. This rubric is underpinned by principles which are enshrined in the various declarations issued by leaders and groups throughout the lifespan of the modern Commonwealth (post 1949). There are fifty-six independent countries which comprise the Commonwealth across Africa, Asia, the Caribbean and the Americas, Europe, and the Pacific, thirty-two of which are defined as 'small states' with a population of 1.5 million or less. Across its member countries, there are 2.5 billion people, with more than 60 per cent aged twenty-nine or under. All members have an equal say regardless of size or wealth.

What has allowed Britain continuously to punch above its proverbial weight, to be uniquely successful, is the contribution of outsiders. Having outsiders entering, be it voluntarily or through force, and adding value is in the DNA of these islands. When we reflect on why Britain is such a melting pot of people from different nationalities, it is because of the historical context that you have just read. To use the title of Ian Sanjay Patel's book 'we are here, because you were there.' This reality cannot change because it is also key to our survival.

Today, the Home Office has what we call a Shortage Occupation List (SOL). These are the occupations where there is a specific skills shortage in the United Kingdom. It is easier for people with the qualifications to do those jobs to migrate to Britain. Mainstays on this list include chemical scientists, civil engineers, mechanical engineers, programmers and software development professionals. Other roles that are inconvenient for politicians to admit and are on the list include health and social care workers. It is estimated that there are 1.67 million health and social care jobs in the United Kingdom, a number that is very likely to keep rising due to the UK having an aging population. The median age is forty in England, and forty-two in Scotland and Wales respectively. 18.4 per cent of England is over sixty-five years old. This figure is due to rise by 5.7 percentage points by 2043, to almost one in four people. Who will look after our elderly? The answer to this question in many other countries is their relatives, but Britain culturally has shifted to preferring to outsource this responsibility to local authorities and the like. There are other economic pressures that have influenced this shift, particularly limited space because of house price inflation driven primarily by a lack of supply.

Meanwhile, the average age of the Indian population is twenty-eight. In Nigeria, the most populous nation in Africa, the average age is just eighteen. In 2001 Goldman Sachs claimed that by 2050 the four BRIC economies of Brazil, Russia, India and China would come to dominate the global economy. South Africa was added to the list in 2010. After the BRICS, the next eleven, also known as N-11, are the eleven countries that are poised to become the biggest economies in the world in the twenty-first century. The next eleven are Bangladesh, Egypt, Indonesia, Iran, Mexico, Nigeria, Pakistan, Philippines, South Korea, Turkey and Vietnam. Note that none of the emerging markets highlighted can be classified as being part of the West. No European Union countries. The internationalists who found the Brexit cause appealing were not necessarily the same as the xenophobic protectionists who do not understand that protectionism has limited long-term value, and that Britain has a long international history that has been the key to its success for centuries. India, which in 2020 was pushed back to being the world's sixth-biggest economy, will again overtake the UK to become the fifth-largest in 2025 and race to the third spot by 2030, according to the Centre for Economics and Business Research (CEBR). At present India does not have a trade deal with the United States or European Union, and for there to be a meaningful trading relationship between Britain and India there will need to be some compromises around immigration rules. This is something that they have made clear. Stay with me, I am going somewhere with this.

A New Silk Road: The Global Stage

Over 100 companies from emerging markets made their initial public offerings in 2021 on local or foreign exchanges. Altogether, they raised $228 billion via listings, about a 31 per cent increase from 2020, according to data compiled by Bloomberg. Meanwhile,

China continues to expand its influence across the world, despite reported human rights violations including the persecution of Uyghur Muslims. The Belt and Road Initiative, formerly known as One Belt One Road, is a global infrastructure development strategy adopted by the Chinese government in 2013 to invest in nearly seventy countries and international organisations. It is considered a centrepiece of the Chinese leader Xi Jinping's foreign policy. This policy is a reimagining of the original Silk Road – a network of trade routes connecting China and the Far East with the Middle East and Europe. The Silk Road was created when the Han Dynasty in China officially opened trade with the West in 130 BC. Routes established remained in use until AD 1453, when the Ottoman Empire boycotted trade with China and closed them. But the routes had a lasting impact on culture and history as well as on trade.

Outsiders Remain the Key

What does this have to do with outsiders, I hear you say? Well, I submit to you that the key to Britain's future, both to remain competitive on a global stage and to meet its domestic needs, will be outsiders – in every sense. Not only will Britain continue to rely on global talent to meet its workforce needs but it will also need people who think differently to help navigate tomorrow's world through innovation. More interestingly, as Britain attempts to build relationships with emerging economies, the diaspora, people with links to countries like India and Nigeria, could play a decisive role in building bridges and helping Britain to grasp opportunities. They will have connections and know-how that money can't buy. We already have some great examples of such people in the world of business.

Lakshmi Mittal is an Indian-born steel magnate based in the United Kingdom. He is the executive chairman of ArcelorMittal, the world's largest steelmaking company, as well as chairman of stainless-steel manufacturer Aperam. In 2005, *Forbes* ranked Mittal as the third-richest person in the world, making him the first Indian to be ranked in the top ten in the publication's annual list of the world's richest people. He sits on the World Steel Association's executive committee and the board of Goldman Sachs.

Manoj Badale is one of the top Asian stars in the UK tech scene, having co-founded more than fifteen businesses since 1998. He is mostly known for his association with the lucrative Indian Premier League, as lead owner of the Rajasthan Royals cricket team. He is also the chairman of the British Asian Trust, one of King Charles's charities.

There is also a new generation of British Asian entrepreneurs creating jobs and value in Britain. One such example is Umar Kamani, who along with his brother Adam co-founded fast-fashion brand PrettyLittleThing in 2012, when he was just twenty-four. PLT, as it is also known, gained significant traction when the likes of Miley Cyrus, Michelle Keegan, Rita Ora, Jessie J and Nicki Minaj were all spotted wearing the product range. Their revenue in 2020 was a reported £516.3 million. The brothers' father, Mahmud Kamani, is the owner of Boohoo, the original and largest UK fast-fashion online retailer. Though there have been a number of controversies around the company, including accusations of modern-day slavery within their organisation's supply chains, there is no doubt that they have been a phenomenal business success.

Another person who epitomises the value opportunity, albeit in a different way, is Samir Puri, the author of the book *The*

Great Imperial Hangover. Samir finished a three year stint in 2022 as a senior fellow at the International Institute for Strategic Studies. He was a civil servant for six years, working in the Foreign Office between 2009 and 2015. We first met while I was in Number 10. I had read a review of his book in *The Times* and his work fascinated me. He was a historian focused on trying to find a way to help people grapple with the legacy of the British Empire without seeking to pick a side or to cast judgement. He had received some criticism for taking such a stance, but I believed he was on to something and was keen for the government to work with him.

We are meeting via virtual conference call as he is currently based in Singapore. To start, I ask if his upbringing was part of why he was so interested in the field of research that he has specialised in, foreign affairs. 'My family is international by background,' he says. 'My parents were born in Kenya and Tanzania, respectively, and they are Indian. As I found out much later in life, it is because of the British Empire that Indians would have ended up in Africa. My mother's parents resolved to send her to London to be schooled in the seventies. It has been three continents in three generations, so thinking internationally is kind of in my blood. And you can't turn away from that. I studied a history and politics degree at university, and I really wanted to use my intellectual passions as I went into the world of work. So that informed all later choices. It still does. It's just a massive privilege to work on issues that I find personally interesting.'

I ask Samir what it was like working in the then Foreign & Commonwealth Office (FCO), widely thought of as the most prestigious department in the UK government. 'I applied to the civil service right after I finished my degrees in 2003. I was twenty-two and had done my masters straight after my bachelors. I never got very far with my application.' In fact, Samir failed his application for the civil service every year for four years. 'That was my annual tradition. Applying to the civil service and failing.' Sometimes he got reasonably far . . . to assessment centres. In the end he got a different job in Cambridge at a think tank as a junior researcher. This experience at the think tank eventually helped to get him into the civil service at the age of twenty-seven. On his experience trying to get into the civil service he says, 'I think for me, it was if at first you don't succeed, try several more times. You find that you just don't quite speak the right language straight away. I always joke with friends that my most valuable qualification is my GCSE in drama. It helps when you hang out with enough people who are from the sort of backgrounds that are more traditionally recruited. So rather than paying for that private education, learn how to talk like that. Learn how to present like them. Because you're not going to get that at home. You're not going to get that conversation at the dinner table. You're not going to have an uncle who is well connected or works in the civil service quite high up or was in the military. You just don't have that. You are kind of starting from scratch in the UK.'

His persistence is admirable, and it is clear that for him the challenge was more to do with not having the know-how when it came to navigating the application process. He continues, 'You've got to build your own networks. You've got to build up a way of presenting yourself that passes an interview. With university you've only got one shot. If you get into university or not, most people don't really delay it, but with your working life, you can keep trying. I was really, really pleased when I finally got a job at the FCO. Getting in after failing four times. They don't discourage you from applying again. I think sometimes they say give it two years, but they don't mind if you apply again.'

I ask Samir if he faced any challenges once he finally got into the civil service, or was it plain sailing from there? 'I'm proud to have worked for HMG (Her Majesty's Government). That's a real source of pride in some respects. What's great is no one can take that away from me. It's like if you'd been in the army for five minutes, you've at least made it in. I was proud to contribute to policy outcomes and meeting challenges like countering terrorism on the ground level. At the same time, I was quite surprised by how old-fashioned the institution was. I should moderate that by saying I did join the year of the financial crash. Departments had constraints, but I really felt that within the civil service, some departments were modernising slower than other parts of British society. In my opinion, if the public institution is public facing, like the police or the National Health Service, they deal with the public daily. If they don't reflect the diversity of that public, they can't function. Sometimes it takes a catastrophe like the murder of Stephen Lawrence to really move them forward, to overcome some of its own inner biases, but with some of the central government institutions, especially my area of expertise, foreign policy, defence, they're much further away from the public. Foreign affairs are not things that people talk about on an everyday basis. They don't have a tangible experience, as they would with schools or hospitals or roads. You just don't have that tangible touch point with it. Those departments haven't had that much pressure to modernise as quickly as a result. And they manage some of the most traditional areas of policy.'

I can relate to much of what Samir is saying. When I was first offered the opportunity to become a special advisor, one of the things that I was told was that even if I was a SpAd (Westminster lingo for special advisor) for five minutes no one will be able to take away the fact that I had served in the highest office in the land. This idea of some parts of society being yet to modernise because they remain largely hidden and the preserve of certain groups is interesting. It's a theme that we will return to.

Samir explains that there are certain unspoken normative expectations of staff, and at the FCO it is easy to see some colleagues fitting in more naturally, whether it's how they dress, how they talk or even down to their family connections. Some will say their father had worked there thirty years ago, or people who went to the same school. 'Now, it doesn't stop you from being there and contributing and working. That's the great thing about meritocracy when it works, but in terms of progression, I'll be very honest. If I had stayed and had a twenty-, thirty-year career at the FCO I would have been part of spearheading the department becoming more diverse rather than following the footsteps of others. I didn't really want those experiences. It can be draining fighting battles. On a positive note, we are at the edge of the wave of increasing diversity, it's going to wash over and no one wants to stop it because everyone understands that the times are changing, but I didn't really want to be in the middle of things. I had enough minor experiences, whether misunderstandings or things that were just second nature to others and not to me, which worked better for a broadly homogenous white public-school-educated entity. Once I had my PhD, I thought, well, I'll take these experiences and I'll use them in a slightly different way rather than being . . . maybe the poster child is the wrong phrase. But being seen as the person who's forging ahead.'

I feel like Samir is holding back on unpacking some of his experiences but decide not to prod. He is being quite the diplomat, pointing to 'misunderstandings'. Whatever they were, they were impactful enough to make this highly intelligent individual decide there was a better path for him to chart, leaving behind a career he had tried for four years to obtain.

It can be exhausting having to be the person who is having to blaze a trail. It's not something everyone wants to do and, to be fair to Samir, on his own journey he has found a fascinating way to contribute to international relations and the debate about British identity. If he was still a civil servant, he would not have been able to do this. Now that he is in Singapore, he is experiencing a different type of outsider status. 'In terms of how Britain is perceived globally, just imagine for decades, possibly even centuries, if you want to go that far into history, the face you recognise representing British diplomacy, military affairs, business has generally been a white male. It makes sense when you consider the ethnic make-up of the nation was largely homogenous for a long time. In Britain, we don't have a Barack Obama figure. His elevation was now twelve, thirteen years ago. We don't really have that reservoir of people like Colin Powell or Condoleezza Rice. It's only now beginning to happen. I did a book presentation in my office here in Singapore. We had some fantastic senior retired Singaporean diplomats. One of them is eighty years old. He was educated in Britain and knows the country well. He straight away mentions Rishi Sunak (who was Chancellor of the Exchequer at the time of the gathering in question). He mentions Sajid Javid (former Health Secretary). In diplomatic fashion, he flatters me, saying we also now have Samir Puri. What he was trying to say was, look, your country is changing and this is a good representation of it, but actually that's very new. I don't think you could have even said that ten years ago.'

He has a point. In 2010 Sayeeda Warsi (now Baroness Warsi), a member of the House of Lords, was the only non-white member of the British Cabinet. We have since had the most diverse Cabinets in British history, and of course the first prime minister of Asian descent.

Samir wanted to go abroad for the next phase of his life. There were opportunities in the Middle East, but he remembered what the perception of him as an Asian in the Middle East would be. 'Nobody's going to believe I'm British. They of course employ lots of Indians, Bangladeshis, Pakistanis to do labouring and low management jobs. I don't blame the Saudis for stereotyping as to what representing Britain abroad looks like. But again, I sort of feel that, if I'm honest, if I was advising students, those are the sorts of nuances I'd encourage them to think about with working abroad. What sort of structures are in place and how are you going to be perceived if you're not white?'

When it comes to increasing ethnic minority representation there is a feeling of urgency among a lot of people, but at the same time there is a counter-argument that Britain is actually on schedule if you look at when people arrived in the country, primarily from across the Commonwealth, and then when people went into higher education. When we break down the data by first generation, second generation, etc, a pattern of progress generally emerges. Post Windrush generation, and then the sixties, seventies, eighties. It would be interesting to do some sort of extrapolation to see where, at this rate of progress, we should be by 2050, for example. I put this to Samir.

'I agree. The chronology that you paint is correct, but it creates a curious paradox, because Britain is such an old country with a long history. Strangely, though, you could argue that though the United States is a younger country, when it comes to this topic the US has a longer direct story, in terms of mass migration of people from diverse backgrounds. It does take generations for people to work through educational opportunities and to maximise chances. Even just our parents' generation's experiences, the eighties, and the late seventies. They faced pretty serious overt discrimination that is less acceptable today, though challenges still persist. Even watching familiar sitcom reruns from the nineties, you see some of the humour. You think, how the hell did you make a joke about that? And there are things like blacking up faces, which were still in sitcoms not that long ago. But it takes work and the desire to put the work in to change things positively. That desire wasn't necessarily there even as recently as the eighties and the nineties. And I think that shifted because there are more people who are deeply embedded into communities, which is different from the experiences of new arrivals. More diverse people in hiring positions. Now it looks odd if you don't have some diversity in the media, or in an organization. Some feel the pace is slow. For me, as long as you get to the destination somehow, that's the most important thing. It takes time, but it also takes work.'

I like that. *It takes time, but it also takes work.* A very perceptive point. I move the conversation on to his book and ask him to explain how it came about.

'It's meant to be a fair-minded view as to what the end of empires has meant for different parts of the world. I took this approach because I work on foreign affairs. I thought I could be reasonably fair-minded because my roots are from outside of the UK, outside of Europe. I was really into World War Two history. My mother would buy me colouring-in books with pictures of tanks. That's the sort of thing I liked and these childhood experiences were filtered through a very patriotic Churchill Battle of Britain lens. Now that I was older, I wanted to add to these narratives by taking in different stories from different parts of the world.'

Samir seems to be in his element now that the conversation has shifted to history. I listen as he continues: 'For me, when it comes to history, there isn't usually a right or wrong way to interpret it. It's normally the stories that resonate most closely with you because those are the stories that are told the most. The ones that are amplified the loudest. I didn't want to write a book only about the British Empire's legacy [that has subsequently been done]. I didn't want to do it because it's not the full story. It lacks context. To say that Britain is the only country that has massive complexities in terms of its population composition, in terms of its history, in terms of its story, I find strange. Sometimes you hear descriptions attached to particular countries as if they're the only ones that have these issues. I can't think of a single country that hasn't had a complex history and that doesn't have some kind of trauma around that. And that has different parts to its population. There are some countries, you can say, which have got quite homogenous populations, but most countries have got a version of this.'

Describing his book, he says: 'The book is meant to be about how the stories feel different depending on who you are. If your ancestors benefited from or took part in the material experience of empire then it doesn't mean that they were necessarily murderers. They could have been missionaries, teachers or administrators. For example, I know a guy whose granddad was a teacher in Kenya at the height of the British rule. He never carried a gun. He was there because the British had colonised Kenya. That's the only reason, otherwise he just wouldn't have been there. And there may be certain types of stories that are passed down through the generations about foreign travel, about how Britain engages with the world. I also felt that there were stories that you are not told if your family came from the former colonies and they're not white or they are not told in their fullness. It is important to give everyone the opportunity to understand a fuller history and the many perspectives. Just taking account of those differences rather than ignoring and washing over them is key. It's not everything, but it's another part of how you move Britain forward.'

Interpreting Britain's colonial history has become a significant area of tension in recent times. I put to Samir that what he is saying is that for both sides of the debate there is a deficit, and both need to overcome it. That those who are very adamant that the British Empire was uniquely evil have not really reflected on what was going on across the world over centuries, if not millennia. And that those who have a very positive view of British history perhaps are not taking a balanced view and appreciating that a lot of people are still living through the trauma of the British Empire across continents. There is still a hangover of sorts. That period was not so long ago. A bit of give and take by both sides is needed.

'You've summed it up very well. I'd also add that both sides have got their champions. They've got their loud voices. They've got some skilled writers and advisors. They can each assemble arguments to make their case look strong, but ultimately neither case can win because these cases reflect different parts of the British soul. We can't just ignore parts of the population. You've got to give them something as well, so they feel included. This is another point we reflected on last year when I fed in my policy paper to the Commission on Race and Ethnic Disparities.'

A New Commission

This is the Commission that was launched in the United Kingdom following the murder of George Floyd in the United States. In May 2020, Black Lives Matter protests had spread across the world like wildfire. The demonstrations in the United Kingdom began on 28 May and lasted for three weeks and three days. The record for the former prime minister Boris Johnson's most watched social media post was his statement in response to the Black Lives Matter protests, with six million views on Twitter alone. This was many times more than when Johnson asked the entire country to stay at home for the first lockdown of the coronavirus pandemic a few months prior. I had given black newspaper the *Voice* the statement in advance as an exclusive. We wanted to show that the prime minister was not ignoring the strength of feeling and was talking directly to black Britons. Their website subsequently crashed as they could not handle the traffic, such was the interest in hearing what Johnson had to say.

I was in the room as he recorded the statement that I helped to write in response to the protests. It began with these words: 'The death of George Floyd took place thousands of miles away – in another country, under another jurisdiction – and yet we simply cannot ignore the depth of emotion that has been triggered by that spectacle, of a black man losing his life at the hands of the police. In this country and around the world his dying words – I can't breathe – have awakened an anger and a widespread and incontrovertible, undeniable feeling of injustice, a feeling that people from black and minority ethnic groups do face discrimination: in education, in employment, in the application of the criminal law.

'And we who lead and who govern simply can't ignore those feelings because in too many cases, I am afraid, they will be founded on a cold reality.'

During the recording I had to stay composed, knowing that Johnson was speaking to the nation, including many people who I shared part of my identity with who had been outside Downing Street protesting. Such was the strength of feeling that people from different backgrounds and ethnicities, who had never marched or protested about anything before, were willing to risk their own safety in the middle of a pandemic. I remember going home one evening during that time. I went into my home office and logged on to one of my social media accounts. The civil rights campaigner Reverend Al Sharpton had just delivered the eulogy at George Floyd's memorial service. I played the clip on my feed. His words pierced through me. 'George Floyd's story has been the story of black folks. Because ever since 401 years ago . . . the reason we could never be who we wanted and dream of being [was] because you kept your knees on our neck. We were smarter than the under-funded schools you put us in, but you had your knee on our neck. We could be running corporations and not hustling on the street but your knee's on our neck. We had creative skills. We could do whatever anybody else could but could not get your knee off our neck.' As the reverend continued, I began to cry, alone in my office. I wept. I am not sure why exactly. Perhaps it was because I could feel the pain of others and felt helpless; even as the most senior black person in Downing Street, I felt disempowered. I was caught in the middle. To some people in Downing Street those protesters were simply the other side of a culture war that they were determined to win. Those protesting were the enemy, and not part of the population they were being paid to serve. For other people who I knew personally, they felt like they could finally release what they had been suppressing inside of them. Not quite knowing how to navigate this unique moment in time, or not feeling like they quite belonged anywhere. They felt like outsiders in Britain, but also outsiders in their parents' or grandparents' homelands. Where could they feel accepted? Where could they feel included? Which side was I to choose? Whose feelings were more aligned to the facts? How could I help to make things better? If I was not at Number 10, would I have joined one of the protests? I was genuinely lost. But we were in the middle of a pandemic; lives and livelihoods were at stake. I had to find the strength to carry on.

The Sunday morning after the prime minister's response to the protests, I woke up to a message that the prime minister had agreed to establish a new commission into race and ethnic disparities, and he wanted to announce it the following day in a column for the *Telegraph*. It was very strange to be launching a commission over a weekend because the prime minister felt it was a good idea, but alas, there we were. We had less than twenty-four hours to establish the initial parameters. I needed to get to work! Once we got through the *Telegraph* announcement and the terms of reference were agreed, the next challenge was to recruit commissioners. People willing to follow the evidence, was the brief. I am the co-founder of an executive headhunting firm, so recruiting senior people to a board (or commission) was something very aligned with my skills. We picked, among others, the chair of the Youth Justice Board for England and Wales, a space scientist and an internationally renowned economist. We wanted people who would follow the evidence. Unfortunately, this principle was not applied in a uniform way. The area of most contention was who would chair the commission. My opinion was that we needed someone like the veteran broadcaster Sir Trevor McDonald or chair of the John Lewis Partnership, Dame Sharon White. I spoke to both. Although they might not have agreed to take on the role of chair if they were offered it, they were the types of people with the gravitas to follow the evidence and bring people together.

A High Court judge was also an option. Others believed that educationalist Tony Sewell would be the right person. I remembered him from my university days, working with his charity Generating Genius to encourage young people from underrepresented groups into science and technology careers. Though I really liked him and felt he would be a good commissioner, I thought that we owed him a duty of care not to make him chair. Others disagreed. I made clear that it would be unfair on Tony as he had written numerous articles that clearly showed he could be seen to have prejudged the findings, and that it was also unfair to put him under the inevitable media spotlight. I could foresee a disaster. I should have spoken up louder – or insisted the prime minister be given more detail. But I didn't. That was a failure on my part. By the time the commission had published their report I had already decided to leave Downing Street (more on this in chapter 6) and was supporting the deployment of the corona-virus vaccines before my exit.

Rightly or wrongly, I decided I wouldn't read the final report until the summer of 2021 so that if asked for my thoughts, I could honestly say I hadn't read it. I had also put so much work into helping to form the commission, managing the various commissioners, and ensuring they had everything they needed to be able to produce something that fulfilled the core mission.

I knew I'd be asked what I thought of the report, but I felt very conflicted about it. When I eventually read it, I couldn't stop myself from reading as if I was still a special advisor with an advance copy, making comments and marking areas where I would have asked for points to perhaps be reflected on or unpacked. I could see that the three-page foreword was what was clearly given to the media in advance. The tone was strikingly different from that in the main text, although that too was far from perfect. Usually, forewords are less than a page in length and very surface-level, thanking those involved and pointing to a positive direction of travel. I would have advised against publishing all the sections at once as it was clear that some sections were at a more advanced stage than others. The differences in length of the four main sections pointed to this as well. I suspect they felt under pressure to publish it all as they had missed initial deadlines, but having an experienced special advisor on their side helping them to navigate this would have helped.

I would have identified the confusing messages linked to their stance on institutional racism and asked them to be clearer. The document affirmed the widely adopted and intentionally broad definition produced by Sir William Macpherson following the murder of Stephen Lawrence, and then offered up a new definition without providing a rationale for how they developed it. It was also unclear which definition was being used for the purposes of the report or which definition they found no evidence of; this was also the main point that triggered a significant backlash. This was also the foundation for the document and meant that they were picking a side in an unnecessary culture-war argument. The document contained several statements that sadly lacked intellectual robustness. I do not know what happened after my involvement with the commission ended. I can only conclude that there were commissioners who could not bring themselves to accept the evidence because it would compromise their perception among the public as 'anti-woke'. I do know that before I had stepped aside, at least three commissioners had flagged what they perceived to be clear evidence of institutional racism. I guess they were never going to win that battle. Privately, people who were sent out to defend the document later confided in me that this was also their conclusion, but they felt they had to support their associates. It wasn't all bad, but with so many people waiting for the commission to fail it needed to be watertight. The government's official response to the report – Inclusive Britain – was received positively by most, demonstrating that the whole episode that sparked the reaction to the report was unnecessary. People can blame Boris Johnson for a lot of things. He has made statements in the past that were clearly inappropriate. But the situation with the commission was not of his making. He trusted people to do a job for him, including myself, and he was badly let down.

A True History Curriculum

There is a challenge for a lot of people around how they locate themselves in Britain's island story. That tension plays out, for example, in academia. Schools minister Nick Gibb regularly argued that there was enough room within the curriculum for people to teach a balanced history, but that is not necessarily what a lot of young people or teachers themselves think is the case. We asked the Commission on Race and Ethnic Disparities to look at this. The objective was to try to find a solution to get the information that is required for a balanced curriculum to be delivered in schools.

Samir and others were asked to be part of helping to make this happen as expert advisors to the commissioners. He tells me, 'It's essential that the curriculums keep up with needs, demands and trends. The British population is more diverse than it's ever been before, so it's got to change. I think it's possible to do it if you also work it into other subjects instead of teaching it in general history. Things like when you deliver PGCE teacher training. I think it is possible that rather than taking a position on the British Empire you can just introduce its existence. Rather than doing a balance sheet, these are the good things, the bad things, you can just point to some of the tangible things that still exist now. I'll just give you two. Number one. Why are there so many people who look like you and me in Britain today? A lot of that came after World War Two, especially when the colonies became independent. Another is why do countries like Australia, New Zealand have a small British emblem flying on the corner of the flags? What is that about? A few hundred years ago, settlers from England, Scotland and Wales went there and established communities that displaced the locals. Many things have happened since, but there's a strong link because the modern Antipodean nations' existence is owed to the British Empire.'

But would this really make a difference, Samir? 'A couple of facts. I know it sounds elementary but, you know, otherwise I'll bet most children simply would not know. I look at textbooks that are available that do a reasonable job of presenting a fair and balanced view. I think the problem with the teaching curriculum is that there are so many kids, so few classroom hours. You've got to kind of cut to the chase on some of these things, while also giving some sense of wider European and world history. That's hard. If you can present some facts versus what I received at school covering the British Empire, which was absolute deafening silence, it could really help to at least lay some objective foundations. Years later, you reflect on this. Like, how did you get through school, and no one mentioned the British Empire? We got loads of Nazi Germany, Russian Revolution history, and we got lots of Tudors and Henry VIII. We got World War Two. But no empire.'

I agree with Samir on there not being enough hours in a week to teach a well-rounded history curriculum and empathise with the challenges for teachers. A project I was keen to put to the prime minister was some form of digital museum that would curate objects from across the country. This would be a digital project whereby a network of museums contributed to a really dynamic platform. All of the wonderful objects that are currently in basements gathering dust would now have a virtual home. It could tell interesting dynamic stories; for example, a third-generation British Indian who wanted to be able to find out how their family arrived in Britain, perhaps using all the various artefacts, would be able to start today and go all the way back thousands of years, visiting many museums through the prism of a laptop. There would also be ways to incentivise actual visits to museums, something that remains a middle-class activity despite most UK museums having free entry.

I think being an outsider is important to a lot of people because it really energises them. Especially if they are not defining themselves by what they are against but what they are for. Many people are attempting to grapple with and understand the past, often through the lens of the present, but to quote Malcolm X, 'The future belongs to those who prepare for it today'. The future of Britain, and many other Western nations, will be determined by how great a relationship they have with emerging markets and how much they can value and utilise those with direct relationships with those nations. Part of that value will mean grappling with history in a much more inclusive and objective fashion, and having environments that allow people like Samir to feel like they can flourish. He chose to leave the most prestigious department in government. That must be viewed as a huge loss to our civil service. One can only imagine how many similar stories there are of demographic outsiders choosing to leave. I am also one such example. Something needs to change.

Chapter 5

Inspire Others

Today, you can be from a disadvantaged background and become very privileged. I am now afforded opportunities that I could never have dreamed of as a child. My children will benefit from the social capital that their parents have accumulated. Despite this progress, many individuals from humble beginnings still find it virtuous to identify primarily with their backgrounds (or their parents' or grandparents' backgrounds), even as they move up the socioeconomic ladder. We hear people extol their working-class beginnings, for example, while it has become very fashionable in the UK to make a big deal about northern roots as the two main political parties jostle to appeal to voters in those regions. Being authentic is easy when it's trendy, but less so when your difference makes you less popular or more open to attack. If you are the only woman in a high-pressured leadership team, or if you are a person of a certain faith (or no faith) during a period of heightened tensions, you may not want to be viewed as different. Imagine how a woman in a hijab feels about leaving the house after a terrorist attack by an extremist has taken place. Her difference becomes more noticeable than it already was – both to her and to members of the public. She pays for the sins of someone else regardless of what she may or may not believe.

This chapter will explore the challenge of remaining authentic as an outsider when it would be easier to fade into the background. It will also show how outsiders have the power to inspire others.

I'm meeting Baroness Sayeeda Warsi in the House of Lords. She served as Conservative Party co-chair between 2010 and 2012, during the coalition government led by former prime minister David Cameron, becoming the first Muslim Cabinet member in the history of British politics. Sayeeda also served as the minister of state for the Foreign and Commonwealth Office and as the minister of state for Faith and Communities (styled as 'Senior Minister of State') until her resignation, citing her disagreement with the government's position on the Israel–Gaza conflict, in August 2014. We sit down in one of the busy tearooms in the Lords and it becomes very apparent to me that Sayeeda stands out. Most members of the House of Lords are significantly older (the average age at the time of our meeting is seventy-one). There are other women peers; I notice Baroness Dido Harding, who led the government's test and trace programme during the pandemic, at the table to my left. There are also other peers with Asian heritage, including Lord Tariq Ahmad, the Foreign Office minister, who we passed on the way in. But Baroness Warsi still stands out. She exudes radiance. Perhaps it's the combination of her strong Yorkshire accent and accompanying vivacious energy that sets her apart. It seems to be something she is also aware of, but not necessarily in a positive way. She tells me, 'I have so many colleagues of colour here in the House of Lords, the Commons as well, who say that the spotlight doesn't leave you and it follows you around everywhere. And if I look back now with some of the things that are happening in government, you know, I couldn't have gotten away with it. I suppose that is what makes you an outsider, the fact that you feel that you're going to be judged by a higher level of standards than anybody else is going to be.'

I certainly remember working exceptionally harder than some special advisor colleagues in Downing Street, which was often noted to me in private. It only became an issue when those same people were being paid more than me, something that was in the process of being rectified before my exit. Part of the root of this desire to prove my value was a combination of my own insecurities and competitive nature. I had come in as a relatively unknown quantity, whereas others had less to prove. Maybe they felt more secure in their position.

Psychological Safety

Psychological safety, as defined and developed by William A. Kahn, is feeling able to show and employ oneself without fear of negative consequences to self-image, status or career. People feel safe in situations in which they trust that they would not suffer for their personal engagement or beliefs. The concept was first illustrated through a study of moments of personal engagement and disengagement in the workplace. The study proposed that individuals oscillate between engaging their true selves at work and defending or hiding their true selves, depending on the present social conditions. When employees felt safe and able to engage in their work cognitively, emotionally and physically, their true self becomes aligned with their role and purpose within the organisation; they are fully engaged in their work without fear of repercussions.

I ask Sayeeda if she thought that feeling like one could not get away with the same things as others was partly because some people would judge her differently, but also partly because some people were just more comfortable with mediocrity. She replies, 'I'm not so sure, when you are the first. And remember I was also the only non-white member of the Conservative-led coalition Cabinet. There was no other person of colour around that table. You visibly look different right from the outset. The second thing was I was very vocal. I was not interested in melting away into the background. I wanted to use my position to bring about positive change, which for some people was uncomfortable. If you don't make people feel uncomfortable, then nobody's going to come after you, are they, because you're not really making a difference. But when the status quo starts to be challenged – it may be just because of your presence, or it may be because of what you're saying or what you're doing or what you're proposing – they make sure that they show how different doesn't work.'

I remember quite clearly the times when Sayeeda was under considerable scrutiny. For someone who had not had a traditional path into politics it must have been very tough. One of the things I remember was when there were suggestions that Sayeeda had connections in questionable parts of the world and business interests with people who were questionable characters. No evidence was found. She continues, 'They also said that people like me don't understand how the system works. You see, what's going on in more recent times, the level of corruption – there's no other word for it – the level of sleaze, the level of rule-breaking, none of that would have even been close to okay for me. You just don't have the privilege of being rubbish, is probably the best way of putting it. We don't.

You can't be as incompetent, and you can't be as inefficient . . . you can't be as crap in any form of high office.'

I can relate in a way to Sayeeda's experience in politics, though her achievements were of course on another level to my own. We both left when it would have been convenient for us to stay in our jobs. We both left on what we felt were points of principle we were unwilling to turn a blind eye to.

An Outsider in Cabinet

I want to move the conversation to her experiences as a Cabinet member. Were there things that made her feel like she didn't belong in such high office? 'Class was a huge issue. I didn't have a great education. I eventually went to a good university, got a great degree, but you know, I hadn't had a lot of grounding. I hadn't learned Latin. I never studied classics. I didn't have the breadth of experiences growing up that my other colleagues had. We never had foreign holidays. I think my class was always an issue. During what they call the water cooler conversation there'd be conversations going on about certain music and certain art that I did not know about. I thought I could either try to blag my way through, or I could just say I did not know about it.' She pauses. '. . . Well, they don't know about what it's like being on the street and know about what it was like growing up, having to fight for every single thing. They don't know what it's like facing gender bias from the day you're born. My experience was valuable, and I had to use that experience at this table. Also, I think what I realised was that by the time I came to Cabinet, I'd already run two businesses and there were people who hadn't run anything. It might not be a lot, but I knew about the Working Time Directive. And I actually knew about payroll. I knew about corporation tax, and I knew about all those things because I'd actually run businesses. I've hired people. I've tried to keep money in people's pockets by trying to keep the business going. I think it's when I stepped back and realised how my life experience may be different, but actually it brings a skillset that is useful around that table. That's when I probably realised that I'm going to talk about things as I see them. I'm not going to just try and understand everybody else's view of the world and try and kind of filter my lens through that. But I'm going to try and show them a different lens because what is the point of not doing it?'

This acceptance of who you are and what you bring to the table has no better visual depiction than Sayeeda's first day in government, when she arrived in a bright pink shalwar kameez, a traditional Asian garment. It reminds me of the image of the late Bernie Grant entering the House of Commons wearing an agbada, an African robe. That image always brings a smile to my face. Sayeeda reflects: 'Even on the day I was appointed to Cabinet, I thought, did I ever imagine that a person like me would end up around the Cabinet table? I had to take that into account and not shy away from my difference. But it must be done in a way that is authentic and genuine. I'm not just going to be an angry brown woman. I don't need to have a chip on my shoulder, but I have to be true to myself. I speak in the way that is natural to me, I dress in the way that feels more comfortable to me. I talk about the issues that matter to me. My humour is rooted in my own experience. I'm going to be that version of me at the table. And I genuinely think with David Cameron, both in opposition and in government, you could do that. He didn't always like it, but I really felt there was a space to do that. I didn't feel like I needed to change. I never thought it was an issue. I attended the first Cabinet meeting in a shalwar kameez. But you know what, that's what I wear in the summer. It was a lovely day. I didn't shy away from my difference; I wasn't ashamed of it in any way. I didn't try and hide it.'

Sayeeda's determination to own her difference boldly reminds me of the founder of progressive conservatism, Benjamin Disraeli. Though he was twice elected prime minister Disraeli always remained an outsider, due to his social status and Jewish heritage. He first gained fame as a writer of novels and then, after three unsuccessful attempts to win election to Parliament, in 1837 he finally succeeded. He was drawn to the Conservative Party, which was dominated by a wealthy land-owning class. Disraeli was an outsider in the party and was often looked down upon as he had a reputation for being ambitious and eccentric. He was known for his flamboyant dress and manners and was something of a character on the London social scene. In the mid-1840s, Disraeli published a novel, *Sybil* or *The Two Nations*, which expressed sympathy for workers who were being exploited in British factories.

The Jewish Question was one of the most fundamental things that underlined his public profile. He had chosen to cope with what was generally regarded as a stigma by openly admitting that he was Jewish by birth. Disraeli had converted to Christianity aged twelve. His attitude was so eccentric and provocative that almost every scholar placed his Jewishness in a central position. He reacted strongly to the attacks on him on account of his Jewish ancestry. It is reasonable to say Disraeli experienced the anguish of assimilation more acutely than other secularising Jews; being in such a prominent position, he had to pay a price for his rapid social advancement in a society that still cherished class and inheritance. Disraeli was always an outsider to the Victorian world and never entirely integrated into it. He managed to advance not because he was popular within the Conservative movement, but because the party needed someone like him for them to succeed at the time. His success can be ascribed to his unique set of skills and characteristics that the Conservative Party lacked, including the ability to improvise and communicate through story.

Box-Ticking Paradox

There is always a perception, expressed or implied, that some people from minority backgrounds are promoted simply as a box-ticking exercise and not on merit. It's an argument often used to counter the implementation of any inclusion programmes within organisations. The irony of meritocracy as a concept, of course, is that we are all benefactors of someone else's actions or goodwill, whether that be a parent deciding to live near a good school or paying for private education, a formal mentor or informal support. It should not be too difficult to conceptualise why people who have less good fortune should receive additional support to level the playing field. There is no doubt that some of the party faithful would have concluded that Sayeeda's elevation was one of those examples of box-ticking. I ask her why she felt David Cameron gave her the opportunity to join his Cabinet.

'I was more talented than some of the people who came through alongside me. It's hard to say that, but you only have to look at BBC *Question Time* performances during that period. To do it over and over and over again and survive. Not just survive but to thrive in that was rare. I could stand up and do a convincing speech on a topic after a limited period of time studying it. I was a lawyer, so this was something I had done before. I was the warm-up before David did his big speeches. So again, there was something in the way I presented. People want to think, oh, it's because you want a brown woman. But I think if I was just a brown woman, I might have been given a role somewhere, but you wouldn't have been given these quite high-profile spaces where you would be front and centre. I think it was definitely because I was talented, but also being in the right place at the right time does help.'

Sayeeda is clearly very confident in her own abilities. I want to know where this comes from. 'My dad came from real poverty in Pakistan but was adamant that you could be anything. You know, if you said to him I'm thinking about making a rocket from some toilet roll he would encourage you to go for it and say when you grow up, you are going to be an astronaut. He made you believe. He has such an amazing sense of self-confidence and believing. So, I think some of it came from that, just the sheer kind of audacity of saying you want to achieve something, why not? I think having confidence in your own ability is important.'

What drives Sayeeda? 'The very clear sense that change has to happen. And knowing that that change is going to be quite painful but being part of that change is going to be assigned to an understanding of history. You might not see the change you are part of bringing about. I definitely didn't start the job and I'm not going to end it, but I have to make sure that during my time I have to keep going and keep kicking the can down the road. I always say to people don't get despondent as long as you think: well, today I've kicked the can down the road a little bit more. That's all you can carry on doing, kick it down the road a little bit. And if progress has been made on gender, race, religion or whatever it may happen to be. I think if you look across the pond to see what's happened in the US, we can't take this slow march towards progressive liberal values for granted anymore.'

But then she did walk away. I ask her to talk me through her thinking during that period.

'I never set out to be the first Muslim in Cabinet, and a woman at that. But I thought when kids write to me and say, we wrote about you in school, we spoke about you in class, it does make you realise the importance of what it represents. At a time when there's quite a lot of angst between Islam and Britain and it doesn't always sit easily. And I was both in the Foreign Office and minister for faith at the time as well as minister for the UN and ICC. I felt that if I was transport minister, I could've said, well, it's not my bag, but at the time when this happened, I was even the minister for human rights too. I was a human rights lawyer before that. I was in the House of Lords answering questions every single day. And I remember being stood at the dispatch box. People said they could see on my face that something was wrong, and I was using language that was not in the briefings given to me by officials. I was going off message. Behind the scenes I was trying everything I could because fundamentally my argument was not that our policy on the Middle East was wrong. My argument was we have a policy, we are supporting international accountability, but we are not upholding it. We have a policy of a two-state solution, but we don't recognise one of those states. The policy is fine, but the way we implemented our policy was complete hypocrisy. There was no basis for it other than the fact that we just chose to turn a blind eye on getting justice. And I thought to myself, I don't want Hansard [the official records of all parliamentary debates] to be read in years to come in my name and for people to think, this is what she supported.'

What needs to be done to build bridges with British Muslims? 'I think when they have equal work, equal value and they're judged by the same standards as others. When the Lee Rigby murder happened, the terrorist attack, I was on the National Security Council. This guy, Douglas Murray, wrote an article in which he said, how can they deal with a war on terror when they have her at the table? The enemy within. My instinct was to say, [expletive] you. But instead, I thought I would own it and that became the title of my book. Then *The Times* got him to review my book. Can you believe that?'

I wonder if Douglas Murray and Sayeeda Warsi would ever sit down for a coffee. If they did, I'd pay for a ringside seat. The experiences of Muslim women often form part of the arguments around why Islam cannot be reconciled with Western liberal societies. Sayeeda does not shy away from this.

'I think mostly Muslim women have had two battles on their hands. They have had to battle from within Muslim communities where, you know, if I go back to when I first started in politics, the thought that a woman would want a leadership position was a new phenomenon in British Muslim communities. Some of those conservative Muslim communities had amazing supportive men as well, but also conservative men who kind of felt like this was the beginning of the end. If you look at things now in the constituency I fought, a decade after the time where one Muslim community felt that I was really out of line for having the audacity to stand, to be a Member of Parliament, they actually elected the first Muslim female councillor, who happens to be the younger sister of a friend of mine. You know, so in a decade, things have changed. And if you go back to where just the thought of a Muslim woman standing was bizarre in 2005, and you now have several Muslim women in Parliament across the political parties, I think there's been change there. Many Muslim women are not even waiting around for the men to give them space any more. They've taken their space. They are brave. They're articulate. They are right there at the front. With all due respect, if you just took all the Muslim parliamentarians, the most impressive are the women.'

Through seeing Sayeeda letting her own light shine, becoming the first Muslim Cabinet member, others have been inspired to do the same. There are ten Muslim women in the House of Commons, and seven men, eight if you count Sajid Javid, who is not a practising Muslim. This progress is a great British story of hope and opportunity. That doesn't take away from the need for more progress for Muslim women.

We turn our conversation to the issue of low expectation. Sayeeda says, 'I used to say that the only time that white men wanted to become allies is when they could fight Muslim men and Islam. They say we want to support you and want you to be independent and articulate and outspoken. But those were the qualities I felt they found most difficult to handle in me. What is it about me that isn't exactly what you're looking for in every single Muslim woman? The truth is it's your version of a Muslim woman that you want. One that talks about how her community is trash and how she needs saving. And everything bad is within her community and everything that is good is what you give her. No, I don't want to suck up to that view that all the people are rubbish within Muslim communities. It's not true. There are rubbish men within Muslim communities just like there are rubbish men outside of it. There are also rubbish men in politics, some that I have worked with.'

I respect that Sayeeda wasn't prepared to play this role of a convenient outsider, where you are basically just used for talking down the group that you have a link to. One should not shy away from challenging communities to do better. You should be willing to call out terrible behaviour, like the former home secretary Sajid Javid has been willing to do around Asian grooming gangs in the north of England. What most people are unaware of is that Sayeeda was the first politician of Asian descent to raise the issue of grooming gangs back in May 2012. In a wide ranging interview with the Evening Standard she called on mosques and community leaders to condemn "a small minority" of their members with racist and sexist views. It is in the interest of any community to raise its game and become better. But it must be done from a position of genuine understanding and of inclusion. One must be part of that change with communities and not simply talk down to people from a high horse. It's counterproductive and breeds mistrust. Anyone can write a punchy column about how Muslims should get with the programme and integrate or author a report that formalises confirmation bias. It requires more effort to build meaningful bridges and to be an active agent for the change you wish to see. Integration is always a multifaceted process which requires action from government, communities, and individuals.

Levelling Up and Modernisation

Sayeeda still lives in Yorkshire, commuting into the House of Lords during the week, so will know more than most about how the levelling-up agenda is being received. I ask for her opinion.

'It's just a new name. Isn't it? Something that every government has tried for the past twenty years. But even before that, devolution, the regional hubs that we created, and before that, even Margaret Thatcher, she had regional firms that she'd put in place. And being able to buy your council home was certainly a bold way of levelling up under Thatcher. It was a game changer for many people. Every government has tried to close that gap to make the whole country productive, particularly when big manufacturing, steel, coal, when they closed down. Every government, since the closure of the pits and the closure of the large manufacturing industries, has tried to recreate a level of economic activity in those regions.'

Are there any policy areas Sayeeda thinks the government should focus on? She returns to her earlier point. 'We now have a government that is socially conservative with the culture wars and economically liberal. And that doesn't make any sense to me because I thought we were socially liberal, economically conservative. Which is what makes me Conservative, but instead we've gone with the other way. It's now about controlling what people can be, who they are, who is or isn't British, it is terrible. I was born in a Labour-supporting family. My dad was a trade unionist and I converted to Conservatism, and I had the zeal because it represented a small state, you know, big society. A low-tax economy. We were increasingly socially liberal, but economically conservative. We didn't spend money that we didn't have. We thought about the future. We believed in the rule of law, we protected democracy, even if it was to our detriment, all those things I feel are being smashed. I look around me and think I'm still a Conservative, but is my party? I'm still standing where I stood a decade ago.'

Sayeeda has a point. Under David Cameron's leadership the Conservatives were able to modernise into a force, given further legitimacy via a coalition with the Liberal Democrats in 2010 before achieving a majority in 2015. But the modernisation agenda was not the brainchild of David Cameron. It was Nicholas Boles, Lord Ed Vaizey, Michael Gove, and others who watered the seeds that were sown initially through Michael Portillo's failed leadership candidacy in 2001. Their work led to the founding of Policy Exchange, arguably the most influential centre-right think tank in the United Kingdom.

In many people's eyes the Tory modernisation agenda is now dead. Brexit has resulted in a political realignment for the Conservative Party, with the red wall offering up opportunities for a new coalition of voters. Many people who bought into the modern Conservativism project now find themselves politically homeless. Outsiders in a way. We are told that the 2019 coalition of voters has much more socially conservative views than the wider population, who are mostly moderately in the middle. Interesting work by YouGov shows us that the evidence for this conclusion is flimsy. What is more certain is that there is some divergence on public spending within this new voting bloc, which may result in increasing friction as we deal with the cost of living. Traditional Conservative voters in rural shires and the outskirts of major cities are more interested in balancing the books, while new converts from northern and left-behind towns are keener on further state intervention.

Demographic changes are not on the side of this new Tory coalition in the medium to long term, with the party only beating

Labour among the over-sixty-fives at present. Britain's ethnic minority population continues to grow and is set to be around 30 per cent of the UK by 2051. Events including the murder of George Floyd, the subsequent Black Lives Matter (BLM) movement and the response to the Tony Sewell report mean they will probably remain less likely to vote Conservative overall – though there continues to be a gap in the market for upwardly mobile black and Asian voters uncomfortable with Labour.

The legacy of Tony Blair's education policy means nearly half of the population's young people enter higher education. These graduates lumped with significant debt and poor student experiences exacerbated by the pandemic are also among those more hostile to the Conservative brand. Both ethnic minorities and graduates (often one and the same) will increasingly spread out of major cities, into shires and other areas that usually vote Conservative. You do not need to be a super-forecaster to see that this presents an existential threat, one very similar to what David Cameron faced in 2010, but perhaps even more challenging in the years to come. The Conservative Party is the oldest political party in Europe. It has been able to form successful coalitions of voters more than any other party in this country. For this to continue to be the case, a renaissance of Tory modernisation is inevitable. The question is – who will lead it?

Ignorance and Knowledge

I ask Sayeeda if she has other examples of when she felt like an outsider around the Cabinet table.

'Probably on a few occasions when there were some conversations that took place about Islam and Muslims, which was in full ignorance. One occasion David had to intervene because he felt a colleague used language that was offensive. I think there were a few occasions where I felt alone. Not always. I remember saying for me this is not policy, it's my reality, what we are talking about here is my children and their children and their future and my future in this country. At times I felt quite angry at the inconsistent treatment that we deliver to different communities. I find it fascinating when people talk about cancel culture. I think what the hell; we've had a government policy of disengagement with the British Muslim community since 2010. They were the first people in this country that were cancelled. Lock, stock and barrel cancelling. We don't engage with most of them because we find a way not to.'

I have grown up a supporter of the country of Israel. Within the Pentecostal Christian expression Israel and the Jewish people have a special position. I also studied the Arab/Israel conflict, which gave me a broad historical context for the current situation. On a visit to Israel for Conservative future leaders I was fortunate enough to visit the Knesset, the Israeli parliament. I also visited the Gaza border, which brought to life a lot of the experiences that I had only read about or seen in the news. During the trip we went into the West Bank to visit Ramallah, a Palestinian city in the central West Bank located ten kilometres north of Jerusalem. We could see how the Palestinian people were attempting to forge a future for themselves. One thing that left a strong impression on me was a young Palestinian woman, who was so smart and clearly ambitious for a more positive future.

That evening we returned to Tel Aviv and sat for a traditional Israeli dinner. A young member of the Likud Party stood up and spoke very passionately about how many Israelis live in constant fear, and how Palestinians were the enemy. He spoke for over twenty minutes uninterrupted. Eventually the conversation was thrown open for questions. I asked if he had ever spoken to a Palestinian or engaged in any formal dialogue with young Palestinians like himself. (The young lady we had met earlier that day was still on my mind.) There was an awkward silence, and then this young man, very likely a future member of the Israeli parliament, confirmed that he had never actually spoken to one of his neighbours whom he so greatly disdained. The room fell awkwardly silent, everyone looking in shock, like I had blasphemed. All very awkward. Then one of the other delegates, who was from Northern Ireland, stood up to save me. He said, 'Samuel asks a very important question. One of the most important parts of the peace process in Ireland was facilitating dialogue between the Protestants and Catholics. Not just between the leaders, but also between regular citizens, the police and others. You can never have true peace if you refuse to engage.' I do not know if those young Israeli future leaders chose to take anything from this interaction. I can imagine it is probably very difficult for someone who is ambitious in Israeli politics to be seen to be talking to the 'enemy'. Perhaps outsiders will play a future role in facilitating this. It is great to see that Muslim and Jewish leaders (as well as Christians and those of other faiths and no faith) in the UK work very closely together on a range of subjects – including tackling anti-Semitism and anti-Muslim hatred.

Sayeeda is right in saying that the government that I was part of had both formal and informal rules in place restricting dialogue between the government and many Muslim stakeholders. The United Kingdom's Muslim population in 2011 was 2,516,000, 4.4 per cent of the total population, while more recent Office of National Statistics sources have it as large as 3.9 million. This is the fastest-growing population in Britain and it is only going to grow in size and influence. Many were born here. This is their home. Politically it is very short-sighted to ignore them. Morally, that lack of dialogue will contribute to isolation, which is a key component for breeding resentment and extremism. The current terror threats are from far right and religious extremists – primarily Islamists. The worry should be that those threats are mostly already in Britain, often represented by people born here. At the root of their belief system is that they are outsiders. They do not belong, they do not fit in, their views are at odds with the majority. That may be true, but the solution must be to deal with the isolation head on. To reach out, to engage, to show not tell that there is a better way.

One of the very last tasks I was given by a very senior colleague in Downing Street was to craft an engagement plan to build bridges between the government and the Muslim population. I would be pleasantly surprised if that work had been carried forward by someone else. But I doubt it has. No one else would have been brave enough to attempt to tackle this contentious subject. There are a lot of ambitious cowards where power lies. The same thing happened with the strategy for the Gypsy, Roma, Traveller population. It was promised, but contentious, so I decided I would take it on.

Progress

I ask Sayeeda what her thoughts are on the progress we have made as a nation.

'We have this conversation in most Muslim communities where people will say, we've come such a long way in terms of women's rights. Yes – we have come a long way from when my mum started. From when I started. And there's no clubs that say no blacks, no dogs, no Irish or whatever. It is not as bad as it was, but if I speak to my kids in their twenties and talk to them about racism and they tell me their experiences, it's sad but we are still talking about racism, in their minds no progress has been made. That is because we continue not to meet the expectations of the next generation. My granddad used to keep his head down. Say thank you, thank you when he was receiving abuse on the streets. My dad's generation used to swear back and that was the end of it. Or my dad or my mum would say things like, well, it is their country. My generation went to football matches. But you know, occasionally you would hear things. You rolled your eyes, and you try and fight it. The next generation, they expect no less than the same opportunities as anyone else, including access to jobs. Expectations across generations change and we must rise to the challenge of meeting them.'

There is a perception of Muslims in Britain that perhaps does not correlate with the reality. That is not to say that those perceptions have not been rooted in any evidence, just that much of the evidence cited is very narrow and outdated. Muslim men and women are progressing academically, economically and, increasingly, socially. Yes, there are challenges that persist, but a lot of those challenges, including women's rights, are not unique to Islam. The ones that are unique, particularly extremism, need an approach that reaches out and does not further isolate those who are more vulnerable to being radicalised. The Muslim population in Britain is large. They can no longer be viewed as separate strangers but should be viewed as part of our social fabric and here to stay. Someone like Sayeeda is exactly who we need to build bridges, but for too long she has been ostracised by the right for having opinions. For being authentic. The good news is she has given so many other Muslim women the inspiration to shine for themselves because of what she has achieved as the first Muslim Cabinet member. That's the power of an outsider.

One final thought. In writing this book I have been conscious not to sound like I have all of the answers, but I have also wanted to ask important and uncomfortable questions. This has been a genuine journey of discovery for me. I am worried about the way we are heading as a nation. People who are moderate, but keen to see a fairer, more compassionate society, do not make good pundits in an age where broadcasters are desperate for the next viral clip. Being kind and compassionate is not good for business, and being able to disagree in a respectful way is all too rare. As a Christian, I worry about how people who profess to be part of the majority faith in this country are often attacked and marginalised. Made outsiders in public life. Perhaps it's easier for someone like me because I am comfortable saying I simply do not have the answers to some of the big questions, but what I do know is that it is important to treat everybody with love and kindness – with no prerequisite or judgement. One of the greatest commandments.

Chapter 6

Family Matters

I guess my story so far is one that is a mixture of the ordinary and the extraordinary. Born into a pretty normal British Nigerian home, with parents who were quite traditional, I am the fourth of five siblings with the same mother and father and have a number of half-brothers and sisters. My parents separated when I was around eight years old, so I was brought up in a single-parent household that struggled financially throughout my childhood. For a large part of the UK population this is a very common story. Eventually I ended up at university, and I guess this is where the extraordinary kicks in. My university experience was a turning point in my life. I literally managed to break my hand on 5 November, Bonfire Night, become president of the largest African & Caribbean Society in the UK, break student union election records, start an organisation, and enter the world of politics . . . all within the space of four years. At some point within those years, I join the Conservative Party, which led to me eventually becoming the most senior black advisor in government. Looking back, I think that I have been very fortunate to have experienced the many things that I have in my life to date. They have helped to shape who I am today, and they are the reason for what I will become tomorrow. They are some of the things that make me an outsider.

A common theme in the study of outsiders is that of representation or what the outsider represents to a group. To be an outsider it must be at least perceived that you are not part of the majority, be it along the lines of social or demographic, psychological or tactical differentiation. This feeling can often begin forming in childhood. Psychologist Ditta Oliker, who specialises in childhood trauma, assessed four different scenarios in which a child becomes alienated within their own family. The first is when the child in question represents physical or emotional differences to the relative homogeneity of the family group; they do not fit in at a fundamental level because they do not look the same, or because they challenge the extant culture of a family. The second is a child who represents some token of resentment already borne by the parent; they may exhibit similar physical features to an abusive ex-husband or wife, or an ancestor who neglected or abused the parent and they therefore become a symbolic representation of that figure, to which deeply buried feelings of resentment are attached. The third is when a child represents that which the parent could not become, nurture or accept in themself. This may involve, for example, emotional sensitivity and intelligence that a father buried in order to achieve a masculine ideal. The fourth and final token of outsiderness for children is the scenario in which a parent has been forced or felt forced to commit to an unfavourable situation such as an unhappy marriage because it was viewed as the best course of action for the child. This demonstrates that outsiderness results from perceived differences (when the outsider does not fit in), blame (when the outsider becomes a scapegoat for an otherwise unrelated issue) or threat (when the outsider represents a challenge to the status quo, or the psychological safety of an individual).

Oliker's assessment focuses on how an individual can begin in the position of an insider and then be ejected from this in-group and become an outsider; it is not a prerequisite for an outsider to have arrived from the outside. Oliker explains the impact of this exclusion: 'to feel like an outsider, the emotional cost is one of deep loneliness and of never belonging', which is a clear violation of the requisite conditions for psychological safety. Perhaps the most damaging experience of outsiderness is one that begins from childhood and is experienced where one should feel most safe, in the place they call home.

It's the day after my elder sister Victoria's wedding and we have just arrived at the luxury villa that she and her in-laws have been staying in. It overlooks the rolling fairways of Barbados's Royal Westmoreland Golf Course all the way out to the clear turquoise-blue Caribbean Sea. The villa is accessed via a long private driveway flanked with royal palms. As you drive through the gates the sheer size of the property is overwhelming. The outside has three levels to it, which have been utilised during our trip for dinners, brunches, and a traditional Nigerian engagement ceremony that took place the day before the main event. There is an infinity pool and an outhouse.

Both family and friends are meeting for a post-wedding brunch. The sun is shining, rum punch is pouring, and all are in high spirits. I take three of my siblings into the outhouse to interview them for this chapter.

Victoria lives in New York, where she is a senior leader and board member in a fast-growing tech company. Rebekah is currently head of finance in a FTSE 250 company, although she is about to take up a role as partner at a venture capital fund. My younger brother Philip has recently started a new role as director at a technology focused bank. All are the most senior black individuals in their respective firms, all are under forty, and all certainly come from a modest background. When you add in me previously having been the most senior black special advisor in government, my parents are understandably chuffed with their lot – although they would rather that I was still in my previous role instead of having taken time out to write what you are currently reading. I'm hoping to discover how my siblings view themselves, what they consider is important in the context of giving back, and what impact their childhood has had on shaping them today. I'm secretly hoping it will help me to better understand some of the things I have been reflecting on since my meeting with Bedford's police and crime commissioner, Festus Akinbusoye.

The conversation starts with me asking if they consider themselves outsiders. I invite Victoria to answer first.

'Yes. The personal reason is pretty obvious, but there's definitely been a journey. It has been a process and a lot of self-discovery and acceptance in that journey. But also moving from the UK to America and starting from the bottom again and trying to find the right way to take the steps to move into the C-suite. Everyone who meets me is like, how are you in these sorts of spaces? I'm unfortunately still always the only woman, and I'm always the only black person in the boardroom, one hundred per cent of the time. Apart from that, I feel like I'm also very comfortable in that sense. And so even that mentality or that attitude of being an outsider but owning it as well is also very different.'

I ask her to elaborate on the personal reason she mentioned. 'Getting comfortable in my skin and what I look like and who I am, and then starting to own that.

Some people maybe thought that me being the lighter one was some form of privilege or something amazing. It was the exact opposite for me. It was not great. It wasn't something that I wanted ever.'

Children and Difference

Victoria is very fair skinned. In our photos as children, she clearly stands out among her darker-skinned siblings. Though Victoria's difference was something I was obviously aware of, I must confess to never really reflecting on whether it had an impact on her feeling like an outsider growing up. As you have just read, one of the four different scenarios of a child becoming alienated by their family includes when they represent physical or emotional differences to the relative homogeneity of the family group; they do not fit in at a fundamental level because they do not look the same, or because they challenge the extant culture of a family.

This difference probably not only impacted her but also my eldest sister Elizabeth, who was not in the room during this conversation. Elizabeth is three years older than Victoria. Having relatives show more favour to a sibling because she is lighter must have been very difficult for a young child to experience. I think of my son, who has had to have constant affirmation that he is also loved as he manages the dynamics with his new kid sister and the unavoidable attention a baby receives. Having a new child often results in siblings feeling displaced or unloved. Variations around age, gender and personality can further influence how a child responds to a new entrant, and the degree to which rivalries develop. It is not uncommon for an incumbent child to attention-seek or for their behaviour to change. Child psychologists advise that parents should prepare their older children for new arrivals, but the journey never stops. Other sibling management tips include ensuring equal treatment, not always intervening or taking sides during conflicts, finding opportunities for distraction, and giving each child their own separate quality time. Ultimately, each child needs to be in an environment where they feel secure and loved.

Colourism

Adding the dynamics of skin colour further complicates. Those dynamics for both Elizabeth and Victoria were certainly never managed or probably understood by my parents, and as a result both sisters have had to deal with the impact. Colourism is a big topic within African and Caribbean populations, but also among most of the Asian population. It is defined as prejudice or discrimination against individuals with a darker or lighter (more often darker) skin tone among people of the same ethnic or racial group. It is a form of discrimination that goes back centuries and continues to be rife across continents. Oscar-winning actress Lupita Nyong'o and the author Chimamanda Ngozi Adichie have both spoken about their experiences of discrimination due to their skin tone. One of the most concerning consequences of colourism is people bleaching their skin to become fairer and – in their eyes – therefore more desirable. Tanning using dangerous UV rays can also be a consequence. The World Health Organization (WHO) has warned of the health risks attached to bleaching due to the inclusion of materials, including mercury salts, that inhibit the production of melanin. Other harmful chemicals include hydroquinone. The producers of bleaching cream across the world continue to evade regulations.

Victoria continues: 'Yeah, it wasn't easy. When I started working in the winter and could afford to, I would use a tanning machine regularly. That's very dangerous, but I was doing it cause I'm like, I'm so white right now. I need to get brown. So even getting past that and being like, okay, that's something that's very dangerous. You shouldn't do that. You get light in the winter and that's okay. Just stuff like that, where you must learn how to get comfortable in your own skin. There's an internal part. Family members would treat us differently. I remember all of that. Or people constantly asking if Rebekah and I were really sisters. Saying we were lying.'

Sharing Knowledge

I want to know more about the comfort she feels in boardrooms. Where the confidence comes from, especially considering some of the challenges and insecurities she has mentioned experiencing growing up. 'I definitely was not born confident. But through my journey I've worked with people who were successful and who had given me bits of advice. I always say that having the humility to learn from someone is a massive, massive key to being successful. If you think you know everything you are going to fail. And so, when I work with successful people, I ask them how to get to their position. I'm always asking questions and I'm sitting there listening to what they are saying, often for hours.'

Her answer is something that resonates with me. At almost every stage of my journey there have been people willing to give me that time to learn about how they have been successful in various fields. That began at university, when I stood with the most successful society president for hours listening to his advice, and it has been the same in business and politics. Most of the reasons why I've been able to experience what I have is because people have been willing to share their knowledge and wisdom with me. Some people would say, well, how do you get to a point where you find someone willing to help? Listening to Victoria, it is clear that we siblings all seem to have an ability to connect with other people, building rapport and relationships that make people open to sharing with us. That is a skill in itself. I don't know why we have it. Victoria's hypothesis is, 'We have five brothers and sisters, five different personalities. You know, I think that helps. And I think we're able to connect with people because we've always had many different people around us growing up in London, many different races. For us, we super-normalised being around different characters, different people, and that makes it a bit easier to connect with people different from us. I could be the only black woman in a room, and it doesn't make me uncomfortable to be fair. If anything, I kind of figured it's a bonus. I'm the different one. I might stand out. But I back myself in that I know I'm smart enough to be there. So, I'm not really worried about that. I know when we get talking, you're going to end up saying, oh my God, you're great, because I have a really good way of connecting with people.'

Class

Keen to get their reflections on social mobility, I ask my siblings if they still consider themselves to be working class. Victoria, who has just spent a small fortune on her destination wedding, jumps in: 'Yes, 100 per cent.' Rebekah, who is usually the most rational, responds, 'Erm . . . you are in the top 5 per cent of earners?' Victoria replies, 'But I need to work to maintain my current lifestyle, therefore I am working class.' She sounds scarily like some Members of Parliament who have been insisting they need a second job for similar reasons.

Rational Rebekah the accountant comes back with, 'That's different to working class. People in blue-collar jobs are what Samuel is speaking about, so no I don't agree that we are working class.' Victoria responds, 'I don't agree. I feel like if you lose your job today and you are not able to maintain the same standard of living then you are working class.' Rebekah says, 'Well, in any case I could probably not work for about three years, and you could probably do the same, so my point still stands.'

Philip provides some helpful context: 'We are literally having this conversation in Barbados, in the hills, in the outhouse of a mansion.' Then Rebekah goes in for the kill. 'How many holidays can you afford to take a year?' At this point I think it's best to bring the conversation back to the topic of outsiders.

Outsiders and Giving Back

Philip, who has been waiting patiently for his time to speak, says he is the biggest outsider because, 'I actually started a tech company, which is the hardest thing to do against everyone's better judgement and all the odds. And then on top of that, I've never had a traditional career path. I've always done something completely different to everyone else. Everyone's gone to get a job. I just felt like there's way more to life somewhere.' Philip also says that he has felt like an outsider when trying to raise venture capital. As we saw in the chapter about Wilfred Emmanuel-Jones, those most able to raise finance for ventures continue to be individuals from privileged backgrounds.

Does Philip still feel like an outsider now he's at a large bank? 'Yes. I'm the most senior black man in the bank. But at the same time, I don't feel uncomfortable anywhere because we have that confidence. That knowing who you are and what you bring. This is what I'm here to do. I'm not going to allow the fact that I'm the only person who looks this way to affect me negatively. I know what I bring to the table. I'm very confident. I know my stuff (he didn't say stuff but I'm keen to keep this book child-friendly). Rebekah adds, 'Philip, as he was trying to run his own business and be a founder, had to be the first person to have done something. Otherwise, what are you doing? So you have to back yourself and be the first. To do something that you have to pioneer, right? American schools, they might not have the best education system, but they teach kids more about having confidence. Americans when they say something they say it with such conviction. We Brits are often so self-deprecating, so imagine if you're being self-deprecating, but you're also black and from a working-class background and a woman. It has the potential to not be helpful at all based on what so many in society tell you about yourself. I feel like that's why we are able to be successful, because we know what we bring to the table.'

I move the conversation to the importance of giving back. Rebekah says, 'It's not always comfortable but it's important. I hate being filmed and public speaking makes me super uncomfortable and I hate doing speeches. It's not my thing. I don't like it. However, I know it's important and it's not about me, so I must make myself visible. Time and visibility are super important. I remember I was talking to some young people. There was one girl who grew up in east London. She had a difficult upbringing. When I told her I didn't go into law because I could not afford to go to law school, her whole manner changed immediately. That was because I'm literally telling her that back in the day, I couldn't afford to do something, and she sees where I work now. She sees how people receive me in the office now, but she can also see that it's not impossible from where she has started too. This is how my life has turned out from not being able to afford to go to law school. So, it's very important that people see you and are able to connect to your story.'

Prior to Philip moving into banking, he had spent time working at Founders Pledge, a social enterprise focused on supporting tech founders to give to good causes once they have exited (sold) their businesses. I'm keen to know how he defines activism. 'I think the best way to be an activist is to be the best version of yourself. I spent a lot of time in philanthropy and working on effective altruism. Thinking about how giving is easy but giving well is hard. The best thing you can do, that's going to have the most impact, is to be the best version of you. In terms of activism being so visible to everyone else, that's the best way to be impactful. There is no greater gift than literally giving yourself, your time, your expertise, to others.'

Victoria interrupts: 'I agree to an extent but would go further. Everyday activism to me also means the little things that help. I think that seeing some people not wanting to give certain people jobs and being able to say, okay, well, let's talk about it. Why do you not want to give this person a job? And they are clearly demonstrating biases linked to common stereotypes. Just being able to break it down and figure out how to change their minds. It may seem minor to just make sure that someone is given a fair chance to have a job, but that's practical activism. Even in that small way, you can still make an impact. I also feel like any day, every day, speaking to people at different levels within an organisation, looking them in the eye when they say hi, and taking time to invest in rich conversations, is also part of everyday activism.'

Rebekah adds, 'I used to lead women leadership programmes, especially at KPMG when I worked there. My activism was I have the best clients on my portfolio. I'm going to put more women on my portfolio. I put them on the best clients. They get good face time with the clients, which means they can put good stuff on their reviews, they get better reviews, more chance of a bonus, and more chance to get promoted. That's my activism. I would put women on my jobs when I was hiring someone to come work in my team and when I saw what she was getting paid compared to men, which is what is industry standard and what's best practice, I would be sure to act. I would say so we're going to push for X. And because we are pushing for X, I will put you in another bracket. Victoria taught me about this.'

Victoria adds, 'I often do market analysis to see what a person should get paid. Women and people of colour come in all the time, and they are always below market. And then someone's like, well, we need to save money. Let's offer them 10 per cent extra knowing they will be grateful. I always push back — the baseline for this job is X and so that's what I'm going to offer this person. Very important.'

Outsiders and the Pay Gap

There is a wider challenge around whether employers should request salary history at all during the recruitment process. In the United Kingdom, 61 per cent of women surveyed said that being asked about their salary history has an impact on their confidence when negotiating. Such practices should be outlawed entirely. The alternative solution would be for more transparency across the board. Scandinavian countries have chosen this approach; in Finland, Norway, and Sweden, all citizen income tax returns are published for all to see.

In Canada, employers with more than 100 workers must publish a report on their wage gap at every level by income band. One of the key policies that members of the Sir John Parker Review board have been advocating for is legislation that would mandate ethnicity pay gap reporting. In the United Kingdom gender pay gap reporting is already required for employers with a workforce of 250 people or more, but there are challenges with simply adopting the same model for ethnicity. For example, depending on where you are based geographically the overall diversity of the population may not allow for statistically significant analysis. If the same model for gender pay reporting was adopted, major cities like London, Birmingham and Manchester, with larger black and Asian populations, would be able to draw more value from ethnicity pay gap reporting than places like Shropshire and Cornwall. It could also result in potentially illegal practices as employers could find ways to manipulate results if their overall workforce was not very diverse. For example, an entry level graduate might not be taken on board if it would significantly skew the overall pay gap results; or they may be paid more than other graduates, for the same reason.

These were some of the complexities under consideration when the government was analysing the results of a consultation into ethnicity pay reporting. They were not insurmountable challenges but required meaningful dialogue with employers and mutual trust with stakeholders.

Before I left my role in Downing Street, I was in the process of designing a solution that most stakeholders, including ministers, seemed to buy into in principle. It would have meant the Office for National Statistics, rather than the Government Equalities Office, would be responsible for coordinating a data collection exercise that not only focused on protected characteristics like sex, ethnicity and disability, but would also look at geographical variances, sector benchmarking and socioeconomic pay gaps using education and parents' occupation as a proxy. This would have resulted in a much richer and less simplistic analysis that would allow employers to compare themselves to their wider industry and policymakers to know where there was a need for further challenge or targeted resources. It is one of many examples where there are solutions if people are willing to try.

Rebekah says, 'It's a shame, because we as women in senior positions are the ones that usually do this. It's another reason why diversity matters, so that there are more advocates, activists speaking up when others won't, when it's more convenient to stay silent.'

Integrity

These reflections remind me of the events that led to my resignation as Boris Johnson's special advisor. I had taken on the
task of ensuring the government was doing everything it possibly could to ensure all communities were taking up the opportunity to receive the Covid-19 vaccination. By late December
2020 it was increasingly clear that there were significant variances in those willing to take the vaccine, across ethnic, regional
and socioeconomic lines. My job was to make sure we were
not just leaving the task of increasing vaccine confidence to the
communication teams; there needed to be a community-led
strategy that was influenced by behavioural insights, and
involved community leaders, trusted voices and medical
experts. It needed to be a campaign led like an election, using
both above-the-line and below-the-line engagement methods.
While the National Health Service and Department for Health
and Social Care received the plaudits for getting jabs into arms,
I made sure the Departments for Culture, Media & Sport and
Communities & Local Government, as well as the Home
Office and Cabinet Office, were able to feed their expertise
into the operation.

I worked closely with the dedicated rapid response unit to
tackle the vast waves of misinformation around the vaccines.
Social media firms were also brought in to play their part.
This was a priority for the prime minister and the most important thing that I worked on in government. But by the end of
February 2021, I had sent the prime minister my letter of
resignation. Why? Because my everyday activism meant that I
could not ignore a young journalist being set upon by a
powerful minister. The journalist, Nadine White, had asked a

very reasonable but uncomfortable question, as many journalists do when they are seeking to hold the government to account. Many times those questions are unwelcome, but we have a duty to respond appropriately. Instead, the minister was forwarded both the name of the journalist who made the request and the original email from the journalist, something that doesn't usually happen. That email was subsequently posted online by the minister, and Nadine White went on to receive a torrent of abuse.

Nadine is someone I have only ever met and spoken to once, at a reception in Downing Street. To this day many people simply do not understand why I would sacrifice so much because of something that happened to a person that I was not close to. But my duty above all else was to make sure that I served the people of the United Kingdom with integrity, and, when these events made it clear that for others that was a secondary priority, it became a problem for me. When no one else was brave enough to speak up when something wrong had happened because preserving their jobs was far more important, I felt it was time for me to go. To be clear, I did not want the minister to lose her job. We all make mistakes, and there were a number of underlying reasons for her actions. It was a very intense period for everyone in government, and we absolutely had to ensure the vaccine deployment was a success. The minister and I had a good relationship up until that point. I just did not think it okay that no one wanted to confront her or even to acknowledge her actions were wrong. There was a lack of desire to uphold standards, which was a worry for me. Rishi Sunak has since staked his premiership on establishing a high level on standards, which is important.

Initially, following internal discussions, I had agreed to remain in post, but that urge to leave remained, and eventually I departed. I lost some friends as a result. The process all happened so quickly, though at the time it felt much slower than the usual fast pace in Downing Street. Almost like watching a film in slow motion. Going back to that walk in St James's Park with the minister who had tried to explain why my friend would never understand my reason for leaving, I think at the time I made the decision it felt as black and white as the explanation that you have just read. However, the journey of writing this book has challenged me to step back and reflect. There was more for me to understand about why I ended up responding in the way that I did. We'll explore this more in subsequent chapters.

A lot of people thought my political career was over. But I have few regrets. We have a political system that rewards ambition over integrity, selfishness over servanthood, division over unity. When news first broke about my resignation letter in late February 2021, the vaccines minister was amongst the people that rang me to encourage me to stay. I will never forget his words: 'Samuel, good people always win in the end.' I'm not sure I believe this to be entirely true, but I do hope that in time good people with the right motives are able to play a more important role in public life. The whole experience was a reminder of what matters most. I was never sure how to respond when people would say that one should not just be against racism, but actively anti-racist, actively against anti-Semitism, but now I get it. Like Martin Luther King Jr once said, 'In the end, we will remember not the words of our enemies, but the silence of our friends.' Everyday activism means looking out for people, even when you do not know them or it does not benefit you. It's being visible to inspire others to be the best they can be. It's opening doors of opportunity when you are in a position of power.

Support and Success

Conscious that I have taken my siblings away from time with guests, I move to the final topic that I want to cover: the impact of growing up in a single-parent home. I want to know if they feel it has had a significant impact on their lives. Not just at work, but in their personal lives too. Philip is the first to respond.

'Well, obviously growing up without a dad is difficult. I mean, it was difficult in the sense that I'd never really known how to interact with older males. So, there's always a bit of friction when it comes to that for me, even till today. Though I was fortunate enough to have, you know, you [he means me] as a role model. You were an entrepreneur, that's why I became an entrepreneur. If you were a policeman, I would have probably been a policeman. Your politician stuff . . . I'm still working on that. Seriously though, I think when you grow up without one parent you feel the absence, right. And especially Mum was also not around as often as we would have liked too, and you are kind of left to your own devices. You have to become your own person. We have seen other people that have both parents in the household. I see how they've turned out and how they've benefited from having that. And certain things that we didn't . . . we weren't fortunate enough to have, but we kind of learned on our own just doing it and just trying to manage it and just learning from one another. So I think there was a disadvantage to an extent, but I think we made the most out of that situation. We might have leaned a lot more on each other for information. Looking at my older sisters getting a job, or Victoria being the first to buy a house. I think you benefit from having older siblings to look to. Maybe because of that I didn't always feel like anything was missing. There is nothing I wish I had because I think even the people who did come up in a dual-parent household, many are not doing as well in some respects too.'

Rebekah says, 'We've normalised it among ourselves because we're such high achievers, but it's not normal. When I was being interviewed for my new job, the interviewer asked what my family did, and what my parents did. When I told her, she was like, listen to your answer to the question. I said, we are a fully functioning, dysfunctional family, but we function one hundred per cent. I said my brothers are the greatest guys I know. I said we all lead with kindness. We're super kind. If you hang out with us, you're going to have the best time. Growing up without a father around. I feel like if that's the worst thing that could happen to us, that's fine. I'll take it. Because everything else since then, it's been the best.'

Philip goes on, 'Victoria grew up with Dad at some point so remembers more. Whereas I don't know what I don't know. You don't know what you are missing out on until you're told you're missing out on something. Growing up I didn't know. I was like, oh, so it's my siblings. When I turned sixteen, Victoria paid for my driving lessons for a birthday present. When I went to New York, I lived with her rent-free. When I came back, I worked for one of your [he means my] companies for a bit. So that's what we did. Became self-sufficient.'

Victoria still adores my father. She tells us that part of this is because she remembers him being a very proactive parent. He was the one that took her and Elizabeth to school every morning. 'He was just so dedicated to being a good dad when he was still with us. You guys never really saw him around. But I remember.'

Rebekah had earlier said that the opposite of love is indifference. I want to challenge that, so I say, 'What would you say to those who say that the opposite of love is actually fear? And do you perhaps feel like you might be afraid of dealing with things that you have not necessarily had to do up until now, as there has been success in other ways?' I'm quite surprised by her response:

'Definitely. I was thinking the other day; I'm not saying I'm perfect. I might have dysfunctional relationships because of the one with my father. But do I really want to tap into that now? Is there anything for me personally that I can gain from this. I've managed to do well or be okay thus far. Is this really going to add anything?'

I respond, 'But isn't there more important things than being successful?'

Philip answers unequivocally: 'I don't think there is, to be honest. What I've learned from Mum is that money is important and without money you have more challenges. We grew up very poor. I've seen the effects of Mum not having money and also having money. So, I'm very driven to be successful.'

I respect his honesty; and, perhaps me having children has softened my own position on this question, but that fear of not having has also driven me like it has obviously driven everyone else in the room.

Philip comes back again: 'I think success is also defined by how free you are to do what you love doing. Although I was not making any money when I was in New York, I felt like I was being very successful doing that because I was actually doing something I wanted to do on my own terms. And then when I came back to London again, I set the terms. I was like, look, I'm not earning less than a certain amount. And I got it. Then a year later I've got three times that. I always tell people; you've got to define success for yourself.'

Rebekah reflects, 'As a single woman, if I was a guy living the life that I live now, travelling all over the world, a head of finance for a listed company, I'd be revered for it. If I was a guy, people would be like, he is living his best life, but no matter how successful I am, people still say to me, oh, you'll really be happy when you get married. I feel like marriage is a good thing, but it's not the only thing. You could get married and it be the best thing. And then you complement each other, and it helps your trajectory. And when I see it going right, I see it going right. But there's other women who get married just for the sake of it. And it damages them. I am a successful woman. I have way more to lose. It's not like I'm just losing a salary now. It took a whole lot of hard work to get to this point. So, I have to be super protective over that, which means that I'm not just going to just get with anyone.'

This conversation with my siblings has reminded me of just how important our roots are in shaping who we become. The first place someone may feel like an outsider is with their family, or if they are not part of a traditional family unit due to being fostered or adopted. I now understand some of the other people I have interviewed a little more. I can see that being able to interact with different kinds of people from an early age helps to shape how we engage with others later in life. Whether you are former chair of Sainsbury's David Tyler (who is interviewed later in this book), who says living in Asia for a period as a child was pivotal for him, or Wilfred Emmanuel-Jones with twelve siblings with all their different personalities, we are better communicators if we normalise engaging with diverse groups.

Growing up I did feel something of an outsider. I was the introvert in the group. The one who did not join in as my siblings danced to the latest music, instead choosing to retreat into my shell. The one less keen to attend social gatherings, and more interested in being at home. Close friends understood this as I was growing up, and as a result my house was where we would meet. As you get older you realise that it is okay to not always get energy from being around people and to prefer to be alone. It does not mean there is something wrong with you.

In Susan Cain's bestselling book *Quiet*, she argues that introverts are underappreciated and that as a result society loses out on the value that they can bring. Where we are on the introvert–extrovert spectrum determines how we communicate, respond to challenges and resolve differences, and often the careers that we choose. The difference between a manager and a leader is that managers are generally taught to treat everyone the same, to standardise responses and ensure consistency. Leaders – including parents – on the other hand, need to understand different characteristics and adjust to maximise output. Whether responsible for a family or an organisation, someone who is not an obvious outsider can end up feeling like one because people do not pay attention to where they are on the introvert–extrovert spectrum.

Reflecting on my conversation with my siblings, I was also struck by Philip explaining that, growing up without a father, he did not know he was missing out on anything until he was told he was. Dads play a pivotal role, as do mothers, in a child's development. The absence of one or both parents does often have a lasting impact, even if we are not conscious of what those impacts are. Choosing not to explore this subject can impact on our relationships with others, including our own children. It is possible for those voids to be filled in other ways, through siblings or role models for example; but unfortunately, there are too many examples of such voids being filled by toxic relationships, including gangs that groom vulnerable children for county lines drugs and sex trafficking. What is clear to me is that despite the barriers it is possible for an outsider to still be successful in life – however you define success. For my family and many others from a similar background, much of our success has been defined by our ability to escape (and not return to) a life of poverty. Confidence is key. A great outsider is also someone who does not forget where they have come from. They are willing to tell their stories to inspire others. They stand up for people even when it is more convenient to stay silent. They are kind and compassionate.

Chapter 7

Confronting Failure

My old boss Alexander Boris de Pfeffel Johnson is often presented as an anti-establishment outsider. This is despite the fact that he was educated at Eton College and Oxford University, where he was a member of the elitist Bullingdon Club. In his professional life he was a senior journalist, rising to become editor of the *Spectator* magazine and eventually a £250,000-a-year columnist for the *Telegraph* newspaper. In politics he became mayor of London in a Labour-voting city at a time when the Conservatives were struggling to broaden their appeal to the very demographics that make up the capital. Despite a failed attempt in 2016, he went on to become prime minister of the United Kingdom. He has been as successful as anyone in politics at positioning himself as a tactical outsider, constantly playing on the idea that he operates by different rules. Whether it is hosting the BBC's *Have I Got News for You*, the seeming lack of care and control of his hair, or being an internationalist who chose to lead the Brexit campaign, he has managed to convince often hard-to-reach working-class British people that he is one of their own, on their side, someone they would love to go for a drink with.

On a personal level, Boris Johnson was always very kind and supportive of me while I worked for him in Number 10 as a special advisor between 2019 and 2021. Whether it was our response to the Windrush scandal, agreeing to my advice to move the Social Mobility Commission back to the Cabinet Office, or my work on vaccine deployment towards the end of my time in Downing Street, his can-do, boosterish energy was always encouraging. Those who have worked with him would also attest that he is in many respects a nice person to be around. Maybe part of the reason for his challenges as prime minister was that at times he was too nice in how he dealt with those around him.

Boris secured his legacy by breaking the Brexit deadlock when there seemed to be no way out. Though there is still great debate around what it means to truly level up the country, he built on the work of his predecessors to give those who feel left behind a voice. I remember our last meeting in Downing Street. A number of officials and I were briefing Boris about a meeting he was due to chair, focused on the vaccine rollout. Once the briefing had ended, he asked for all of the others in the room to leave so that he could have a private word with me. Once they left, the prime minister asked if I was okay as he had read my resignation letter and the various reports in the news. Before I could speak Dan Rosenfield barged into the room and took a seat. He was the chief of staff at the time, and it was within his gift to come into a room to be present when people were speaking to the prime minister. But he was also someone who I did not know well enough to trust; I could speak freely to the prime minister but was hesitant about doing so in front of Dan. This was potentially going to be the last time I had a chance to explain to the prime minister what the situation was and what I felt he needed to do. But I instead chose to play it safe, and just said I was fine. He asked if I still intended to leave. I wanted to say I felt I needed to continue, but for some reason chose to say I would be gone by May as originally planned. The prime minister said he did not think my work would be done by then. I did not respond. There was an awkward pause. Dan broke the silence by saying I had been doing an excellent job on the vaccine deployment and the whole building was aware. We then left for the meeting that the prime minister was chairing.

Having now had time to reflect, I think I should have been more honest in that conversation, despite Dan's presence throwing me off. I owed it to the prime minister, who I worked for after all. I should have stayed and continued the things I was working on. The Civil Society Unit (CSU), which I helped to lead, was set up in 2019. It was an attachment of the Policy Unit (PU) and as a result staff within the CSU were part of most PU activity. My role could only be executed effectively if I had the trust and respect of the various other teams. That included Private Office, Events & Visits, Press, Custodians, Domestic Communications Unit, and more. I also had to have a good relationship with special advisors across government, ministers, and relevant officials who would help to get things done. I was always busy but always had a clear plan.

At its core the Civil Society Unit existed to engage a wide range of stakeholders with Number 10, ensuring that there was two-way dialogue at all times. The CSU was the temperature check for civil society (charities, social enterprises, community interest companies), faith communities, and the black, Asian and minority ethnic population. In my role as a special advisor, I was able to deliver on my main objective of managing stakeholder engagement while taking on more policy-related work where I felt necessary. This was not part of the original brief set, but I was able to do it as a result of build-ing relationships with colleagues within the PU who were happy for me to 'share the load'. When I left, a lot of the things I hoped to achieve for the government and the country were paused, scaled down, or not delivered in the way that they would have been had I remained in post. Not staying and fighting for what I believed was right was a failure on my part. One I will continue to regret.

Failure and Resilience

When I told my wife that I was working on a chapter on fail-ure for this book, she laughed and said, 'That will be hard for you, as you don't talk about failure.' Surprised by this state-ment, I replied, 'Don't I?' If ever there was the risk of me believing my own hype, my wife has always been readily avail-able to offer a dose of perspective. She has been with me since the very start of my professional journey and is of course acutely aware that there have been many failures along the way. She constantly reminds me of the need to stay grounded and not to forget that our roots are humble.

In the culture we both grew up in, failure was not some-thing that was ever discussed. To be fair, most things were never really discussed. We are both Brits of Nigerian heritage and grew up within the evangelical Christian expression. Though there were often sermons about 'the righteous man falling seven times and rising', the prodigal son returning and many other principles that would stand anyone in good stead, failure was only fine if it were an experience for somebody else or a relatively intellectual concept explored from a pulpit during a Sunday service. I was brought up with an internalised desire not to confront those inevitable moments when things did not go to plan.

In politics, becoming an advisor to the prime minister would suggest that I have managed to overcome enough failures to reach such elevated status. In some respects that is true. I failed to be selected for a local council seat before being elected to a council nearly a decade later. I was a failed parliamentary candidate (a safe Labour seat I was never going to win, to be fair to myself) and would also call myself a failed parliamentary staff member, as I didn't last too long in what was previously my only paid role in politics. It is not uncommon for parliamentarians in the United Kingdom to have failed on many occasions before finally being elected. In fact, it is a rite of passage for most of the political class. Boris Johnson failed to be selected as the Conservative candidate for Holborn and St Pancras, the seat now held by the Leader of His Majesty's Opposition, Keir Starmer. Boris went on to contest Clwyd South seat in North Wales in 1997, which he lost. In 1982, Tony Blair failed to be selected as a candidate for Hackney Council in east London and then in the same year contested Beaconsfield as a parliamentary candidate, where he was also unsuccessful. Failing to be selected or elected helps to toughen you up, and to prepare you for the inevitable battles ahead should you become so fortunate as to one day hold elected office.

We must all endeavour to harness a spirit of resilience as we navigate life. But for an outsider, who may already feel like even lifting their head above the parapet is an act of faith, failure can often feel like the end. In fact, one of the main reasons why I was initially hesitant about the idea of becoming a special advisor to the prime minister when asked was because of previous failures. I had to grapple personally with the power that both the risk of failure and actual failure can hold over someone. I set up my first business as a nineteen-year-old from a poor background. Though I had seen my mother engage with enterprise, I was never exposed to some of those challenges, and learned very much on the job. Like most businesses in the UK, my first enterprise failed. It shook me to the core. I thought that this failure would mean that I could not go on to achieve all that I had ever dreamed of doing in business and politics. That an experience in my twenties would weigh me down for the rest of my life. This feeling is one that many feel much earlier in life, when they perhaps do not achieve the exam grades they hoped for in school or are rejected by their first-choice college or university. Sometimes it is forgotten, but at other times it is so difficult to let go, to see a bright horizon.

Learning from Failure

My first business failed, and I had nothing to fall back on. Was my failure worse than the failure of someone with deep-pocketed parents? No. Did it make me feel worse? That's difficult to say. Did I feel like I could still be all that I wanted to be? At times no. Around one in five businesses in the UK fail every year. That means that there are many individuals who have been in the same position as me, yet as a country we are so focused on shaming those who have failed so spectacularly that we do not reflect on what impact it could have on people who could be future innovators. Does that fear of shame prevent them from taking the leap? I have lost count of the number of articles I've come across about Victoria Beckham's fashion business, which has been going through challenges. Not one of those articles has focused on the resilience and commitment she is showing in the midst of a tough trading environment. She has faced these challenges despite the resources at her disposal.

While looking at people who achieve phenomenal results, we must never ignore the underlying current of them learning from mistakes and rebounding from failure. Arianna Huffington once said that 'failure is not the opposite of success, it is part of it' and that it was 'ok to fail'. War hero Winston Churchill famously said, 'Success is not final, failure is not fatal, it is the courage to continue that counts.' If there is one lesson that can be universal, it is that failing in life is inevitable. Something at some point will always go wrong. Sometimes it could be because of our own acts or omissions, sometimes it is because of the acts or omissions of others, and sometimes it is both or neither. Experiences are supposed to strengthen our ability to make better decisions, to better understand what will help us win, and hopefully to give us the opportunity to help others to achieve outcomes with greater information on what it will take to succeed.

We are our failures just as much as we are our successes. We all fail. We are all fallible human beings. The most impressive people can dust themselves off and go again after experiencing a setback. I have already talked about two-time world heavyweight champion Anthony Joshua in 2020 losing his world title belts to Andy Reiz Jnr. The strength of character that Joshua showed was something that should be studied in school by every young person today. Not only was he gracious in defeat, refusing to offer up an excuse, but he learned from the experience and went on to regain and defend his titles in style.

Everyone can learn from Joshua's experience; but he arguably had the benefit of learning from so many other great champions who had returned to the ring after a setback. For outsiders, if you do not have stories like these that are close to home it is key to find them elsewhere. Do not grow tired of learning about how others overcame similar obstacles, even if you cannot find examples of people with a similar background to yours. My first mentor Catherine Muirden was from Edinburgh. When we first met she was Director of Human Resources for one of Britain's largest banks – a world very far from where I was coming from. The people that have opened the most doors for me have had quite different upbringings.

One of the challenges for an outsider is not quite knowing how to handle failure in an environment that is less familiar. Not knowing who to call on if a crisis needs to be managed. Not having influential allies who will fight on your behalf when a mistake has been made is where being an outsider perhaps has more of an impact on how resilient you are when the inevitable failure happens. Not having access to someone who has been in your shoes before to let you know that 'this too shall pass' is one of the biggest handicaps to being in a new environment. It is therefore so important to have allies. Being loyal and being intentional in making sure you have built up an alliance of people who are on your side is key to navigating such moments. Of course, not everyone you think will be by your side will be, and it is in the midst of a storm that you know who really is in your camp. Often it is those people who knew you before you arrived at any real point of prestige. Nevertheless, I would say cast your net far and wide; you never know who may be surprisingly loyal.

The world would be a better place if we could hear more about where people fell short and how they were able to overcome, but of course such openness comes with risks. Some cultures are more comfortable with failure than others. The United States is a place where so many successful entrepreneurs have not hidden away from stories of bankruptcy as they bounce back. Former IBM head Thomas John Watson Sr once said, 'If you want to increase your success rate, double your failure rate.' In the very recent past the United States has had a president who was a known bankrupt. The United Kingdom on the other hand is a place where failure is not so much embraced. The British media's thirst for breaking news is partly to blame for a culture so averse to failure. This stifles creativity and competitiveness, as people opt for safer paths to avoid making headlines.

Failure and Disruption

A former colleague of mine, Dominic Cummings, will go down in history as both a person who divided opinion and one who was disruptive enough to achieve things that many thought would not be possible. Though we were never close, the one thing that struck me about him was his keenness for the risk of failure to not be an impediment for someone trying to do something that would improve an outcome. He understood that Britain needed to be bold if it was to remain competitive globally, with many emerging markets increasingly better positioned to exploit future opportunities.

One of Dom's legacies in government is the Advanced Research and Invention Agency (ARIA). This £800-million investment fund will take risks that could result in some of the most critical technological developments in the future. It will very likely help Britain to get up to par with the United States Advanced Research Projects Agency (ARPA). Inventors will be able to take risks without the fear of scrutiny that often comes attached to the checks and balances linked to government bureaucracy.

Such tenacity is of course not necessarily conducive to an environment that arguably needs stability – such as government, where 400,000 civil servants are trained to understand and mitigate risk. To cover their own backs, to avoid saying things that would embarrass the government should a freedom of information request be lodged, to preserve one's reputation at all costs. If anyone was to ask me what the role of a good special advisor was, I would say it is to be the one willing to present crazy ideas that ministers would otherwise not be aware of, and to then ensure that those ideas do not disappear into the 'blob'. Of course, if all special advisors are recruited from the same place, then such examples of radical thinking become rare. Do not get me wrong, there are excellent civil servants who would be keen to do more or to go further, but the need for political cover and to avoid being stifled by colleagues is often a great barrier to taking risks and sticking your neck out. It is not always viewed positively if a civil servant has helped to push a radical idea forward. In doing so they may themselves become an outsider, in the tactical or psychological sense. But that is no bad thing.

Being Allowed to Fail

There are other types of failure that society is increasingly averse to accepting or understanding. So-called cancel culture has meant that there is a constant witch hunt for the next scalp, fuelled by self-righteous keyboard warriors who are unwilling or unable to afford the same grace to others that has been bestowed upon them. A few days after the resignation of now former chairman of KPMG Bill Michael, I spoke to a friend who worked there as a senior consultant about how Bill was viewed within the organisation. He was quite upset, but not in the way many would think. He said to me that as a black man in KPMG he always felt as though Bill was a good person who cared about the organisation and staff. Following the death of George Floyd, Bill had organised meetings to discuss race in the workplace and the protests that were taking place across the world. My friend told me that Bill was extremely empathetic. Bill of course went on to host the car crash town hall meeting after which he resigned, where he was dismissive of the idea of unconscious bias and failed to demonstrate empathy for staff who were having a tough time during lockdown, sounding like he thought they should simply consider themselves lucky because they were still in employment.

Bill clearly made a mistake in not showing that he understood that people of all backgrounds and employment statuses had suffered to some degree during the pandemic. He was probably also attempting to dismiss the efficacy of unconscious bias training and not unconscious bias itself. Either way, the damage was seemingly irreversible. He later apologised, but it was not enough. Commercial imperatives meant that KPMG could not risk further damage to its reputation and subsequent loss of clients, and therefore Bill had to go.

This culture has had disastrous effects on free speech, as people say less in pursuit of self-preservation. It has also influenced our ability to reason with and learn from each other.

Nations are divided because people feel like they cannot speak or be heard, and populist leaders emerge as a beacon of hope for those who feel silenced, when in fact very often there is a better way.

Our establishment is also steeped in disdain for failure. From my experience in government, you were less likely to receive an honour from Her Majesty the Queen (and I am sure now His Majesty the King) if there was evidence that you had failed in business. This does not only apply to people who have become bankrupt. Let's just reflect on this for a moment. If you have been brave enough to step out, leave the safety of employment and risk it all, and have somehow fallen short, it will count against you. Why? Because in Britain we are more concerned about media headlines and political correctness than we are about being open and honest about the realities of life.

Of course, I am not defending some of the most damaging acts of negligence that have led to the collapse of some of our country's most famous high street brands, but I do think that we should celebrate those who have stepped up, even when it has not quite worked out. In a global pandemic many people will have lost jobs and closed businesses through no fault of their own and despite trying their very best to stay afloat. For the next twenty years at least, they will have to wonder how people will react to the knowledge that they are one of many who had a business that did not work out. This is very strange when you consider someone with a county court judgment will have their credit file cleaned after six years, and for people who have actually committed a crime the possibility of a spent conviction exists. I totally agree with second chances and new beginnings. But the question is, why is that same level of grace not afforded to business leaders? Most will never be as rich as

Richard Branson. Transparency is good, but often the impact that society attaches to knowing someone has failed makes one wonder if there is a need for a veil to cover our collective nakedness at times. The Scandinavian model of extreme transparency, and associated laws, simply would not be conducive to British culture, because we are not very gracious.

Outsiders and Failure

Failure can be debilitating. One can often be less willing to try again, and doubt can creep in about one's ability to achieve a goal. Many enter a depressive state that becomes difficult to break out of. The emotional scars of failing at something are often never fully dealt with. The fear of being found out, or the risk of shame, can often stifle. The challenge for an outsider is not necessarily that failure can have a more significant impact on you than someone else, although it must be said that those with deeper pockets will have a better cushion to fall back on if things do not go to plan. Philip Green, former owner of Arcadia Group, may be going through a tough time now that his retail empire has closed, but it is very unlikely that he will ever be worried about where his next meal will come from.

Sometimes there is also a feeling of inferiority that can make you feel a failure through no fault of your own. During the 2019 general election I went for dinner with colleagues. As discussions progressed it emerged that I was one of only two people at the table not to have studied at Oxbridge. It was the other person who hadn't who kindly helped to point this out. Being the child of a world-renowned historian, he did not seem too fazed by his newfound minority status. He was so confident in himself that he not only raised it but went on to informally chair a conversation about this revelation. I had to remind myself there and then, as I was eating my plate of Chinese food, that I was someone with value and my story was one not to be ashamed of.

Being a second-generation migrant who was now a special advisor meant that I should not view myself as inferior or a failure because I could not quite reach the highest heights in education. I was not there because someone had arranged for me to have an internship at party HQ upon graduation. People had helped me along the way, but my course was different and in many respects the advice I could give was richer for it. To expect to have the same level of privilege as others was not healthy and it was a reminder that though I was a minority at this table, in many other ways I was part of a majority. This experience is one many can relate to. The very regular occurrence in the corporate world of those who have attended Harvard Business School exchanging pleasantries as others wait for the intimate moment to pass is a story that has been told many times. In fact, I once visited Lagos in Nigeria as part of a research exercise and found myself in the middle of such an occasion. Harvard Business School snobbery is truly a global phenomenon.

So, what advice can I give to outsiders dealing with failure? Firstly, prepare for failures by building social capital in advance. You may not, in your hour of need, be able to rely on everyone who calls you their friend, but it helps to have several options. I was surprised by some of the people who reached out to me after I left Downing Street – and was also surprised by some of the people who didn't.

Secondly, owning failures often makes people more human and relatable. In January 2021 Britain reached a sad milestone that no one could have predicted back in March 2020 when we entered the first lockdown. At the beginning of the Covid-19 pandemic we were told by experts that 20,000 deaths in the United Kingdom would be considered a good outcome. Even at that time many could not quite comprehend what we were being told. Fast-forward nine months and over 100,000 people had sadly lost their lives due to coronavirus. This had all been presided over by Boris Johnson, who many would have expected to have suffered a backlash from the British public as a result. The first thing that he did on that infamous day was not to justify decisions made or explain how we got to such a devastating figure. Instead, the prime minister swiftly apologised, and the following day every single national newspaper, even the most hostile to the administration, carried a photograph of him with a melancholic expression, giving the apology to the nation. That apology was clearly accepted by most people, as subsequent polls showed that the Conservative Party had bounced back from a previous dip and were ahead of Labour. Of course, part of the reason for the bounce was the successful rollout of the vaccine programme, but it should not be ignored that owning a failure and apologising can often help to nullify any subsequent consequence. Contrastingly, Liz Truss became the shortest-serving prime minister in British history and left office defiant, refusing to apologise for her contributions to the suffering many households were facing as a result of her mini-budget.

Thirdly, you should be aware of the impact that your current actions may have on your future aspirations. That will mean you are more careful about what you put on social media, places you visit or who you associate with. It may also mean you are more careful with what you put in writing or who you choose to offend. There have been unfortunate examples of people who had posted comments when they were much younger that then resurface when they become more prominent. It may not be right for someone to have to pay for comments that may no longer reflect their views, but again the best way to manage such situations is to remember that the internet keeps receipts, be upfront and explain that your views have evolved. We have seen occasions where someone who is clearly from a background where it is likely they are under-represented in certain spaces has been forced to leave because they have not been adequately advised about how to manage a situation. Or sometimes, even if they are advised it is still felt best for them to depart. The National Union of Students seems to have a conveyor belt of newly elected officers who have said anti-Semitic things via social media when in their early teens. It is strange that on no occasion has there been an apology followed by a proactive form of reconciliation. No meeting between the offender and a Holocaust survivor. Instead, said young(ish) person is eventually relieved of their duties with no evidence of an opportunity for a teachable moment taken. I know this is a slight oversimplification of the issue. But I suppose part of the challenge is that many student leaders have become so averse to engaging with people with opposing or controversial views, that they are afforded less grace when they are the offending party.

Renowned fashion editor André Leon Talley died in January 2022. During his four decades at the magazine publishing house Condé Nast, he wrote landmark features, including Michelle Obama's *Vogue* interview after she became first lady, and oversaw some of its most iconic shoots, including Naomi Campbell as Scarlett O'Hara for *Vanity Fair*, inverting *Gone With The Wind*'s racial dynamics.

He was a 6ft 7in larger-than-life African American with a heavy build, constantly encircled by slender white women. Talley's book tells the story of his life, which is often the story of the women who have supported him, including his grandmother, who raised him while his parents worked in another city. For decades he was the only black person on the front row at fashion shows.

A significant number of people who work in fashion come from a relatively privileged background. The barriers include the notoriously low (or no) pay at entry level, coupled with the obvious expense associated with trying to keep up with fashion trends. His relatively poor background made his accomplishments extraordinary.

He was then the most powerful black man in fashion, although he has now been overtaken by Edward Enninful, editor of British *Vogue*. When Enninful got that job, he wrote to Talley to tell him: 'You paved the way.'

Talley's death at the age of seventy-three, two years after his biography was published, came following his falling-out with Anna Wintour, his boss at American *Vogue*. She was his mentor and key supporter. Some argue that his failure to move with the times and adapt to the digital age was part of his demise. Others argue that at seventy-one he should have been more prepared to take on the role of an elder statesman in the industry. Talley once said, 'I am seventy-one years old, and I take my story with me wherever I go. The past is always in the present.' He perhaps felt he could go on for ever and did not plan for the autumn and winter of his story. It is important to be prepared for all eventualities as best you can.

It takes courage to be able to go again after failing, and the more confidence someone has the easier it is to navigate those moments. Our level of resilience is often based on our experiences as children. Parents play a vital role in helping us to navigate and respond to failure. Every child is different, and so treating everyone the same is likely to be the first problem when trying to improve a child's resilience. As we grow up, our experiences in education and extracurricular activities will also play a role in how we are able to deal with failing. Relationships will also matter. Ultimately, outsiders must find a way to be comfortable in the power of taking pride in their own story. Outsiders must learn to accept that they cannot change their background, and in many ways their journey is what will be a source of inspiration for others. Failure is inevitable and universal. You must not be overcome by the guilt attached to falling short; you are not alone. But you must own the failures, learn from those mistakes, and make sure you go again with more determination to do better.

Chapter 8

Variables

When I left Number 10, many people checked to see how I was doing. Some of those people are in the chapters of this book. But it is those who were silent that I remember most clearly. Again, I think of the words of Martin Luther King Jr which so resonate with me: 'In the end, we will remember not the words of our enemies, but the silence of our friends.' Some of the colleagues who I had no personal issue with, who I had worked with day and night, side by side, during the toughest moments trying to respond to the coronavirus pandemic. Their silence was deafening. I am not naive enough to think that one makes many true friends in politics, but I think it is important to be empathetic when it matters, or at least courteous. Every time a colleague from my team left Downing Street (be it through their choice or not) I took it upon myself to send them some words of encouragement. It can be very debilitating when you leave high office, crashing back down to earth with nowhere near as much power as you once had. Quite a few former colleagues have suffered with mental health challenges, both while working in Number 10 and after. It is a high-pressure environment. Most former advisors would never tell the truth about their experiences in government like I have in this book because they believe it would impact their ambitions to become parliamentarians or to be recruited to a future administration. They may be right, but it's a little depressing that being open and honest is seen as detrimental to being able to serve in public life.

Attending Conservative Party conference in 2021, six months after my resignation, was so interesting. Some former colleagues were afraid to speak to me in public in case I was cancelled. One in particular, the special advisor for climate change when I was in Downing Street, was so remarkably cold, I wasn't sure how to respond. Not only did we have the same first name, but I remember we were in good spirits at the final rally in London before the 2019 general election. We never had any issues with each other, so it was so strange to see that he had turned so frosty. The political class can be remarkably petty. It was clear that I was an outsider in many people's eyes by the time I attended the conference, so I decided I may as well own it. Ultimately, it is more liberating for me to be myself than to try to conform to being something unnatural for me. Besides, as we have already established, being a political outsider is often not a disadvantage.

Fast-forward to the autumn of 2022, nearly a year since I began writing this book, and I can't help but feel like something is missing. Doubt begins to creep in about this journey I have been on. I know that once this book is published there will be no turning back. Plenty of people will unpick the merits of the conclusions that I have made. Some will now decide that they can finally put me into a box or assign me to one side or another in relation to current debates around how society should function. These reflections are what led me to this chapter. I needed to find a way to confirm some of the things that I had discovered and to answer some of the questions that I still had about how I should respond to what I had learnt.

To help with my thinking I wanted to speak with someone different to anyone that I had spoken to before, and identified Eleanor Southwood, the former chair of the Royal National Institute of Blind People, more widely known as RNIB. She is also a local government councillor in the London Borough of Brent. I thought someone like Eleanor would be able to show me beyond any doubt what it truly means to be an outsider and the value outsiders bring. This after all was the premise of the book. I had worked with RNIB in the past, helping them to recruit new members to their board, both during and after the organisation had faced regulatory challenges. I knew that their constitution required the majority of their board to be blind or partially sighted. Though I had never met Eleanor my assumption was that as the former chair she would at least be partially sighted, but most likely blind. Eleanor had led the RNIB, a multimillion-pound royal-chartered institution, and I felt that she would hopefully have a unique combination of strategic-level insights and personal-level experiences to draw from.

We met on Tuesday 6 September 2022, the same day that my old boss Boris Johnson officially left his role as prime minister of the United Kingdom. A strange backdrop to the interview I was about to have. In a parallel universe I would have been one of the advisors clapping for him as his administration came to an end, the same way I had clapped in 2019 when he entered through the famous black door of Number 10 with the largest Conservative majority in recent history. Instead, I was sitting in the coffee shop in the basement of the Royal Society of the Arts (RSA) preparing this interview.

Eleanor was born in Manchester before moving to Walthamstow in north-east London. When she was eight her family moved to Derby. Eleanor and her younger sister Matilda were both born blind, with the same congenital eye condition called Leber's Amaurosis. She tells me it's 'all to do with the communication between the optic nerve and the brain.' There is nothing physically wrong with their eyes. There's nothing physically wrong with their brains either. The issue is the communication between the two. She can see light and dark and nothing much else. I'm immediately gripped by Eleanor's contemplations. 'I think disability is really challenging for people,' she says. 'We hold within ourselves, particularly in the West, a very deep-rooted disgust. I'm not suggesting people look at me and think, yuck. But think about the people in the Bible who are blind, it's either a punishment or you're awaiting a miracle to be cured. You are not whole, there's something wrong. There's something broken. All through our cultural heritage, the West in particular has blindness down as either a punishment or something to be cured and that stays with societies for a long time.'

As a Christian myself I am challenged by this. Why are they not whole? Often when you don't have one of your senses, it means that perhaps you are more sensitive to seeing and feeling things. You have to live your life in a different way. Eleanor explains: 'People always say to me, oh, you must have amazing hearing. I don't. But what I do have is hearing that I use in a different way to how you use yours. And you'd use yours in the same way if you couldn't see. When I use my hearing, I'm using it to figure out what's around me, all the things you are doing visually, or what's happening over there or what's happening with the coffee machine. I'm doing that in my ears.

It's an orientation thing rather than supersonic hearing. People would've monetised it by now if it was a real thing.'

I ask what she thinks needs to happen that isn't happening for blind people to flourish and what the biggest barriers are for people who are blind. 'The opportunity to work is a massive one, and everything that flows from that. To have a meaningful job and dignity of work. Being able to look at what your assets are and what you can bring to the table.' A lot of blind and partially sighted people spend a great deal of their lives feeling like a burden to others and feeling like people are doing them a favour by assisting them. I think there's something really powerful about the dignity of knowing your own value, not just financially, but whatever that means to you. Eleanor says, 'Blind people should have the right to define for themselves what they would like to pursue. I think probably pilot is off the list, but you know, I just think there's a lot of pigeonholing of disabled people through people trying to be helpful.'

Establishing the value that outsiders bring appears a consistent theme throughout this book, and so is the importance of confidence to making people thrive. It is no different for disabled people. Eleanor confirms this: 'The kind of flip side of that is the skills and confidence to work. You know, I am incredibly fortunate in growing up in a household where it never occurred to me that I would not be successful. It literally never occurred to me. There are people who've lost their sight as well, who are also experiencing the need to learn, to do things differently with a feeling of loss. A lot of people just don't have the confidence to work. I can't do that because I'm blind. I can't be that because I'm blind. And so, it's both sides of the equation, I suppose it's the skills and confidence. That's where a lot of projects have sort of fallen down in the past. You get one side, but not the other.'

Both of Eleanor's parents were actors and so the financial consequences of leaving London were severe for the family. But they were very keen for their two daughters to go to a local mainstream school. Eleanor thinks she may have been the first blind child in the county she lived in to go through to the age of eighteen in the mainstream schooling system. 'There is a debate raging still about specialist schools versus mainstream provision. I think I'd have been very pro-mainstream, based on my own experience, but I chaired RNIB for three years and I was a trustee for ten years. I met lots of families for whom, for lots of different reasons, mainstream wasn't the right option.'

This is the challenge when trying to respond in a uniform way to circumstances that people find themselves in. It's all well and good to try to take firm positions on how people should interact with the world, but the reality is that external factors like quality of provision coupled with internal factors like personality mean that one size very rarely fits all. Just because one person was able to flourish in one circumstance, doesn't mean another person with the same characteristics will as well.

Eleanor went to a comprehensive school and was the only blind child in her year. It wasn't a school that had a particular specialism, but her parents fought incredibly hard for her to go there when she was eleven, because it was where everyone from her primary school was going. She went on to read politics, philosophy and economics at Oxford University. She tells me that many people were on hand to help her and her sister along the way. People were not afraid to learn alongside the family in terms of how they could offer support. 'My friends were always super helpful. This is before audio description was as prominent as it is for most films. Now, if you go to see a film, if you go to certain performances, you can wear a headset and get the audio-described track kind of relayed into the headset. This was before that, so friends used to describe what was going on, including, you know, all sorts of things that occur in films that teenage girls go to see. When we went out dancing together, occasionally one of them would give me a shift to make sure that I wasn't dancing with a totally different group that we didn't know.'

The family left London in the late 1980s because options for schooling in the mid-eighties were not great for blind children. The Warnock report had been published in 1978, which promoted the integration of children with disabilities into mainstream schools; however, there was still very patchy provision for children with special needs.

Disability Rights in History

The disability rights movement in the United Kingdom can be traced at least as far back as the late fourteenth century, when the 1388 Statute of Cambridge (otherwise known as the 'Poor Law') was passed. The statute made the distinction between 'deserving' and 'undeserving' poor people in the context of eligibility to claim alms, with disabled and older people being among the groups considered 'deserving' and therefore being eligible for charity. However, it was not until more recent times that the organisation of disabled people, for disabled people, started to take form. In the late nineteenth century, the British Deaf Association and the National League of the Blind were established as the first two recorded organisations of disabled people. This was a key development because movements recorded prior to this development can be distinguished as organisations for disabled people, movements that were run by non-disabled people to 'provide' for disabled people.

This laid the groundwork for many future developments, and a timeline of activism that has seen many significant subsequent developments in the attitudes towards and treatment of disabled people in the personal, political and professional spheres. As early as the 1920s, disabled people began protesting against discrimination and derogatory attitudes towards them, with the National League for the Blind leading a march to a rally in London in order to demand improved working conditions and remuneration. This action was directly linked to the formation of the Blind Persons Act 1920, the first disability-specific legislation in the world and an early antecedent to the Equality Act of 2010.

Activism by disabled people reached new heights in the 1990s, with previous movements having amplified the voices of pressure groups and other activists. In this year, Mike Oliver also published his seminal dissertation 'The Individual and Social Models of Disability', thus becoming the first professor of disability studies in the world. This was also a significant development as it started the tradition of disabled self-advocacy within the academic sphere and carried forth the famous slogan of the 1970s, 'Nothing about us without us'.

From 1993 to 1998, the Disabled People's Direct Action Network (DAN) staged over 100 protest actions, continuing the campaign against inequality for disabled people. Alongside DAN and other protest groups, now Baroness Jane Campbell featured heavily in lobbying Parliament to introduce commensurate legislation. This eventually led to the incumbent Conservative government, led by John Major, passing the Disability Discrimination Act 1995. The bill received its second reading on 22 May 1995, and received royal assent on 8 November. The act, now superseded by the Equality Act 2010, provided protection for disabled persons against direct discrimination, failure to make reasonable adjustment, and victimisation in the areas of employment and occupation; education; transport; the provision of goods; and the exercise of public functions.

The act was the first of its kind to protect disabled people from multiple kinds of discrimination and was a testament to the fact that organised self-advocacy as well as direct action have the potential to effect radical change at the national level. Disabled people today have legal rights to be treated with dignity because of the pressure from activists.

I find Eleanor's reflections on activism so powerful as she turns to me and says, 'You know, we're not politically aligned, but I'm sure there are comparisons. On the left, not being an activist is an unpopular thing. The fact that I approach my political life from wanting to get into committee rooms and being around the table, being a decision-maker. That does not always go down well. People want me to be weighed down. It's quite challenging sometimes.'

Eleanor's career began in public policy before she went to the Confederation of British Industry, where she worked on public service reform, and did a stint at a communications company who ran public policy conferences. She also worked as a headhunter, and now says, 'I really loved it. I mean, it is the best job for people who are curious, right? Not only can you say to people, yeah, but what do you actually do? You can also say, and how much do they pay for that? Meeting so many fascinating people and thinking about the difference that leaders make in organisations was really fascinating to me.'

Her journey to becoming the chair of RNIB stemmed from her willingness to challenge decision-makers. While recruiting trustees, the then chair of RNIB had a meeting with one of Eleanor's colleagues in her office. 'They were like, oh, we have to introduce you. And I was thinking, oh, yeah, random blind man. This is an hour of my life I'm never going to get back. We've got nothing in common besides both being blind but sure. I spent an hour telling him how useless I thought RNIB was and how it was totally irrelevant to me. How I just thought they were totally behind the times, very uncool. And he of course called my bluff and said, well, you've got a choice then. You can shout at me for another hour or apply to be a trustee, be part of changing it.' She was on the board for ten years, including three years as chair, and has since taken on a number of board positions where she has a seat at the table to effect change. But the pressure to become an activist has continued. 'There's a lot of criticism of disabled people who are not weighed down being activists all the time. Not calling out things all the time. I really feel strongly that it's entirely somebody's choice about whether they do that or not. I'm hugely grateful to people who've gone before me. Who've chained themselves to railings so I don't have to. That is an amazing thing. But you can be grateful for that while at the same time living your life and finding your own ways to influence the world around you.'

Outsiders, Responsibility and Expectation

My question as I listen to Eleanor is how I square that circle myself. I am a black man from a working-class background. People will – rightly – say I have become quite privileged, and that privilege is partly because of other people who were activists and challenged the status quo. Just like those who fought for disabled people's rights, there are countless people who have fought for racial equality, from bus boycotts in Bristol to protests outside of the Palace of Westminster. What is the responsibility for anyone who is standing on the shoulders of giants, to quote Sir Isaac Newton? My conclusion after speaking with Eleanor is that it is a personal thing and not for others to prescribe. For some people, it means they need to really be high-profile and talk about inequality all the time; or it might be that someone makes sure that every week they offer an opportunity to somebody who wouldn't have otherwise had one. It might be both of those things. There'll be some people who do nothing, and that's life. It's very tempting, especially in politics, to decide that one has a right to judge how someone should engage with certain topics. Senior black Conservatives have historically avoided speaking about race and have been attacked for doing so. Though I take a different approach to them, I do not think anyone has the right to decide how another person should live their lives or what interests they should take up. It's reductive; and actually a sign of true progress is people having genuine choice in how to spend their time, regardless of their background.

I sense Eleanor wants to say something that she fears will be quite controversial. I ask if she has further thoughts on the subject of outsiders. 'I think we need to be a bit careful about how we talk about this, and it may have come up in other conversations, but there are a lot of people I meet who live their lives through an expectation that they will be discriminated against.'

I ask her to continue. 'If I kept a journal of every time I was mistreated I would have loads of things written down. Some of it might be about gender. Some of it might be about disability. Some of it might be about politics. I think there's quite an important choice that certainly I observe in people. I'm not suggesting these things don't happen and I'm not suggesting they don't make me angry. I'm not suggesting I don't have days where I go home and you think, oh God, that was really hard, you know? All of that happens. At the same time, I just walk out of my front door, expecting to engage with the world. I don't expect the world to discriminate against me. Sometimes it lets me down, you know, but the thing is, in my experience, if I look at the world through a prism of everything that is wrong, I just think it would destroy me. I honestly do.'

This is the most fascinating part of the conversation for me. I can tell Eleanor wants to say more but at the same time she recognises that she has privileges, saying, 'I am an Oxford-educated, white woman, living in the capital of one of the largest economies in the world.' This is of course what many people who do not like what she is saying will say to shut her down. The reality is Eleanor has a right to speak her truth as a blind person from a working-class background. Not only that, but she is a councillor in the most diverse borough in the capital and has chaired the leading organisation advocating for the rights of those who are blind or partially sighted. To use a modern colloquial term – she has receipts.

Eleanor has resolved to not allow other people's ignorant

behaviours to weigh her down. For this reason, some may label her the 'wrong kind of blind person'; but I wonder if she is the one with the issue, or whether it's other people's own biases and insecurities being projected onto her. I have always felt very sad when I hear someone say that they are exhausted because of the impact of constantly being let down by society. I just don't think a time will ever come when we are not let down by others, and so Eleanor perhaps is on to something with her outlook.

She continues, 'Just trying to make it easy for people feels important. I think sometimes naming things helps people as well, because actually if I'm the one with the lived experience, in a way I've got the upper hand because I've got the legitimacy to talk about it and in a way, it is my responsibility to. I think a lot of people still have a lot of anxiety around language and they don't want to get it wrong. It's all very well to criticise people about how they talk about disability or how they offer assistance. But the thing is that we have got the advantage on them in a way. This is my life. It's what I know. I can't possibly assume the same level of competence or fluency from people who do not have the same experience. Plus, everyone's different. If you met ten blind people, we'd all tell you something different about what really winds up blind people and what doesn't, and there's no accounting for that in public discourse today.'

With that my interview comes to an end. What Eleanor has cemented in my mind is that all of our upbringings play a vital role in crafting how we are able to respond to the things the world throws at us. Even as a blind person from a modest background, her confidence clearly came from her parents reinforcing the fact that she could be whatever she wanted. Eleanor's ability to flourish is at least partly because people, including friends and her wider community, were willing and able to help her along the way. She has been able to build bridges, to challenge policymakers, and hopefully to inspire others through what she has achieved. But the biggest takeaway from her story is that there are variables, often hidden somewhere in our individual stories, that will determine how outsiders will respond to their outsiderness. It is wrong to simply say that because one person with a certain difference responds in one way, all others should be expected to do the same.

Eleanor's story is inspiring but not every blind person will have access to the things that have made her so impressive. In an ideal world they would have things that would build their confidence and sense of value, because that would allow them to better deal with life's obstacles and to fulfil their full potential. If a black or Asian man or woman can become a Cabinet member within a Conservative administration, that does not mean that those activists who still feel the need to push for progress are behind the times. Again, there are intersectional variables, notably the school somebody goes to, that mean there is still a need to push for progress. This goes both ways. Not everyone who is blind or from a minority background will feel they must take on the role of an activist, and that is okay. We all have our own path and there should be mutual respect and perhaps less pressure on people to conform to any weight of expectation.

Disability and Representation

What stays with me most after my conversation with Eleanor is this idea that disabled people are viewed as not whole. I can't stop thinking about how this idea needs to be discussed more and challenged. While there has been extensive research about the value of diverse teams, most of those studies have focused on ethnicity and gender. The area of research focused on disabled people remains underserved. McKinsey & Company have released a series of reports that encompass the business case for diversity. Their 2019 study found that companies in the top quartile for gender diversity on executive teams were 25 per cent more likely to have above-average profitability than companies in the fourth quartile – up from 21 per cent in 2017 and 15 per cent in 2014. They also argue that *the greater the representation, the higher the likelihood of outperformance. Companies with more than 30 per cent women executives were more likely to outperform companies where this percentage ranged from 10 to 30, and in turn these companies were more likely to outperform those with even fewer women executives, or none at all.* The differential is substantial, at 48 per cent. Gender diversity is not the only factor that impacts positively on company performance either. McKinsey & Company argue that ethnic diversity is also crucial to successful organisations – in the same study, they found that 'top-quartile companies outperformed those in the fourth one by 36 per cent, slightly up from 33 per cent in 2017 and 35 per cent in 2014'. Diverse employees with various backgrounds and thought processes can bring unique expertise to organisations that can optimise problem-solving. This can also be said of having people from different age groups involved in decision-making. We will explore neurodiversity in a later chapter.

My conversation with Eleanor has challenged me in many ways. We need to recognise the value people who have a disability can bring.

Chapter 9

Understanding Ourselves

On 25 February 1964, a certain Cassius Clay – who would later take the name Muhammad Ali – shocked the boxing world by defeating defending heavyweight world champion Sonny Liston. His victory took place in Miami Beach, a place where we would reasonably expect a twenty-two-year-old newly crowned world champion to remain for celebrations into the night. Icons like Frank Sinatra, Sammy Davis Jr and the rest of the Rat Pack were known for regularly cavorting around Miami Beach's glittering nightclubs. But this was a time of Jim Crow's segregation laws, which prohibited African Americans from mixing with white Americans. Ali would not be allowed to stay. Instead, he went to the Hampton House Motel in Miami's Brownsville neighbourhood. The hotel was a famous location for prominent African Americans not able to stay in Miami Beach lodgings. Martin Luther King Jr is thought to have given an early version of his famed 'I Have a Dream' speech at the hotel. Accompanying Ali were his friends Sam Cooke, Jim Brown, and one Malcolm X. They spent the evening together in what many call a once-in-a-lifetime meeting of legends.

Directed by Regina King, the film *One Night in Miami* offers up a fictional account of the four icons speaking about their roles in the civil rights movement. We will never know exactly what was really discussed that night; Jim Brown is the only one of the four still alive. Malcolm X and Sam Cooke were both killed within a year of that evening. But many of the subjects of conversation in the film are true to the biographies of Brown, Clay, Cooke and Malcolm X, each of whom were then at a crossroads in their professional lives. They were all outsiders of course, but how they chose to respond to that status was different.

Malcolm X, the civil rights campaigner and prominent spokes-man for the Nation of Islam at the time, preached a message of black empowerment and separatism. He was very critical of Martin Luther King Jr's message of non-violence and integra-tion. The Nation's vociferous message angered whites and split blacks. Malcom's views softened towards the end of his life after he had left the Nation of Islam because of his disillusion-ment with the leadership. Muhammad Ali on the other hand would go on to join the Nation of Islam shortly after this meeting, and his friendship with Malcolm X ended. Sam Cooke was at the time creating music that would appeal to white Americans. He saw a greater value in trying to be part of the world of those with power, much to the disquiet of Malcolm X and Ali. Sam had begun his career in black gospel music, before crossing over to secular music and white audi-ences. In 1957, his future classic 'You Send Me' hit number one on the Billboard pop charts. In the film *One Night in Miami*, Cooke is the only one who could stay in a hotel in Miami Beach. How? He got his white manager to book a room for him. It wasn't that he did not care about civil rights; Cooke was also a campaigner in his own way. Inspired by Bob

Dylan's famous song 'Blowin' in the Wind', he wrote 'A Change Is Gonna Come'. Economic empowerment and normalising the entering of places you were told weren't for people like you were his methods, which he thought was a much more impactful approach.

Finally, Jim Brown, who played for the Cleveland Browns at the time, was one of the best running backs in American football. He also believed in black empowerment, but his brand of activism was not explicitly separatist as that of Malcolm X and Cassius Clay. When he was invited to the White House to meet with the newly sworn-in president Lyndon Johnson in 1963, he used it as an opportunity to talk about race relations. Later, when sharing his reflections on Martin Luther King Jr, Jim opined, 'I didn't think much of Dr King. I mean, I am not trying to put him down, but if you think about the majority of the rhetoric, it's about what's being done to us. It doesn't have damn near anything that says what we're going to do for ourselves.' Brown attributes his views on self-reliance to having grown up on St Simons Island, a community off the coast of Georgia where he was raised by his grandmother and where racism did not affect him directly. Decades after the 1964 meeting at Hampton House, Jim, a friend of Malcolm X, Muhammad Ali and Sam Cooke, would declare his support for Donald Trump for president of the United States.

What this story shows us is that outsiders do not have a uniform response to being on the outside. The four were among the most famous black men in the world at the time. They were all outsiders, but how they responded to this status was entirely different. As part of my sabbatical when writing this book, I went to visit Hampton House with my sister Victoria. We were given a private tour, which included walking into the room that Martin Luther King Jr frequented. I closed my eyes and tried to picture what this place was like back then. An oasis of pure joy in an age of struggle. A safe place for outsiders to feel human and valued. A place of rest for those exhausted. For all those things that it represented, it was still just a hotel. Temporary by design, meaning those who visited would have to return to their reality before too long. Just like I would have to.

Outsiderness, Responses and Psychology

We usually have three responses to being an outsider in group dynamics. The proactive response is when people want to be part of a given group and take what they think are the right actions to ensure that they can be properly embedded into that group. Like Sam Cooke. For example, coming to a new country and embracing the whole culture; the good immigrant, so to speak. The passive response is when people are inactive or indifferent about engaging with a group. But by doing so, often they are not going to be embedded or included in that group unless somebody proactively drags or compels them in. This is often where we have debates about the integration of some groups, for example communities where significant numbers of people who have been in the country for several years do not speak English. It is important to note that there are sometimes barriers that make someone passive, including socioeconomic or cultural factors, that must be overcome. At other times the passive choice is based on personal priorities. Though Jim Brown has been passionate about empowerment for his community, there is a sense of indifference about whether that empowerment required ever being accepted or part of an inside group. The final type is the rooted response, when someone seeks to stay outside. Sometimes a tactical decision, but often one that is steeped in a deeper-rooted story. Perhaps they or people they know have had experiences that make them feel unwelcomed or unwilling to come inside. Historical examples of racism may still feel all too raw, or maybe there are very recent events that make them feel alienated.

I did not grow up in America, segregated under Jim Crow, but it isn't too difficult for me to understand why the Nation of Islam would have been so appealing to people who had witnessed lynchings and police brutality. Today, the issue of disproportionate stop and search rates is a less extreme example of a subject that creates this kind of tension. Other times there is a fear that to be inside would mean compromising too much of who you are. One's identity, culture, or heritage. Muhammad Ali's style often rubbed people up the wrong way, but when you discover that he was born and raised in Louisville, Kentucky, home of the Kentucky Derby, his vivacious style and seemingly natural desire to stand out makes more sense. We are not very good at understanding each other. Perhaps part of the reason for this is we are not very good at understanding ourselves.

I am off to the British Museum to meet with Dr Shubulade Smith, a consultant psychiatrist and a visiting senior lecturer at the Institute of Psychiatry, Psychology and Neuroscience (IoPPN), King's College London. She is recognised nationally and internationally for her approach to psychiatric care, focusing on the complex interactions between the biological, psychological and social aspects of a person. Dr Smith is a clinician with a strong academic focus who has published over sixty journal articles, research letters and book chapters in the field of psychiatry. We first met when I was still in Downing Street. I had arranged a round table to discuss mental health ahead of the publication of the Mental Health Act white paper. Her contributions left a lasting impression on me and so I asked for her to return for a private meeting. We speak about the white paper and reflect on the progress that has happened. There's been a lot of activity and it's very pleasing to see that improvements are noticeable. Things are changing as mental health becomes less of a taboo subject in the UK.

This is the most challenging conversation I have had on this journey of understanding outsiders because I am having to reflect on what Dr Smith is explaining to me as one of the pre-eminent experts in the field. I'm also seeing if I can relate it back to my own experiences and the experiences of the outsiders I have already interviewed.

She begins by saying, 'The thing about being an outsider is that people may not know if they want to be an outsider, but there's something that we do know about people, which is that they definitely want to be an insider. We will often hear about people working to make sure that they can fit in with others.' That makes sense to me. She gives another example: 'You will have the area where you grew up Samuel, Peckham?' I correct her assumption: 'Barnet'. She says, 'That's definitely not inner-city south London, and in that grouping in Barnet just like with Wilfred Emmanuel-Jones [the Black Farmer] you will have had settings where you were not like the people around you. Some of those groups you will have worked actively to be part of, and some of them you may have decided that you were not going to join. Or you might have just not bothered. So you weren't doing anything but by passively not trying to be part of one group you have actively decided to be outside of it.'

She is frighteningly correct. I remember arriving in East Barnet secondary school as a thirteen-year-old boy. I started on the same day as another black boy, which doubled the total number of black boys in the year group to four. There were some groups that I did proactively seek to join, like the football team, but the other new boy and I were quite passive about joining other groups. Probably because we had a more familiar companion in each other. It meant that eventually we had enemies, boys who were intimidated by the new guys who were a bit different from the other black boys, who were already well integrated. Without proactively trying to assimilate into a group or to normalise your presence within it, you are making a decision, even if it's not a proactive decision. So those people who say I don't know why I am not included . . . Maybe it is that they haven't actively tried to be part of the group, and therefore they are separate, which might allow them freedom to get on and do their own thing, but they must recognise it was a decision nonetheless. This is a countercultural position to take, but it is only when we try to look at human behaviour from a new perspective that we will be able to understand ourselves.

As I understand it, everyone wants to belong to some kind of group. People want to be insiders. There are many different groups that shape our individual lives, some of which overlap. Actively deciding to be an insider of one group can make you an outsider of another. You can't be members of two political parties. You can also be a passive insider just because you're born into a group. Being a passive insider is the fourth way. Dr Smith explains, 'It's what requires the least amount of effort for reward and affords you more options and privileges. That's the most common condition. In fact, what everyone kind of wants in many ways is to be a passive insider.' The likes of former UK Independence Party leader Nigel Farage are passively an insider because he was born to an upper-middle-class family. He went to a posh school, Dulwich College. He understands the things associated with being part of the establishment. When he sits down for dinner and there are five settings, he understands what cutlery to use because he is naturally already on the inside, albeit passively so. Yet he has actively worked to place himself on the outside. A tactical outsider.

There are certain groupings that people want to be part of. For example, wanting to be a celebrity, because that's where it looks like all the good things are. The reality is often very different. There is now no longer a need to even have talent as a prerequisite for fame, with the rise of the social media influencers. Once you are in you have choices. More privileges. An example is the comedian Dave Chappelle, who famously quit his television programme, *Chappelle's Show*, after Comedy Central reportedly used old material to create a third season against his wishes. You can choose to be an outsider in the comfort of the knowledge that you have already been able to be in the inside group, and remain an insider in some ways, even if passively. Chappelle was still invited to premieres, still had celebrity friends, and was able to have access to things that others don't. He was also able to return to television screens on his own terms. I will always be a former special advisor to a prime minister in the eyes of the media, unless I do something to eclipse my work at Number 10; but that is an incredibly high bar. I was once inside, which has even afforded me the opportunity to write this book. Despite this, Dr Smith explains that though outsiders can become insiders, in some ways they will continue to remain outsiders: 'I think about you as a person, Samuel, you've got the establishment group of Number 10 and the Conservative Party, at one point you were well embedded within them. With all that that brings. I'm sure you would have gone to Conservative meetings, in Tunbridge Wells or something, and someone would have stopped you at the doors and said are you sure you're in the right place because you are different from their usual members. On the one hand you're properly in there, but there would be some people that won't fully accept you, so you'll still be partly outside. But then in Number 10 you had your colleague (the health special advisor) who went to Oxford and Cambridge. Rowed for both. He would be someone who will be in a separate grouping in Number 10 that you would not belong to. Even if you were doing the exact same thing, he would have his public-school mates who he would hang out with.' To be fair I have never been asked if I was in the right place, but I was mistaken for a black former Conservative Member of Parliament, Sam Gyimah – which is the main reason why I insist on being called Samuel and not . . . Sam.

You may ask why this is all important. Well, it's important because of what psychologists call conflict and ambivalence. Think about all the different groups that you can belong to and then the other groups that you want to belong to. Then the groups that you actually belong to. If there's a coherence between all the groupings, then that's fine. If you belong to a social group or groups that are lauded and admired, then that's also fine. However, there's no point pretending that there aren't social hierarchies – there are. If the group that you belong to isn't an admired group, if it's a castigated group and what you want is to be part of an admired group, then there is a conflict. For example, a black man walking down a quiet road on a cold November evening may wish to help an old man with a Zimmer frame (I tell the story in the next chapter), but his grouping might create inner conflict because he is unsure how his act of kindness will be received. Dr Smith offers a more extreme example: Cass Pennant – one of Britain's most notorious football hooligans, who ran with the Inner City Firm (ICF) associated with West Ham football club in the 1970s. A six-week-old Pennant was abandoned by his mother, and he was placed into care. His upbringing and the constant racism and bullying he endured had made him feel worthless as a child. Racial tensions were high in the country during the 1970s and 80s with a number of riots taking place. Football hooligans were known for racist chants and violence during this period. Although he maintained that ICF were not racist, it was thought that Pennant put up with regularly being called racist names.

This may be an extreme example, but less extreme versions of it happen to lots of people because what they want to be and what they are is not congruent. Dr Smith says, 'Maybe they want to be part of elite groups, but they are from a working-class background. That can lead to conflict within themselves. There is also the ambivalence. If you do end up being able to inveigle your way into the inside group, especially if you are a visible minority and so you are not usually there, then there's always an uneasy kind of recognition that you don't quite belong.' When there is uncertainty, uncertainty produces anxiety. If you're in a slightly anxious position fearing that someone will point out that you are an imposter, you as an individual may feel the ambivalence of that potential situation. 'So there's ambivalence, which relates to anxiety. And anxiety is part of the human condition.'

Resolution?

How you resolve that anxiety is what the challenge is. What Wilfred Emmanuel-Jones did was to say, I am making a proactive decision because I am never going to belong anyway. I don't feel the same as my siblings. I know I'm not the same, especially when growing up, coming over as part of the Windrush generation. I'm just going to go and do my own thing and make my own way in life. Within the boundaries of my imagination, where I can make my own rules, I don't have to be anxious. But then, Wilfred is an entrepreneur, afforded the luxury of creating his own domain. I put that to Dr Smith, who replies, 'Go back a minute. When Wilfred was growing up with his twelve siblings he wasn't an entrepreneur.' I respond, 'Was he not? He was independent-minded, ambitious. He was used to having autonomy, a high locus of control, his own domain on his father's allotment. With his first job at the BBC, he was definitely underqualified for the job on paper, but he was very proactive and entrepreneurial in securing it.'

Dr Smith comes back, 'I would be careful in saying that he had those qualities because he was an entrepreneur. I would instead say that he had those qualities and as a result was able to become an entrepreneur.'

Me again: 'Okay. Fine. But nonetheless, he has a rare set of qualities that has allowed him to be an entrepreneur.'

Dr Smith says, 'Hold on, hold on. How do we know that those qualities are rare? We don't. What we know though is that this process is fluid, based on where people are in their lives. This need to be inside, outside, it's a dynamic situation, it changes. There are certain times in your life where you'd be keener to belong than others.'

This exchange reminds me why I value conversations with Dr Smith so much. She provides a degree of challenge to my thinking that I rarely experience. Well, of course she would – she's a psychiatrist!

To be inside, integrated, does not mean that you are no longer an outsider. This is something that is very paradoxical and perhaps difficult for many people in public debates to grasp. As a result, many outsiders do not want to own their difference once they come inside. In fact, they hope no one will notice. I think about Margaret Thatcher and how she received vocal training to obtain a deeper voice and never wanted to be dragged into debates around gender equality. Other people who are different, like Sayeeda Warsi or Wilfred Emmanuel-Jones, use their difference as a strength. To make a different type of contribution. People often want to be inside the group but not distinctive, because that's what we're taught. That's what we have been conditioned to think is correct. Where the happiness is. This is where you won't be upset. You don't have to worry. If you fit in easily, then that's fine. But if there are characteristics about you that set you apart then at some point you will have to come to some sort of acceptance. Not only you, but those around you too. That's the benefit of a family grouping – acknowledgement of an unconditional bond despite difference. Dr Smith gives her workplace as an example: 'I'm responsible for a group of doctors. Around thirty, who are brilliant. But we've got a couple of them who are quite quirky and can be a bit difficult. We accept that and we know what they're like. You can support them knowing that if we don't support them, then we'll lose them. The benefit they bring far outweighs their little quirks. We treat them like family.'

On overcoming conflict and ambivalence, the first phase is for people to have some sense of acceptance of their difference. Whatever that might be. Getting to a point where you can say, well this is me. I'm an introvert, I have a different upbringing, this is my accent, my cultural heritage is different. We must also accept that whether we like it or not the human brain is conditioned to record experiences and information in order to build patterns. Biases, no matter how inaccurate or unhelpful, are based on evidence, albeit sometimes flawed evidence. If a group of Englishmen travel to a Spanish island and drink until they become drunk and disorderly, then that will become how Englishmen are perceived abroad. The president of the island government in Lanzarote has recently announced the desire to replace British holidaymakers with more Germans – because of how they are now viewed. The Germans are perceived as more 'quality' tourists who spend more and engage in less anti-social behaviour. If there are weekly images of young black boys being victims or perpetrators of violent crime, then that is the image many will have of this group despite most of this demographic not choosing such a path. This is why representation in the media matters. It has an impact on how different groups are perceived. If someone asks us a question as we may be the only person they know from a certain background, I think it is better we help to shape their view than for their brain to download information from unhelpful sources. This might not be ideal as in a perfect world we would all be judged as individuals. We all love the famous extract from Martin Luther King Jr's speech about being judged 'by the content of your character'. But very few things in this world are in an ideal state. We must be aware of the reality.

Self-Negation and Denial

Being an insider can sometimes require things that fundamentally negates something about yourself that you think is a good thing. This is another place where problems can arise; where people are more likely to either decide they are going to stand alone, or have some form of tipping point about it later on. Everyone's different. In politics there seems to be a consistent thread, though not for everybody. We have had Sayeeda Warsi, Sajid Javid, Sam Gyimah and, most recently, me. There comes a point where there was a conflict and then there was a reaction. At face value Sam Gyimah's tipping point was a bit different as it was over Brexit. But he wrote a piece in the *Financial Times* a year or two later where you could kind of see the conflict that he was grappling with. He spoke about not knowing how to navigate being a black Conservative MP, and the challenges he faced experiencing racism but not wanting it to overshadow his career. I worked in Parliament briefly while he was there, and I could see that he wasn't quite himself. But we were not close, and I was very junior in comparison, so it was not a conversation I could initiate.

Sam Gyimah was on the way to becoming a Cabinet member. It was a sad way to end a political career. Reconciling the different facets of who you are should not mean not being able to function in certain environments. I suppose the question is, how do you then overcome that conflict in environments that are high-pressured? Some would argue that my strong reaction over a minister's spat with a young journalist was also a strange hill to die on, or that Sajid Javid resigning because of the employment of special advisors who could have just been replaced was also strange. Other ministers have had their special advisors removed, but everyone has something that will trigger a response that others may not understand. They won't understand because people do not ever know your full story, including the things that you have seen or experienced that have left a lasting footprint on your soul. Like Festus Akinbusoye in the first chapter, whose father's life and death were so pivotal to shaping his character.

Dr Smith thinks that there will come a time when another politician needs to deal with their own conflict. 'I think at what point it will be when they can't reconcile things with themselves. Someone that has kind of always been around the establishment. Maybe an Eton scholar, obviously a clever individual. But he's still black. There'll be times when he'll be in meetings or a party or whatever, and someone says something terrible about black people, which he probably copes with for himself. I remember when I was at university, and the rugby players would be around singing in the bars. Some of the songs, I mean, were just frankly racist. People would just sing along with these songs. I would be thinking, oh God, you didn't realise I'm here while you are singing this. But they did realise. You can somehow live with the ambivalence of that. Particularly if he has a son, his son will be at least mixed race. When his mixed-race son is fifteen and walking down the road with his white mate called Andy. They're both called Andy. Andy and Andy are walking down the road and the police decide to stop one of them. Then what does he do? If he's like his dad, he's going to be big and tall. He's going to be walking through Kensington, the policeman will say this black guy fits the description of a crime committed nearby. He shouldn't be on this road. I think sometimes what happens is when people start to see, my child is being affected by this, that's when they start to think, I can't reconcile this anymore. I suspect that will happen again to someone. There'll be a kind of George Floyd type moment. And they'll be the one who's rolled out. But he'll be there, and it will be such a conflict that he'll find himself in. Like you during the BLM protests.'

To counter this rather sober reflection by Dr Smith, I would say a positive thing is that most people function in whatever work setting they are in without constantly feeling like having to hold their breath because they can't be themselves. They somehow reconcile it and there's now discussions about bringing your whole self to work. There are exceptions to this rule. If you are a nudist, it might not be wise to bring your whole self to work. It is also wrong to think being yourself means everyone must adopt your world view. That is not true inclusion. The social infrastructure that we have needs to be such that it can encompass everybody. It should not be that it excludes people because it requires you to be what you are not in order to fit in. The world is a diverse world, the country is a diverse country. Different ethnicities, different types of people. If you want to be successful, you must be able to reach different people to win. I ask Dr Smith how organisations and groups develop environments where people can reconcile who they are in a meaningful way and still contribute productively.

'Ideally what happens is that you are clear about what your aim is for your organisation. Leadership is really important because it's the leader who sets the tone about how to behave. In my world, I'm making it clear I am very egalitarian, and, know certain staff from particular backgrounds could easily be quite negative about certain people's backgrounds, but I'm very clear, no homophobia, no racism, zero tolerance. I nip the small things in the bud. When someone's coming in and it would be clear that this person is a gay man, we make it clear that we will not condone any homophobia, because it's going to be really easy for people to slip into certain conversations that then isolate others.'

Outsiderness, Segregation and Mixing

Slipping into making inappropriate comments or having biases are not simply accidental anomalies. We are all human. No one is perfect. This is the reason why we need those checks and balances to make sure that mistakes or 'misunderstandings' are kept to a minimum. Dr Smith continues, 'There's also a need to recognise the role of a facilitator. For any entrepreneurial endeavour, if there's someone who lets you through, gives you access to capital or customers, that's a facilitator. With Venus and Serena Williams, they eventually found a coach who ensured the family was supported financially so that the two of them could train in Florida. A facilitator will give you the green light to flourish as yourself. It could be as little as a word of encouragement from a leader, giving you exposure, or making sure there is fairness in a process. Sometimes people will forget, but usually the facilitator gives outsiders the ammunition to belong and thrive.'

Being on the outside and being on the inside are opposite things, but the interaction between the two positions is complex. In all this analysis we must not forget that the most powerful way to ensure someone remains outside is to segregate groups, to stop them from mixing. For centuries it has been the key to avoiding meaningful integration. It's worth looking at some of the theory behind this subject.

Foci are defined as 'social, psychological, legal or physical objects around which joint activities are organised' such as work, a neighbourhood, a school or a household. These foci systematically constrain the ability of individuals to choose their associations, but also provide the antecedent conditions by which choices are homogenised. For example, associates of a workplace tend to have joined an organisation due to similar interests, such as career goals or company purpose. Another example is that of a school; sharing catchment areas with individuals who share the same socioeconomic status or bringing together individuals with similar experiences growing up. People who share foci also share experiences, which further entrenches social homogeneity. Short interactions between individuals foster homogeneity, as the cumulative effect of this interaction is common points of reference that self-strengthen over time; this means that foci notwithstanding, different subgroups of individuals can become homogeneous if they are exposed to one another long-term. When trying to overcome difference, the impact of engaging regularly with people who are viewed as different should not be underestimated. That's the secret to integrating communities. Politicians, the media and other stakeholders who are genuinely interested in avoiding division should contribute to creating opportunities to bring people together, both socially and structurally.

We must not forget that when migrants arrive in Britain – as far back as the *Empire Windrush* on 22 June 1948 or as recently as those arriving from Hong Kong through the British Nationals Oversees (BNO) visa scheme – they have settled in clustered areas and not been encouraged to spread out, particularly into more rural settings. It is rational to want to live next to friends and family when relocating to a new country. Cost and accessibility to job opportunities and knowledge of locations within a country will also be contributing factors. Arrivals as part of the Windrush generation also faced discrimination when attempting to secure a place to live – further restricting their mobility. Today, ninety-five per cent of all ethnic minority people live in urban settings, with a particular concentration in major cities. Social mobility is helping to change this as people seek more space for their families, but no government has had a meaningful plan for integrating communities.

We can't even be honest about our continued reliance on migrants or our long-term need for economic growth, partly because of our aging population.

Confirmation bias also contributes to social homogeneity. First coined by Peter Wason, the term describes the tendency of individuals to interpret new evidence as confirming their own theories or be drawn to accepting evidence more readily as long as it confirms the individual's pre-existing beliefs. Individuals who encounter others from different foci or backgrounds may react in self-defence by self-affirming. The same can be said for situations that present a change or challenge to an individual's views; they will seek out evidence that confirms their views instead of facing the discomfort engendered by heterogeneity. I have lost count of the number of times someone has shared with me an article that affirms their view on a certain subject. It means one is unable to learn another perspective or even strengthen their own arguments against an opposing view. My own politics were shaped as they were partly because all the other students in the group in which I studied my postgraduate degree were different shades of socialist. It allowed me to both better understand their position and also critique my own. It has also given me the ability to engage with people who I may not agree with in a productive and empathetic manner. A consequence of similarity-seeking behaviour is echo chambers; 'environments in which the opinion, political leaning, or belief of users about a topic gets reinforced due to repeated interactions with peers or sources having similar tendencies and attitudes'. This results from the individual's choice to engage in selective exposure, interacting with sources of information that are congruent with their existing beliefs – a sister phenomenon to confirmation bias.

To truly understand the outsider phenomenon and to find ways to overcome associated challenges, we must understand human behaviour. Often people with good intentions try to explain why the world is the way it is simply through the lens of historic events, missing out the psychology behind the choices that people made in history and still make today. History can only offer up limited pointers towards being able to truly grapple with important subjects. We need to better utilise experts who understand the human mind when trying to improve outcomes.

We need to listen to experts like Dr Shubulade Smith. Surely understanding how the human mind works is the key to achieving what we want – and what the world needs?

Chapter 10

Broadening Audiences

Baroness Sayeeda Warsi's words about her experiences at the water cooler with other Cabinet members has really struck a chord with me. Not being exposed to certain elements of art and culture growing up puts you in a precarious sort of position as you rise through the ranks. Sayeeda opted to acknowledge that it was not the world she came from, owning her difference. Many others simply smile and nod, hoping nobody notices . . . but they do notice. The question in my mind is why we should accept that certain things continue to remain the preserve of the privileged? Should we be comfortable with children no longer being able to learn an instrument for free in school, for example? These are some of the things I am thinking about as I head to Nottingham to meet with Kadiatu and Stuart Kanneh-Mason, who have invited me for dinner. They may not be names that many people would recognise straight away, but on 19 May 2018 their son, Sheku Kanneh-Mason, shot to global fame playing the cello at the wedding of Prince Harry and Meghan Markle, now known as the Duke and Duchess of Sussex respectively. Sheku is one of seven siblings, all classically trained gifted musicians. They are award winning and have played in some of the most iconic venues around the world. There are many things that make them unique, in addition to their phenomenal talent. These include the size of the family, the modest background of their parents, their age, and their visible difference, in the world of classical music, as black artists. I'm hoping to learn about their story and maybe better shape my ideas on how to engage with a world that often seems so foreign to outsiders.

It's a cold dark November evening. As I get out of the taxi, I notice a very old man with a Zimmer frame. He is outside a house, shouting, obviously trying to get the attention of the inhabitants. I don't think he lives there. Something might be wrong. The homes are on a steep hill, and I am a bit worried about what will happen to this old man who looks a bit lost and in distress. I pause and wonder what to do, wanting to help but also conscious that it is very dark, and I am a black guy alone on a road lined with large houses. They probably know everyone on the street, and it's clear that I don't live here. Eventually I decide to walk up to him to ask if he needs any help. He says no thank you and that he's fine. As I walk away, he continues to shout at the house. No one responds. I walk back and insist on helping him. He directs me to a window that I could knock on to get the attention of those inside. I knock and see the silhouette of someone getting up. My work is done; now to get to the Kanneh-Mason home, five minutes late because of the unplanned detour. As I approach their door and look through the window, a young-looking person holding onto a very large-looking instrument is in a large room alone, practising. It must be Mariatu. She is twelve, the youngest of the Kanneh-Mason family, and she plays the cello and piano. I'm at the right place!

Kadiatu, called Kadie for short, was born in Sierra Leone. Her Welsh mother had moved there at the age of twenty-two to marry her father, who was one of forty-five children. Following the death of her father Kadie moved to Wales where she lived in a rural area that was dominated by steelworks. The only reason she learned the piano was because her mother was a primary school teacher and there was an old upright piano that the school were going to put out on the rubbish heap. Kadie's mother arranged for it to be brought to her home instead; and that's how she learned to play. Kadie tells me that pianos are 'expensive things'. Her mother initially taught her and then she had piano lessons. She went to a deprived comprehensive school, but they had free music lessons. There was an orchestra. There was a school show. It was all just part of everybody's education in school. That was her introduction to music; but Kadie never went to concert halls. In Wales, for lower-middle-class and working-class people back then, learning the piano was all to do with chapel. It was one of those things. If you got any kind of music education, learned to play the piano, then you were sort of linked with the church and the chapel. There were no such things as concert halls unless you travelled thirty-odd miles to Cardiff. Kadie says her family would never have thought to go somewhere like that anyway. She says, 'You just learn to play to a certain level. I nearly got to grade eight piano and grade five clarinet. I never would have thought of studying music at university or anything like that.' I ask when the first time Kadie went to a concert was. 'With my children. It would have been when they were younger to a concert here in Nottingham, that was the first time.'

Outsiders and Broadening Out

Outsiders often have the power to broaden audiences. The Kanneh-Masons have begun to inspire a generation of young people. The world of classical music in many respects remains the preserve of a specific demographic of listeners and performers. The Audience Agency's modelled age breakdown suggests that classical music audiences nationally are much more likely to be in middle and older age groups: 42 per cent are likely to be aged forty-one to sixty and 37 per cent aged over sixty-one. Just 7 per cent are likely to be aged under thirty-one. The oldest Kanneh-Mason sibling, Isata, at the time of writing this, is just twenty-four. In 2015 the Kanneh-Mason siblings made it to the semi-finals of *Britain's Got Talent*; an audience of millions of people seeing young classical musicians was important. Although the producers of the show were keen for them to perform mainstream songs, the siblings wanted to be authentic and play classical pieces. As a result of this difference of opinion they were not given the same levels of promotion as other semi-finalists; but the impact that they had despite not winning has been remarkable. Sheku winning BBC Young Musician of the Year, the first black person to do so, was also an important moment for the family and the world of classical music.

Before the pandemic, by far the highest proportion of classical music concert attendees (67 per cent) went just once over a two-year period. Only a quarter booked two to five times and just 8 per cent were very frequent attenders, booking six or more times over two years. Classical music needs to do more if it is to broaden its appeal, particularly to younger people. Its global influence over centuries is perhaps not fully appreciated by those who have not been engaged from a young age. Nigerian musician and political activist Fela Kuti took lessons in piano and percussion before studying classical music at Trinity College London. While in London, he encountered various musical styles by playing piano in jazz and rock bands. That exposure to classical music made Fela's sound distinctive and his music disruptive with many layers. But again, he was exposed to classical music from a young age. The challenge is where do you start if it is a foreign world? Ideally there would be friends gracious enough to help you, assuming you are confident enough, like Sayeeda Warsi, to admit it is not something you have engaged with much. Kadie mentions that the family also relied at times on YouTube for insights into the world of classical music.

The Value of Outsiders

Andrew Lloyd Webber has long been calling for the United Kingdom government to recognise the transformative effect that classical music can have on the lives of children in disadvantaged communities. He said, 'We do know music empowers children. The evidence is that it absolutely improves academic standards [and] all aspects of behaviour because they're having to take part in something . . . with other people and think of other people . . .' Broadening appeal for arts and culture is not simply an altruistic objective though. There is a commercial imperative too. The UK has a creative economy worth £27bn and culture brings £850m to the UK, through tourism, each year. Our leading cultural institutions are a calling card worldwide and have important trading links with other countries, from the US and Germany to China and South Korea. Theatres, museums, galleries and libraries are at the heart of our towns and cities. Not only do they bring prosperity, but they also bring communities together. Each year, UK orchestras play to over 4 million people in over 3,500 concerts and performances in the UK, and give over 400 concerts in 40 countries across the world. Unlike orchestras in European countries, which receive upwards of 80 per cent of their income from public funding, the average for British orchestras is just 30 per cent, meaning they are far more reliant on earned income to survive. The government set up a Covid recovery fund to support the sector during the pandemic, but there will inevitably be a lasting impact. Broadening audiences will be key to recovery and survival.

Stuart's mother introduced him to music at the age of six, when his parents could afford to buy a piano. He says, 'Back in those days there was the Inner London Education Authority (ILEA). You could get a scholarship to study music.' He would go every Thursday evening to the Blackheath Conservatoire and have lessons there. His father used to take him. When was the first time he went to a concert? 'When I was twelve, I think. It was Daniel Barenboim. My parents drove me up to the Royal Festival Hall. After that I couldn't stop practising.' His exposure to classical music inspired him. It just shows you the impact of seeing somebody at the highest level play. Stuart also took up the cello at one point and played in the local Goldsmiths College youth orchestra, which was free to join. He would go there every Saturday with his cello, but piano was his main love. 'I don't know if I could have done music professionally. When I was about ten or eleven the head teacher suggested that I to go to a specialist music school, but we didn't really understand what that meant. I just said to my parents: they probably don't do football, and that was sort of the end of it. My parents just said, okay. There wasn't really a sort of network of people you could discuss it with.'

Kadie and Stuart met at the University of Southampton. Kadie, who chose Southampton based on a picture of the sea on the prospectus, studied English while Stuart studied physics. As both played instruments from a relatively young age, I want to know if they still felt like outsiders once they began to engage with the world of classical music. Kadie is the first to respond: 'I definitely did. I mean, you could learn it at school, but becoming a classical musician was something other people did. I barely even got to listen to it let alone consider it. We had one classical music recording. Handel's Water Music and Handel's Fireworks Music. And that was it. I had no way of understanding what it was. We used to play it and I could hear these sounds. One time I said to my mum, what's that song? She said, I don't know. That was it.'

In Kadie's beautifully written memoir *House of Music: Raising the Kanneh-Masons*, she speaks about how her first child Isata took to music quite naturally, and in our discussions both Kadie and Stuart point to classical music being a path that was very much self-directed by their children. Kadie tells me, 'I think we were lucky because we had seven of them and they kind of inspired each other. And I think when they were able to play together, that was a whole new dimension. They found that it was like a kind of conversation with each other.'

Stuart offers a different perspective. 'When Isata was young, there weren't seven, right. But it was clear she enjoyed the sound. She used to play a lot and she used to sort of improvise.' Kadie says: 'She would improvise to the harmony. And she would change it to the minor key and . . .'

Stuart goes on, 'play some sort of jazzy music.'

Kadie adds, 'She was very, very mathematical. At school she was just off the scale with maths, and she was also off the scale with reading. I think those two things, language and maths, go very well with music. At school she was just bored and didn't know what to do. When we put that into music, it became a powerful outlet. That's probably why Isata got into music, because we both understood music, but also because she was able to channel all of that energy into it.'

Though they have a beautiful house, sizable enough to house its nine residents plus additional guests, they are not from exceptionally well-off backgrounds. I ask what it has been like entering a world that is usually the preserve of the establishment. Kadie says, 'It hasn't been easy. There are financial difficulties, as well as cultural difficulties. If you're in a world where people are privileged, they've all got their instruments, which are really expensive. For a long time, we could not afford a full-sized cello for Sheku. He was trying to do competitions and everyone around him had a full-sized cello. Their parents could buy them. It was things like getting a good enough instrument that was always a frustration. Also, not having the knowledge of where to go. There's a whole network of things that people know that if you're not in that world, you don't know. Like what courses there are and where to find the instruments or where to go to learn and what teachers there are. There's a whole network. You have to be willing to engage and have conversations. It was the only way.'

Stuart adds, 'I think the fortunate stroke for us was probably when I was looking for a good place for Isata to go to learn classical music. We discovered the Royal Academy of Music. When Isata auditioned and she got in, we would go there every Saturday. We sort of learned on the job. Got a good teacher, and we talked to people. That's when we started to learn about the environment, then the kids would do more competitions, which again gave us more exposure.'

The family would wake up at 4.30 a.m. every Saturday and head to London from Nottingham in order to attend lessons at the Royal Academy. Kadie says, 'To take that leap to go all the way to the Royal Academy in London every Saturday from Nottingham. I think it was worth it.' Stuart concurs: 'I think it was.'

Kadie goes on, 'But it was a massive risk. I worried about it. We couldn't afford it, but we just did it somehow. We had to keep believing it was going to be worth it. You can't think too far ahead. One Saturday at a time. One competition at a time.'

Stuart says, 'To be clear, this was not necessarily believing it was going to be worth it in the sense that Isata was going to become a classical musician. But it was more about building that confidence. I always said to the children, you will meet very few people who, as adults, will say, I used to play the piano or guitar, and I'm so glad now that I am shot of it. Most people say either they're still doing it, or they'll say I gave it up and most people will say, I wish I still played. That was probably the one thing I said to them. I said, you won't regret it. So regardless of what you do, it's a good thing to have in your life. I played to a sort of good standard, but I do wish I'd kept going a bit longer. Instilling that belief that you won't regret pushing yourself to go further is what was always worth all those early Saturday mornings.'

Discussion about the value of arts to society has grown around moments of change in arts funding and policymaking over the last two decades. The debate tends to polarise – around 'excellence' versus 'access', 'high' culture versus 'low', 'popular' or 'common' culture, and around the notion of 'extrinsic' and 'intrinsic' value. In the past, arts and culture became a tool for achieving wider policy goals including regeneration, economic development, social inclusion and health. Academics like Dr Abigail Gilmore at the University of Manchester argue against 'instrumentalism'; this is when policymakers define the value of the arts in terms of their economic value and their contribution to defined policy objectives, rather than their broader value in improving the quality of contemporary life. The maturation of the National Lottery, begun in 1994, has helped to resource arts and culture as the level of government funding has diminished, but there continue to be calls for more funding.

Kadie reflects, 'I think as a parent as well, I didn't want to say no. I thought Isata couldn't get into the Royal Academy of Music. I thought it was impossible. But I didn't want to say no, because when you say no, it's just not right. Somehow then, you're already saying to a child, okay, that's not your territory in the world. It comes down to whether you are brave enough to let your child fail, because that's what we were facing. And we both thought, well, there's no way she can get in, but we've got to let her try. Allowing your child to fail is really important or allowing them to face challenges. I lost out on the things that I didn't have the courage to try when I was younger because I felt they were not for me. I don't know if I'd ever have made it. I didn't want that to be the same for my children.'

On auditioning the two boys for the Primary Academy of the Royal Academy of Music after Isata had joined, parents at the school gates in Nottingham would say it was wrong to take two black city boys out of their natural environments. But Stuart's response was, 'Who said the environment of the Royal Academy couldn't be their environment?' They believed the kids belonged on football pitches with their friends. The parallels with Stuart's own story when the opportunity to go to music school came along in his own childhood are striking. But this time Stuart supported his children in taking a different path – to venture outside of comfort to explore their unbridled brilliance.

Outsiders and Networks

I want to delve into the idea of networks and so I ask if people were willing to help them along the way, particularly in terms of telling them things that they might not know about because they were outsiders in the world of classical music. Kadie says, 'You seek out the people who are helpful. Your friends. People with positive roots. Of course, there's always the ones who want to try and stop you, who say that it's impossible, but you have to be resilient and ignore those dissenters. Stuart was better at that than me. I would dwell on it, and I would worry, and it would make me lose my confidence. And Stuart would just say, they are ridiculous. And sort of steer us off to people who were more positive.'

Stuart adds, 'I think in life, there are always positive people and the people that are positive can be remarkably positive and remarkably helpful. And remarkably generous. I think you must seek those people out and then the negative people, you must know who they are and manage your engagement with them accordingly. I think also you must listen to advice. Of course, you need to filter what you think is sound advice, but it's important to listen to constructive advice even if it doesn't feel nice. I remember once we went to a competition. Someone came up to us afterwards and said, Isata is very good, but you know, there's this lack of understanding of opera and Mozart was all about opera. I didn't even know what he was talking about. We went home and began to listen to opera. I had never been to the opera before then. So, I think it's also about listening to advice. I think that's definitely helped.'

Kadie adds, 'But there are some things you can't do even if it's helpful advice from someone that may not understand the limitations of your background. We listened to opera, but we couldn't take the children to opera because it was too expensive. We could take them to concerts because they were five pounds for anyone under the age of twenty-five or whatever. But opera was thirty pounds a ticket. No way. We just listened to the radio.'

Both Kadie and Stuart entered the world of classical music as outsiders. However, their eldest child Isata began playing from the age of six, and the rest of the siblings were arguably born into the world of classical music. I wanted to know to what extent their seven children felt that they too were outsiders.

Kadie thinks. 'Hmm. That's an interesting question. Isn't it? I think they definitely do. I mean when they went on every course, they were visibly different. I remember when Isata started the junior Royal Academy of Music, she was the only black child.'

Stuart adds, 'You can't not notice it. Of course, they do. But also, there's no value in kind of ignoring the obvious difference or not talking about it. And their eyes are very wide open to the country that they live in. The world that they live in. I've always thought that every time they went on a stage in a competition or a concert, they were having to fight a negative view because people thought they were going to be rubbish. You'd sort of hear it in the background. Often before they went on stage, someone would say, oh, bless you, and, that's very sweet. You know, there'd be this patronising tone. I was very aware that they had to be three times better than the person before them, before they could break through that perception of not being an equal or not being there on merit. We were very rigorous about ensuring they had to be absolutely prepared for everything they did.'

He goes on, 'Later on, they took that sort of semi-humorous side of it from us. I remember once when Isata was probably seventeen or sixteen at the Royal Academy. When people audition, they have a pianist as an accompanist. And one of the accompanists was sick so Isata was asked to fill in. There was this mother with her child and she saw that Isata was the accompanist and looked like she was going to complain. Then of course Isata had to do a run-through with the child. I still take great delight at the change in the air after she heard Isata play. The mother was really enthusing and keen to engage with us after.'

I find this story interesting. It is when a person is under pressure or strain that you find out what is inside. For that mother, having her child pass the audition for the Royal Academy was so important that it was difficult for her to remain composed and hide her prejudice. But of course, she is not the only person who would have had those same reservations or reacted like this.

Stuart is quite diplomatic. 'Sometimes prejudice is also born out of ignorance. It is not that people are always just choosing to be bad. For example, someone might be surprised to see a woman taxi driver – not because they don't believe a woman can be a taxi driver, but because it is something that they have not come across before. In London, less than 3 per cent of taxi drivers are women. So, you know, stereotypes are difficult things to overcome.'

Kadie says, 'If you ask the children they'll say, well, I never saw many other people like me but knew I could do it because I saw my siblings doing it. They say that they do not feel alone. There had to be a first one, who was Isata, but she was focused on the music and then they all looked at each other and said, well, I can see everybody else doing it. They never felt alone.' Stuart agrees. 'As long as you believe it, then they will believe it. There are some worlds where despite all that you do you just can't break into it. I think we've had some fortune along the way as well. Winning the right type of competitions, for example.'

Each sibling practises for hours each day, perfecting their sound. Stuart says, 'I suppose we were very clear that if you want to do something, you have to go through the rigour of it. You know, I think if you want to do sport, yes, you can be naturally gifted, but if you're not prepared to be fit you won't go far. We have seen many talented young players not quite fulfil their potential. I think if I had a child who said, I want to be a football player and I saw they genuinely were passionate about it, then I would probably say, well, you're going to have to be fit. And if you want to be a football player, have you ever thought about trying to use both feet? Some of the greatest footballers – and I don't know why all players aren't two-footed, but the greatest ones are – so maybe I would probably tell them the story of George Best, who for like a month only played with his left foot. Then maybe that might trigger something. It might not, but at least I'm saying it would sort of encourage you that way. Whereas, if you don't, if you don't let them understand what's involved, then I think they won't fulfil their talent. Giving them honest feedback is important.'

Barriers and Advantages

The Kanneh-Mason children have achieved global fame, touring across continents. They are clearly exceptionally talented. I do wonder if their visible difference has also led to their success. In other words, if part of what gives them a unique selling point, what has propelled them ahead of so many other classical musicians, is that they are outsiders. A family of seven children, from modest backgrounds, and of course . . . black. I pose this question to Stuart and Kadie. Stuart says, 'Yes. But they also take their role as role models quite seriously too. I'm sure they've inspired a lot of young people to enjoy classical music. Now, obviously when they were young, they weren't thinking like that, but now they are older I can see they reflect on it more. They have a media profile, and they get invited to schools quite a bit.'

Kadie adds, 'What's lovely is after concerts, you see people bringing their children, many from diverse backgrounds coming into the concerts, and they will come up and they'll say, the reason we are playing is because of you. There is a change that you see happening, you know, it might be small, but it matters.'

She goes on, 'Places change slowly. The culture changes slowly. Sometimes it takes a generation. You look at the Junior Royal Academy, for example. There are more children from diverse backgrounds there now than there were when Isata was there. It's not always great when you're the first one, but you would have said that about black footballers in the seventies. There used to be presenters who would come on the television and say, well, there'll never be any black footballers in the then First Division. It was a narrative that we had that black people couldn't play football. So it happens everywhere. The hope is of course that in classical music in twenty years people will say, oh my goodness, look how far we have come.'

Stuart says, 'Saying this has perhaps lost a bit of its meaning, but it's also important to dream big. I remember when Isata did that first composition, did this concerto. She was like ten and we took it to the Academy, and they were fine. But then I remember I wrote to every orchestra around the country. I said, look, you may not like it. I wasn't saying this is amazing. Then one orchestra wrote back. It was an amateur orchestra in Angel, London. He said, I'd love to do that. And he said, but in return, we're struggling with venues. I just so happened to work for Hilton at the time. I contacted the general manager at the Waldorf Astoria in London and said, could you do this? He said, you can have it for free for the night because it's empty. Believing in your children and just giving that opportunity is important.'

I say to Stuart, 'It doesn't sound like barriers are something that you have allowed to hold both of you back.' He replies, 'Don't get embarrassed. I think you should go for things and then fail. There are people, unfortunately, who are going to be better than you, whatever that means, but I don't think you should not try things. You should do it. And then if it doesn't work out okay, you reflect and either think that's not for me or you see how to improve to get better.'

Kadie adds, 'I think my background is different because Stuart was born in Britain, born in London. Very much in a black community. Whereas I was a mixed-race child in a very white area. I don't think I had the same amount of confidence. I think we felt a lot more isolated. My early years were in Sierra Leone. Despite having a Welsh mother, coming to Britain, being viewed as an immigrant, the shock of that was very traumatic. I love Wales and I love the Welsh, but we were never quite allowed to be Welsh. You always felt that you weren't quite part of them. It was horrendous. When I was at school, nobody was mixed-race. People would see us with our mother and thought that we were adopted.'

Outsiders and Parenting

The last thing I want to speak to Kadie and Stuart about is their parenting style. Raising seven high-achieving classical musicians is no mean feat. Their children are known for being particularly well mannered, and in Kadie's memoirs she speaks a lot about them having a very clear routine. Kadie says, 'Yes. I think we were quite old-fashioned. I've always thought that if you have structure and routine, that's actually incredibly reassuring for children. It gives you a sense of a safety net. You kind of know where your boundaries are within that. I think if you give children a sense of not quite knowing what's going to happen every day, then it makes them lack certainty. We were very strong on routine and discipline. Discipline sounds like a horrible word, but it's not. I just made a kind of sense that they kind of know that you're there. You're very strong. And I think it's having a sense of parents who were very strong and they know what's right and what's wrong. I think it's good to have that sense of they're your parents.'

Successful creatives do have structure and they are creative in that structure. Freedom within boundaries is often a very difficult concept to accept, but it is a secret of some of the greatest artists. Kadie calls it 'freedom without chaos'. Stuart adds, 'I think structure allows you to be creative. You can only do what you think is right. I would never say to another parent, this is what you should do, but for us, that was what we wanted, and we were aligned on that. We were both brought up in that way.'

As a father, I often worry about how I will be able to help my children to navigate life. This is partly because of my own personal experiences, struggling with my behaviour at school. I was expelled from nursery (yes you read that correctly), and in secondary school was excluded three times. I found out during my postgraduate study that I had dyslexia and dyspraxia, which explained a lot.

I think about where my children will grow up, which school we will choose for them to go to, what extracurricular activities they will do. Should they be in a school with a smaller class size but with not many people who look like them? What impact, if any, will that have on shaping their identity and confidence? Should they instead go to schools where perhaps they may not have access to the best facilities, but will be able to mix with a more diverse range of people where they can be in a class and not necessarily feel like they are different because there are other kids that look like them? Where there are parents who perhaps might be more like ourselves? (Whatever that means, considering the complexities of us no longer necessarily being working class.)

I think about how to communicate with my son, considering the fact that my father wasn't around during my formative years. Like me, he is always asking questions. I am not completely certain about what good or bad fathering looks like. I constantly wonder how I make sure that my children have the love and support that they need, but also structure and discipline.

I think about all these things. I want to make the right decisions. The right choices that will help my children to be the best they can be. What does that mean in reality? How do we make sure that we have children who above all have good character? With technology being the greatest distraction and influence of our time, can we as parents remain the most important factor in our children's lives? I hope so.

I'm determined that my children won't see the world of the arts and culture as the preserve of the privileged. Its survival is dependent on the broadening of audiences. The cost is a real barrier for engaging with some parts of it; however, many things are accessible, including affordable concerts and free-to-attend museums. Yes – you should be honest during your water cooler moments about not being aware of certain things. But at the same time there is a world steeped in rich history and passion that we all should have the opportunity to experience, even if we were not exposed to it as children.

Of course, it is not just the arts where outsiders are able to broaden audiences. Another example of siblings who have broken barriers, mentioned briefly already, are the Williams sisters. Their contributions to the world of tennis are unrivalled. Venus and Serena have over 122 titles between them, including thirty grand slam singles and thirty-two grand slam doubles, plus eight Olympic gold medals.

Their father Richard started giving Venus and Serena lessons when they were four and a half in public tennis courts. The Williams family moved to Palm Springs in Florida in 1991 so both sisters could enrol at the famous Delray Beach Tennis Center. Here, Venus and Serena would spend around six hours a day, six days a week on court practising and honing their skills. Venus turned pro at the age of fourteen and beat her first opponent ranked in the Top 20 just a year later. Meanwhile, in 1997 Serena (aged sixteen) became the lowest-ranked player to defeat two stars inside the world's Top 10 at the same tournament, the Ameritech Cup Chicago. In 1997 Venus made history at the US Open, becoming the first woman to reach the final on her debut since 1978 and the first unseeded player to do so in nearly forty years. On this occasion, she went on to lose the final to Martina Hingis but would return to win the title twice – in 2000 and 2001.

Richard worked nights as a security guard, and the Williams sisters' mother, Oracene Price, was a nurse. Their children – along with Venus and Serena, Yetunde, Lyndrea and Isha – led highly structured, intensely monitored lives. Their success was no accident. Richard is believed to have written an eighty-five-page plan for Venus and Serena before they were born, charting their course into elite tennis. He chose tennis because he could see the opportunity to disrupt a sport that was the preserve of the upper and middle classes. In the film biopic *King Richard*, Will Smith, who plays Richard Williams, depicts a father with a clear idea about what he wanted to accomplish and guiding principles of discipline, hard work and determination. In the film the coaches can see Venus and Serena's potential as athletes, but only within the limitations of a status quo that the sisters will soon dismantle. The Kanneh-Mason parents perhaps did not have the same ambition as Richard Williams at the start of their inspiring journey, but they certainly had the same guiding principles and never limited their children's horizons. Like Venus and Serena's parents, Kadie and Stuart have had to contend with other people believing that they were not doing the best for their children as they helped them along the way. The world is a better place because they were able to ignore those dissenting voices.

The success of the Kanneh-Mason family in the world of classical music, as outsiders, is based on several factors. Stuart and Kadie's unwillingness to limit their children's horizons, while being very honest about the commitment needed to succeed, is important. The dedication of the virtuoso children to the craft of music, coupled with both parents having previously learned music themselves, was pivotal. But I think the decisive factor that stands out the most to me in the Kanneh-Mason story is the willingness of people, often strangers, to help them along the way. This help came both before and after they became well known. Cellist Julian Lloyd Webber (the brother of Andrew) is a source of great advice for Sheku. He once said to him, 'You are not just an important black cellist, you are an important cellist. Never forget this.' Sir Elton John agreed to financially support Isata's study at the Royal Academy. Fashion designer Paul Smith has been dressing Sheku for concert performances for years; and many more individuals have been there to support the Kanneh-Mason family on their journey. People are keen to do good. We should look for the good in people – as what we look for is what we will find.

Chapter 11

Facts vs Feelings

On 27 April 1994, Nelson Mandela became president in the first democratic elections in South Africa with universal suffrage, marking the official end of apartheid. The word apartheid comes from a word in Afrikaans meaning separateness. There is history before apartheid that is important because it's a different history than that of a lot of other former British colonies. Before the British the Portuguese and then the Dutch had inhabited parts of the country. The Dutch East India Company arrived at the Cape, at the southern tip of South Africa, in the mid-1600s. They saw it as a refreshment colony, a place where their sailors and merchants could stop on the way to making trade deals around the world. The Dutch known as Boers settled there in the seventeenth century. The British arrived in the next century and gradually took control of the country, leading eventually to the Boer Wars between the British and the Dutch. After some time, the British were able to establish it as a colony, coexisting with the Boers. Black indigenous South Africans, though the majority, became the outsiders. The resistance by black South Africans was constant, including the Anglo–Zulu war between 11 January and 4 July 1879.

Apartheid in South Africa was a form of racial segregation, but it was not a new thing. It was merely the reinforcement of established practices. Though slavery was banned by the British Empire in 1833, there was still the indentured servant system, a form of labour in which a person is contracted to work without salary for a specific number of years. Black people also had to have passes if they were travelling anywhere in the colony. They were being treated like outsiders even before South Africa became a union and achieved its own independence in 1910. The South Africa Act banned black representation in parliament. In 1913, the government passed the Natives Land Act, limiting black African land ownership to 7 per cent and restricting black inhabitants from buying or occupying land, except as employees of a white master. Over three decades later, this practice of racial segregation was given the name apartheid and was extended under the government of the time.

During the Second World War, the Dutch Boers in South Africa were less keen to support the British war efforts. An alliance occurred between the British population and the 'coloured' races to form what was called the United Party. The unintended consequences included a huge explosion of black South Africans migrating to cities for jobs because the whites were all going to fight the war. This created racial friction. The result of this tension was the election of the Afrikaner National Party in 1948. The party was very nationalistic and played on the fears of white South Africans. Upon election, they implemented apartheid, which allowed for lawful segregation using racial divides. The policy governed South Africa for nearly fifty years. The party's goal was to separate South Africa's white minority from its non-white majority. They did this by putting in place hundreds of race laws touching every aspect of life, preventing non-white people from having equal opportunities for basic human rights; this included dictating where they could live, work and go to school. Interracial relationships and marriages were illegal and, perhaps most importantly, non-whites did not have the right to vote. Remember – keeping people from mixing is the most powerful way of maintaining division. For if people mix, they will find out that they have more in common.

The Race Classification Act put people into four different categories: white at the top followed by Indian, coloured or of mixed descent, and black at the bottom. Within those groups were subgroups, further segregated by ethnicity and tribe. A number of pseudoscientific tests were used to classify individuals suspected of not being European. For example, the pencil test involved putting a pencil in an individual's hair. If the pencil fell to the floor, they passed the test and were considered white. If it stayed put, they were considered coloured or black. South Africans were forced at all times to carry identification, known as a passbook. Resistance to apartheid laws came in the form of mostly non-violent political engagement. Freedom fighters like Nelson Mandela, Oliver Tambo, Walter Sisulu and Ahmed Kathrada started to play an important role for both the African and Indian National Congress Parties. In 1952 they began a defiance campaign, calling on people to purposely break apartheid laws in order to get arrested.

People of colour got onto white buses, used white toilets, and entered white areas. Their hope was that the high number of prisoners would cause the system to collapse, but it didn't. Thousands ended up in jail. And in 1953, the Public Safety Act and Criminal Law Amendment Act were passed to impose even more severe penalties for demonstrating against the law. On 21 March 1960, a protest against the use of passbooks turned violent in the black township of Sharpeville. Police opened fire on unarmed protesters, leaving nearly seventy dead and 180 wounded, including children, a state of emergency was declared nationwide and opposition political parties, including the ANC, were banned, forcing many to move their fight underground.

A Personal Perspective on Apartheid

I have been to Johannesburg and visited the Apartheid Museum. To think that such a thing as apartheid was so recent that I was actually born when it was happening is very difficult to fathom. To help me to understand this period further I have gone back to visit my secondary school – East Barnet School, north London. I'm meeting with Beveley Smith, one of my teachers, who was born in apartheid South Africa. I have never had the opportunity to ask her about her journey to Britain, and was keen to see what reflections she had about growing up during apartheid, and also her experiences now. There is something therapeutic about going back to see someone who knew me before I had achieved all that I have so far in life. Perhaps there were things that she could see in me as a young person that might help me to better understand myself.

Beveley tells me she was a bit of a rebel growing up when it came to questioning the status quo. 'My upbringing was quite secluded. I was very protected in my little bubble of what South Africans call coloured people. Everybody I knew was coloured [in the terms of the Race Classification Act]. I couldn't understand why everybody in my area looked like me but when I looked on the TV, nobody looked like me. I always questioned that. That is what drove me. I think many of the generation before me were less interested. They were just so indoctrinated by apartheid that they accepted it. I made up my mind to find out a lot about where we come from, the make-up of South Africa. I read a lot. At the same time, I always had a one-sided view because obviously everything I read was either against the apartheid regime or was from teachers that wanted to teach me about how good South Africa is and how good the system was.'

Beveley received a scholarship to one of the best universities in South Africa. It was a white afrikaans medium sized university. She says her experience there was 'awful'. There were only thirteen non-white people she knew of on the whole campus at the time, out of over 20,000. They formed their own clique as no one else spoke with them. Beveley would be in a class of 300 students in a lecture and nobody would speak to her. 'My name is Smith, and the teacher would ask "Ms Smith" a question. I would think he's talking to me, and I'd answer, and people would laugh because they thought, why is she speaking. Somebody else next to me or down the aisle would be the Smith person that he was referring to. It wouldn't be me. It was never me. Lecturers didn't speak to me and neither did any of the students. So that was my first experience of university.'

Eventually Beveley did make a white friend. She was from a rural area and spoke to Beveley like she was a normal person. They became good friends. Beveley explains, 'I would invite her to my house for dinner. She always said, no, no, no, maybe we shouldn't do that. And I couldn't understand. Then one day she invited me to have dinner at her house, and her family wouldn't allow me in. They knew that Beveley Smith was coming, but they didn't think that Beveley Smith with an Anglo-Saxon name would be a black person. So they wouldn't let me. The table was laid, but they wouldn't allow me in. I couldn't go in. So my friend decided to walk out with me and she said, okay, now we're going to your house. We went to my house.' It was not common to have a white person in their house. Beveley's parents began to act differently. 'They tried to be what they weren't. They weren't behaving normal. My parents wanted everything to be clean and everything to be perfect for this white person. My dad is now ninety-three and he's still like that. The first question he asks me if I say I am with a friend is, are they white? When I ask why is that important, he'd say, oh, I don't know. I'm just asking. But to him, it's not nothing. The way he grew up was so different from what I've experienced.'

Beveley tells me she grew up in a period where many young activists had run-ins with the police during anti-apartheid protesting. She knew of people who would be arrested and left in a cell without being asked any questions, before being released the following day. Her life changed when her brother, who was also her best friend, died in a car accident. 'It rocked my world. Me coming to Britain was a personal thing because that just destroyed my world. I could not cope with anything. Nothing made sense anymore. Nothing mattered. The shock and horror of my brother dying. That was probably the thing. It just changed my life. I was a staunch devout Christian before my brother died. And then when my brother died, I hated God. I went from the one extreme to the other.' She has since returned to attending church regularly.

The head teacher of Friern Barnet County School had flown to Cape Town in late 2001 to recruit teachers. There was a big advert in a newspaper, which Beveley saw. 'These beautiful brochures. I can't tell you how beautiful it was,

Samuel. It was something from out of this world and you are sold and you're just thinking, wow. At the interview I asked what are the class sizes like? And he said to me, there's about twenty, twenty-five max. Most of the classes are quite small the higher it goes up, which wasn't true. I was thinking I'm teaching a class of forty now and forty is a small class here. Twenty-five is nothing.'

The following day she received a call to confirm she had got the job and was off to the UK. 'When I came to the UK I partied a lot. A group of South Africans had come over to teach at the same time and we became good friends. I loved it. I didn't realise that I was just physically in the UK, but I was living with South African friends. I didn't get to know the culture at all. So that first seven months, that's what happened. And then I had to decide, am I going back or am I staying? I thought, I'll stay for another year, but I needed a contract because I couldn't just stay here. I applied to East Barnet and the rest as they say is history. I met my first British friend in East Barnet School. For seven months I only had colleagues. I knew them only at school. And when I was out of school, I knew only South Africans.'

Mr David, another black teacher, was the very first person Beveley spoke to when she arrived in East Barnet School, the place where I studied and where she taught me. 'He was probably rolling his eyes at me, thinking what the hell are you talking about. But he was the only one I felt comfortable talking to. Because now it was back in the white majority environment, like when I was at university.' She speaks fondly of the former head teacher of the school, Mr Christou. 'When Mr Christou left, I wrote him a long note about how he gave me confidence to stand up. I had confidence in South Africa because I was always with a crowd of people. Supporting me in any fight that I had about race. There was always a crowd of people supporting me. He gave me that confidence to speak up because I was so unconfident when I came here. He kept giving me opportunities to maybe just speak for two minutes in the assembly about things that I like to speak about or to mentor somebody that is white because he knew I would never have been able to mentor somebody that was white in South Africa. I never had the opportunity.'

I notice that Beveley uses black and coloured interchangeably when describing both herself and her experiences in South Africa. Coloured is a term that we do not use in England as it is deemed offensive, so I really notice when it's used. I ask her about how she describes herself. She explains, 'I always say we do low-grade racism in Britain. Racism in South Africa, they segregate you properly. Where I lived would be a coloured area. So, everybody there would be coloured. The white people made you aware that you have maybe better features, sharp features, slightly better. Coloured people were said to have better hair than black people. You were better than the black people so that we could look down on them. The coloured Indians was slightly higher of course. My ancestry is Indian, but my dad's coloured. So the hierarchy was clear.'

I ask if she can remember what I was like in school. 'You were never rude, but you were cheeky, very cheeky. And you always had to have the last word. Always questioning things, why do I need to do this, miss? You came as a managed move, I think, to the school. So, you were moved from one school to the school in year 10, wasn't it?' Prior to attending East Barnet School, I had been at two others within a two-and-a-half-term period, so this was my third school in less than a year. The moves were largely due to a combination of bad behaviour and limited adult supervision. East Barnet School was essentially my last chance as GCSE exams were on the horizon. Beveley says, 'I don't think you got into that much trouble with us. Maybe people were slightly more tolerant of you. I don't think you got into that much trouble, because you eventually came into sixth form, which is where I got to know you. By that time I think you were focused. You hated your accounting and finance module, but wanting to study accounting and finance at university, which is also something I don't understand. You questioned everything. But I would allow you. I suppose I allowed you to just say anything. You were clearly a favourite.'

She is probably right that the school was more accommodating. I always tell people Barnet is the best place in the world. That is because I am aware that if it was not for me ending up in that school in that area I probably would not be where I am today. They gave me a chance, they were patient with me, and I owe them so much for it.

Outsiders and School

Does Beveley think she is still an outsider? 'The reason why I feel like an outsider is because I identify as South African. There's a lot of things in English culture that I've got that I like. I love football, you know. I can speak about football for days. But I hate the pub culture, for example. There's a lot of things in the school that I still don't do because I just won't do certain things. So I still think I'm an outsider. I still have different ideas to other people. Although now maybe I'm not outside anymore. I'm also comfortable because I've been here for

twenty years and I kind of know everything. There's a familiarity. I'm one of the oldest members of staff. I'm also very
comfortable being in the staffroom. I'm still a bit of an outsider,
but that can just be because there are big cultural differences,
and I may be still a bit old-fashioned.'

Has her feeling about being an outsider stopped her progressing? 'I've not applied for higher positions. I just love teaching.
Somebody spoke to me about not applying and I said, you
know what? I've not applied because I don't ever think I'm
going to get the job. That's why I just don't apply. And they
said, why would you think you're not going to get a job when
you clearly would qualify? It comes back to not being confident in my own abilities. I'm happy to speak my mind, but I'm
not happy to put myself out there and that it's a character flaw,
isn't it?'

My final question for Beveley is what she thinks needs to
happen to build bridges between groups that often feel divided.
She replies 'When my daughter comes home and tells me she's
upset because of something someone says, I always advise her
to communicate. What she must understand is there needs to
be communication. You've got to communicate with him or
her why you don't like what they said so that they can understand, because if you don't tell them and you're just angry at
them, how are they going to know? That's the biggest thing, is
trying to make people aware of how it affects you. And it
doesn't matter how you meant it. It matters how I received it.
That's what matters. So don't address what you meant. I don't
care what you meant. Address my own feeling. Next time you
say something, you think twice before you say something that
might offend me, because if you don't know it's going to offend
me, you're not going to stop. If somebody calls me the N-word,

you can't tell me that they didn't really mean it, it was just a joke. I don't care whether it was a joke. It's no joke to me.'

Beveley makes an interesting point. These days when we discuss how someone feels in the context of communicating a position or dealing with a social issue, it can be viewed through fairly reductive lenses. On one side we have a school of thought that argues that how one feels should be the main or only consideration. If one feels they have experienced a racist or homophobic attack, then that must be accepted as the reality. Others believe that 'hurt feelings' should not be a significant deciding factor in any context and facts should always be the prevailing influence for how we deal with a situation. Borrowing from a famous mantra in court one must 'prove beyond all reasonable doubt' that something has happened or that an issue really exists. Stick to the facts and not feelings.

Reflecting on how we overcome this conundrum of facts vs feelings takes me back to antient Rome. Marcus Tullius Cicero [3 January 106 BC – 7 December 43 BC] was a Roman politician, lawyer and writer. He was an outsider from a background more modest than some of his famous contemporise like Julius Caesar and Mark Anthony. He had no distinguished ancestors and came from a family of modest economic means, achieved no military distinction, and often struck others as being vain and self-centred. But he managed to rise to the highest political office in the Roman Republic. How? Through his exceptional oratorical skill. In fact, many believe him to be the most accomplished orator in history.

Central to Cicero's approach to persuasion was one fundamental principle: This was the belief that people are primarily ruled by emotion. He argued that if you are trying to persuade an audience then your goal is not necessarily to appeal to logic or reason. While these things are useful, the most essential goal is to stimulate an audience's emotions. He argued that if you can get an audience emotionally invested, then they can be made to believe whatever you want them to.

When we think about the main reasons why the majority of the British people voted to leave the European Union in 2016 – at its core it was feelings that had the greatest impact. People felt left behind in traditionally Labour voting areas. Others felt a sense of nostalgic longing for a period when Britain was an economic and military superpower – in control of its own 'laws and money'. Even in places heavily reliant on EU subsidies like Cornwall, a significant majority voted to leave the European bloc. The facts on this subject were and remain relatively opaque for the average Briton. Most do not know about the complex nature of the European Union. The role of the EU Commission vs Council vs Parliament. How the European Central Bank functions. The European Court of Justice as an institution may invoke some feelings in public debate, but its overall efficacy is not something that most people would opine as evidence beyond a few divisive subjects. Remain campaigners failed to address these feelings in a meaningful way. In 2023, just like in 2016, and in ancient Rome, feelings still matter. The facts, of course, do and should matter too. Whether or not you meant offence when making a statement should be a consideration. But ultimately, the best communicators are able to engage with people's emotions as well as logic. It is not either/or because we are not robots. In terms of what comes first, it probably depends on what your objectives are. If you genuinely care about trying to build bridges then how someone feels will matter to you. To quote Nelson Mandela, 'If you want the cooperation of the humans around you, you must make them feel important.' It's important to be kind, and to consider others as we go about our everyday lives. That does not mean we should not defend the right to freedom of speech, or that we should not speak truth if it risks offending. Often, it is those willing to speak the truth who are the ones with our best interests at heart. However, being considerate is how we can live more harmoniously. It costs nothing to be kind. This nuance is often lost in public discourse. Free speech is not a licence to be unkind, while being upset is not a good enough reason for not confronting facts or engaging in important debate.

When I started the journey of writing this book, I would never have imagined that it would feature some of the stories that I have covered, including what I have just heard from Beveley. I reflect on the publication of the Commission on Race and Ethnic Disparities report and think that those responsible for writing it probably had the same conundrum. To what extent do they relay the evidence that they have received, especially when for many of the commissioners it would contradict some of the things that they had been known to have said in the past? Maybe they felt it would have hurt their reputation or career aspirations. It would have been immoral for me not to write about the things that I had heard, uncomfortable as they may be for some readers. We still have a long way to go to truly be cohesive as one nation. It is sad to hear about the experiences that people still face, particularly young people in schools, but we must all work together for a better future. Like Samir Puri said in our conversation, progress takes time and takes work.

One thing that concerns me is just how much and for how long a period victims often pay the price for other people's actions. There is no good to be derived from being bound by other people's actions. Those who do wrong often move on and are able to continue with their lives while the ones who have been wronged are weighed down. Healing from trauma isn't easy but we only live once, and we must try to use our time wisely. Forgiveness can be hard, but it liberates us. It is okay to seek justice, and it's okay to challenge and for people to feel discomfort about wrongs and history. But true emancipation can never come from someone else. It comes from within. Eleanor Southwood, former chair of the RNIB, was correct in her assessment that we would be weighed down if we held on to every time we were wronged. Again, Nelson Mandela perhaps put it perfectly when he said, 'As I walked out the door toward the gate that would lead to my freedom, I knew if I didn't leave my bitterness and hatred behind, I'd still be in prison.' People shouldn't be able to live rent-free in your head. Since leaving Downing Street, I have lost count of the times I have been contacted when a former minister I had tensions with was in the news for something controversial. People reaching out to look for a reaction, perhaps some back-biting. The truth is I genuinely couldn't care less about what said minister was up to. I'm free; I have no bitterness whatsoever towards any of my former colleagues or the minister whose actions sparked the events that led to my resignation. Holding unforgiveness would only weigh me down.

My visit to East Barnet School has been a humbling one. Beveley says that I haven't changed; I am still that cheeky young man who questions everything and perhaps makes decisions that people do not understand. She is a teacher who has a very special place in my heart because I knew that she cared. I suppose it is rare for people to go back to their schools or even to still be able to connect with a teacher many years after leaving, but it is an important thing to do when possible. In my darkest hours I often find myself wanting to go back to those places in and around Barnet where I would go as a child. A park or the streets of the many homes my siblings and I lived in as children. I would go alone and simply pause, trying to recentre myself, taking deep breaths for a period before returning to life. This visit has been one of those pauses, albeit in a different way.

We end the interview and I am given a tour of the school facilities, which have changed drastically since I last visited. The school is on a hill, and the new library has a panoramic window that when the skies are clear allows you to see as far as the tall commercial buildings in Canary Wharf. I can imagine it is a great source of inspiration for the students as they study. A reminder of the possibilities that their hard work could offer them. I had never even heard of Canary Wharf until I went to university. Perhaps that exposure through this window might have impacted on my behaviour, and choices, as a young person. Who knows.

Chapter 12

Holding the Pen

We have all heard some iteration of the statement 'those people coming over here taking our jobs'. A worried native feeling like their opportunities will be somewhat diminished because an immigrant or someone from another region has arrived. It is responsible for all countries to control their borders, not least for security reasons. As someone elected to a local government position myself, I recognise my own responsibility to ensure the people I represent can access local jobs and opportunities. I am very grateful that the likes of Tesco, the largest supermarket chain in the land, have chosen to have their headquarters in my district, employing many local people. However, the economic reality is that Britain has been enjoying a period of stable mass employment for the best part of the last decade, and therefore the prosperity of an individual in most cases is not threatened by the arrival of people competing for employment. There is more to the story. In fact, I would argue that any country's ability to improve its standard of living depends almost entirely on its ability to raise its output per worker, its productivity, and not simply how many people are in work. Tangible increases in living standards and well-being depend on sustained growth in productivity. More people need to become knowledge workers and deliver more value and innovation, which improves earnings, spending power and quality of life. The $10 million question is how do you increase productivity? There is no silver bullet but, for a start, the opportunity to develop new skills at any stage of your life is important as economies evolve. We also need to ensure we continue to value our elder citizens, not writing people off once they pass the age of fifty.

Outsiders, Productivity and Wealth

Relatively low productivity remains a significant challenge for the British economy, with productivity levels having remained flat since 2011. To give more context, matching the United States' levels of productivity would raise UK GDP by 31 per cent, the equivalent of an extra £21,000 per household. With record levels of unfilled vacancies, and the jobs market rapidly bouncing back since the start of the coronavirus pandemic, getting more people into work is too simple an answer to the challenge of boosting economic growth. Though of course there is a challenge of many over-fifties being economically inactive. We need to find ways to expose people to higher output possibilities. We need to get more opportunities into regions that have suffered from a post-industrial aftershock. Areas that feel left behind. We need to make sure that everyone can realise their full potential. That is what levelling up should mean in British political discourse. Boris Johnson repeatedly said that talent is spread evenly but opportunity is not. The nation wins if more people can win. That includes outsiders getting a bigger piece of the pie. This does not necessarily mean others receiving a smaller share (though we should be uncomfortable with some excessive wealth); in productivity terms, you can grow the pie so that more people can receive a bigger piece. A win-win situation. Emerging economies like India and China are great examples of increasing productivity and growing the pie. 'Growing the pie' is a phrase Liz Truss elevated to the national stage when she was elected prime minister. Unfortunately, the disaster of the 'mini-budget' a few weeks into her premiership has perhaps tarnished the reputation of the term; but it is an important argument nonetheless. Truss's argument sounded too much like trickle-down economics. She led with lifting the cap on bankers' bonuses and not with turbocharging housebuilding to create jobs and to tackle house price inflation. Her investment zones idea was interesting but needed more detail. An inclusive pro-growth message is one most of the nation would back, but the pitch must be comprehensive, and the presentation delivered in a way that is inspiring.

We have established that there is a clear economic imperative for people from all backgrounds, including outsiders, to make the most of their gifts and talents. The question is, how do you succeed if you are not from a background that gives you access to the networks and knowledge required? There are many great books about people who would be categorised as outsiders. I enjoyed musician, author and activist Akala's bestselling book *Natives*, for example. He charts his journey as a mixed-race person from a single-parent home growing up in inner-city London. He is now a successful thought leader. My challenge with some of the content of books like these, is that you are often left with the notion that the success of the protagonist is because they have simply been more fortunate than others. Why does one outsider perform better than others from the same area, socioeconomic grouping, and family structure? I regularly hear and read about people saying they were simply one of the lucky ones. The exception.

This unwillingness to explore why people from particular backgrounds, afforded the same opportunities, have different outcomes is often influenced by one's world view. Sometimes there is a reluctance to reflect on the extent to which choice was a key determinant. Good fortune is undeniably a factor at times. But I am not convinced that exceptionalism is accurate in most instances where it is thought to apply. Rather, there are principles that successful people consciously or subconsciously apply that lead to their achievements, coupled with some character traits that are debatably natural but more likely learned through one's environment.

With these reflections in mind, I'm off to meet David Tyler, who a few years ago agreed to act as a mentor to me. David is one of the most experienced non-executives in the United Kingdom and is best known for being chairman of the second largest supermarket chain in the country (J Sainsbury's), between 2009 and 2019. He previously served on the boards of other mammoth companies including fashion powerhouse Burberry and consumer credit reporting agency Experian, and has recently stepped down as chairman of Hammerson – the real estate owners of London's Brent Cross and Birmingham's Bullring shopping centres. Guiding Hammerson, who were already adapting to changing consumer habits due to the growth of online shopping, has meant that his chairmanship during the Covid-19 pandemic would have been particularly challenging. Of course, he would be the first to say that he is more fortunate than the many who have lost lives, loved ones and livelihoods during this most testing of periods for the world.

David is very much a traditional high-powered executive. There was a time not too long ago when there were more men called David on a FTSE 100 board than there were women in total. I suppose he is the first typical insider I have spoken to for this book. It's important to have different perspectives to avoid potential confirmation bias during any line of enquiry. As I'm walking along Baker Street in London to meet David, I look on my phone to see if there is anything in the news about him that I should probably know before we meet. I see that he is now chairman of home decor and furniture retailer The White Company, and has also agreed to chair Imagr, a European tech start-up that allows retailers to brand their own autonomous checkout solutions. He is still the co-chair of the Parker Review, an initiative established under the coalition government to improve the ethnic diversity of FTSE boards.

I finish my rapid research exercise and head in for our meeting. The plan was to see if I could get some interesting reflections on the power of relationships, particularly mentors, in assisting someone's success. My assumption was that David would agree that the most significant factor in someone rising through the ranks in any environment is the network they have around them, and that he would then explain how one can go about establishing that web of people. Our conversation starts in the usual way: I update him on what I've been up to, and I ask him about his own endeavours. We then somehow end up at Brexit. David, like many senior business figures, is very anti-Brexit.

We then get on to me asking questions for this chapter. I ask David what he feels is the most significant factor in his and other people's success. 'There's an element that is really important to my career, but also to many other people's careers,' he says. 'That's having self-confidence. You need that if you are going to be successful. But it's important for it not to turn into arrogance. Very often, but maybe not always, people that are most successful are confident.' Confidence has been a constant theme throughout this book, and so I suppose I shouldn't have been surprised by David's response. Reflecting on my time in Downing Street, one thing that stood out to me very quickly was that most of the other special advisors, particularly those who clearly had a different upbringing to my own, had a confidence that was very visible. I was always taught to be humble and have quiet confidence, but what I was observing in Number 10 was very different. People pushing themselves to be on attendee lists for meetings instead of waiting to be invited. Making sure their names were on notes to the prime minister, even when they had not really been involved in the work, and constantly briefing the media about how great they were instead of focusing on simply being great. I had to learn very quickly that if I was going to be successful and influential in the job, I could not afford to not have self-confidence, albeit in my own way.

Outsiders Holding the Pen

This wasn't the first time in a political setting that I was reminded that my style was perhaps not appropriate to the environment. When I attended an assessment board for potential parliamentary candidates in 2017, I had an experience that would stick with me for the rest of my life. We had a group exercise that was part of the assessment. We all walked into the room, then the facilitator explained what was to happen. After the explanation he said we could begin, and one gentleman straight away picked up the notepad and pen and said that he would help to take notes. In holding the pen, he had subtly but firmly assumed command of the whole activity, bringing the rest of the group in one at a time, guided by him, the note-taker. On a number of subsequent occasions, I observed how someone more alert than me was able to take charge in a political setting simply by pushing themselves forward to 'hold the pen'. I had to be more direct than I was used to, and, if I am honest, I needed at times to find a way to become more confident.

When someone is confident in their capabilities, they are more likely to set more ambitious goals and to continue a journey despite the challenges. The likes of David Cameron and Boris Johnson perhaps never doubted that they would one day become prime minister of the United Kingdom. Despite many setbacks and personal shortcomings in Boris Johnson in particular, they were able to still achieve that objective. Many less confident people would have given up in similar circumstances. That belief in one's abilities also inspires others to have belief in you. It is what often determines how much someone is valued, what salary they can command, what promotion comes their way and, yes, if one can be elected in a democracy. Confidence extends to who you can interact with socially, and who someone chooses to invest in or partner with.

People often have imperfect knowledge of their own abilities, and there is an optimum level for confidence. After this level is crossed the likelihood of adverse consequences becomes greater. Confidence or morale can play a significant role in dealing with challenges; conversely, when people expect to fail, they fail quite effectively, and that failure can often have a lasting impact, as we explored earlier. Confidence has long been regarded as a personal asset, with psychologist William James (1842–1910) focusing on ideas of 'believing in oneself' as a key to individual success. There is in modern times a whole industry full of self-help gurus who publish books and deliver motivational talks focused on developing people's self-esteem. However, the fact that confidence plays such a significant role in the outcomes of every person means that managers who want better output from staff need to ensure that confidence is built into their teams. Governments that desire higher productivity must also ensure that confidence is part of the development of young people from all backgrounds. It is not just that individuals benefit from a workforce that has confidence; whole ecosystems prosper as a result.

Having self-belief makes it easier to convince others (rightly or wrongly) that you are as good as you say. It is not only privileged people who may have imperfect knowledge about their abilities. We all have the same challenge. It is often said that to lie most convincingly a person must believe his own lies. In the Hollywood film *Catch Me If You Can*, Leonardo DiCaprio plays Frank Abegnale, a teenager who turned into a con artist. The film is based on the memoirs of the real-life Frank, who is said to have successfully performed scams worth millions of dollars by posing as a Pan American World Airways pilot, a Georgia doctor and a Louisiana parish prosecutor. DiCaprio presents an individual who exudes so much confidence that he is able to get away with some of the most outlandish deceptions for a long period of time.

In business, there is evidence that there is a cost saving of self-confidence from a signalling perspective, where those who are more confident have a lower cost associated with convincing others of their product or service value. Confidence also has a significant motivational value. Liverpool Football Club attacker Mohamed Salah was asked about whether or not he felt he was the best player in the world following his excellent goal against league rivals Manchester City during the 2021/2022 season. His response was very direct: 'It's always the ambition to be the best player in the world. I don't have to lie. It's something that drives me to work really hard and just try to be the best version of myself. In my head, I'm the best player all the time. I'm trying to have that confidence in my head. It doesn't matter if some people agree with you or not.' The comfortable acknowledgement of his ambition, the require-ment of hard work to realise it, and the affirmation that he is delivering on the promise is a great example of the confidence needed to make it to the very top.

There are many interdependent factors that self-confidence works alongside. Author David Lawrence Preston says, 'When we talk about self-confidence, self-image and self-esteem are close associations. They are related to self-confidence. Self-image is how you perceive yourself to be. It consists of three core feelings: self-worth or the value you put in yourself. Competence or your capability to succeed, work out hard-ships, and the ability to think for yourself. Belonging or others' acceptance and respect.' Leaders in businesses tend to be more self-confident, having stronger beliefs in their own abilities and opinions, allowing them to more effectively guide and manage employees. High levels of social self-confidence may lead a person to emerge as a natural leader with an ability to influ-ence the decisions of others. Their confidence can be what inspires people to follow them. Conversely, low confidence can put someone into a lower position than their ability merits. Society often views elites as having superior abilities, when the reality is very seldom the case. Perhaps this has something to do with elites being able to invest in their own reputation management. They are more clued up about how to use the media to their advantage, which results in the development of an enhanced image. It's only when you get closer to those people that you realise there is nothing superhuman about them at all.

For those who are seeking to be more confident, my advice would be to find ways to win every day, one goal at a time. At a recent event the former Conservative Party chairman Jake Berry said his one piece of advice he would give to anyone seeking to be a Member of Parliament was, 'Apply, because if you do not take that first step it is impossible for you to know how far you can go.' If you do not apply for that job that may seem impossible for you to get, you will never know what is possible. When a striker has a goal drought, confidence can dry away. The way to overcome this is to keep on shooting, and eventually one goal comes, and then another, and with every goal the confidence returns until eventually that confidence results in an overall better performance. But if a striker stops shooting, they will never score.

That's the same with anything in life. Set daily goals, keep shooting, and your confidence will grow. You should also find people who will give you helpful feedback, aiding you to do better but also giving you the confidence to push on. I used to be very sceptical about professional coaching but now I see the value in having someone helping you to be the best you can be, giving you the confidence to do the things that you were born to do well. I suspect Mo Salah probably has someone who has helped him to work through his mental toughness to be so confident about being the best. Confidence is not just about knowing what you do well. It is also about knowing what you don't do well and having the confidence to lean on others who are better than you at certain things. A truly confident person is not afraid to let other people shine because they know what they bring to the table themselves.

Outsiders and Building Confidence

Returning to my conversation with David, he is clear that overconfidence or confidence alone is not sufficient for achieving great things. 'Have a nice balance. You obviously must also be competent, but successful people are comfortable in their own skin. They have an ability to back themselves and the ability to get outside of themselves and look at themselves from the ceiling. Someone who is always 100 per cent sure of himself or herself has gone too far. Somebody who never has any confidence in themselves and is not as comfortable in their own skin, again, will probably also not get as far as they could. And this isn't particularly to do with business itself. It's in general about leadership in organisations where there's more than one person.'

I'm keen to know more about the things that helped to build David's confidence.

'I gradually gained self-confidence through my childhood and youth, if you like. And then once I was in the serious world of work, it was a series of activities that came up in my working life that made a difference. For me, to some extent it was built as my level of competence gradually grew. I'm a good leader because over a period, I've learned lessons in many different environments. And there isn't necessarily one story where some people would have where suddenly there was a kind of revelation or the road to Damascus or whatever. For me, it was a series of things that built my confidence.'

Though David has had a more traditional path to his current status, successful outsiders will have had a similar journey of building their confidence through different experiences at different stages. On my own journey, being involved in student politics was a game changer. It exposed me to the world of governance (including boards and committee structures where strategic decisions are made) and allowed me to engage with senior people from an early age. This gave me the confidence to forge my own path, as I learnt to engage with senior leaders. I have gone on to set up Inclusive Boards, an organisation that supports people from underrepresented backgrounds to have the same exposure. It's a similar story for many people. For those not young enough to take that path, obtaining some sort of governance role can still accelerate that journey. Opportunities that are readily available include becoming a governor of a local school, joining a local public health board or being involved in local government. As David has said, confidence can be built over time – and, no matter who you are, it is a vital thing to have.

I take the conversation onto the theme of relationships and ask David if there were people in his career who played a part in developing his confidence. He responds, 'One thing that is really important is having senior people who you respect giving you approbation. Saying you did a great job there. I was really impressed by the way you did a or b. I was aware of how you are on the back foot here, but you've got out of it well. Those sorts of things give you a little measure of confidence and I've been very conscious of that throughout my leadership career. Find a way of tapping someone on the shoulder when he or she did something right. You don't want to only be talking to people when you're putting them out when they do things wrong. I learned the lesson, particularly when I made mistakes. It was really important that if my boss, or whoever the right person was, took me aside and said, "Look, you didn't do that. This is the reason why," but at the same time in that same conversation was the fact that "I've still got confidence in you, you've got these great attitudes or capabilities or whatever." Finding the opportunity to say to somebody you've done that very well, but also when he or she makes mistakes to pull them up about it as soon as possible after the event, when it's very fresh in the moment. It's not something just to talk about in an annual appraisal nine months later or something.'

I want to know who the key people are that have helped David to get to the point of being one of the most successful business leaders in the land. 'My advice to people is to have a partner. It might be a wife or husband, but it could be all sorts of other relationships where you can openly and easily share. An environment where you feel you're loved and respected. You can say to them, this is what I was worried about. This is what's gone wrong. So right away, you can simply share things with that partner who feeds back to you as well. I think that's the most important thing. It doesn't have to be one person, but for many of us it is one person. It could be several people who you might approach on different things.'

I explain to him that for some outsiders, keeping people close from their past is a difficult thing to do when they progress. I remember reading a particular article where the Mayor of London Sadiq Khan bumped into an old school friend serving a sentence during a prison visit when he was justice secretary. That story could easily be my own. There are also questions around to what extent someone can keep their accent in different environments. David replies, 'I think that does happen to some people. It might make them feel a bit rootless. People who come from a working-class background, and maybe they're white, maybe they're black, but you know, some of them absolutely retain that background, including the accent. It might be a northern accent. There must be some people who at some point find a mismatch somehow because the kind of people they're mixing with, they can't talk about the same things, public-school boys, for example, maybe somehow talking a different language than someone who went to a comprehensive school. It's difficult to bridge that gap. I am very conscious of that. I am always working on that, so I'm sure some people don't do as well as they should potentially because they are constantly second-guessing if they are doing the right thing.'

Did David have any mentors? 'When I was a child. Yeah. Well, teachers, if you like, obviously members of my family. I knew older men and older women, I suppose, who would generally be family friends probably apart from teachers. I've never had a formal mentoring relationship with anybody, but obviously got on well with some much more experienced people. And, you know, I talked to them and asked, what do you think about this or that? But yeah, not really in the way that I've been a mentor to other people over the years. There are some individuals at work that I would certainly go and talk to. It was probably easier for me because I was probably seen as someone who was going to be successful and rise to a senior level in the organisation.'

Formal mentoring schemes have become commonplace within organisations, something we will speak more about later.

David's experience of mentoring receiving a mixed reception is not unique. Some recognise the vital role it has played on their own journeys, while others believe being given the opportunity to participate in a formal mentoring scheme might be seen as a sign of weakness or inadequacy. Others believe that mentoring can be used as a substitute for more substantial actions to reduce inequalities. I remember having a discussion with a woman during the 2019 general election about the manifesto. A minister had mentioned the desire to have a mentoring programme for women in business written in. When I stated this to the person I was speaking to she was mortified. I think she felt that offering a mentor to a businesswoman was patronising. Many people argue that entrepreneurs from under-represented backgrounds have been over-mentored and under-funded. Contrastingly, in a US study of senior females and their CEOs, 91 per cent of female executives mentioned having a mentor, and many saw this as the 'single most critical piece to women advancing career-wise'.

Though it is probably reasonable to argue that businesses can do more to improve things like access to capital for women in business and that mentoring alone is not the solution, to dismiss its overall value is wrong. On my own journey I have had many mentors who played a pivotal role in helping me to navigate new environments as an outsider. From mentors in my church, to mentors in business and politics, I realised very early on that I needed to learn from people who had gone further than me or were more used to environments I was entering for the first time if I was going to succeed. Thankfully, there have been many willing to help. Without them, it is very difficult to see how I would have got so far.

It is also important to view mentoring as a mutually beneficial activity that offers learning and development growth for both mentors and mentees. Mentoring is often portrayed as an asymmetrical relationship in which the mentee is the main beneficiary, and the mentor provides more support than he or she is likely to receive in return. At a very basic level, mentors can often benefit from personal satisfaction, organisational recognition, and the development of a base of support from mentoring. A mentee will also have access to information as they are closer to the ground within an organisation or perhaps more in tune with different generations, cultures or technology. There are even studies that have found mentors reporting higher salaries as well as more rapid promotion rates and stronger perceptions of career success than those who choose not to mentor. I have on several occasions received thank-you notes from mentors after I had given them useful advice or helped them along their own journey. I've even been a reference for one of my mentors for a non-executive board position on a listed company.

Mentors are important at all stages of life. The type of mentor can be material to how successful the mentee will be in their chosen profession. A good mentor can encourage and promote their mentee in growing not only as a professional but also as an individual. People often outgrow mentors as they become more experienced and learn to trust their own decisions without the need to have someone validate their choices. The mentoring relationship will be positive only if mentors also strive to develop professionally and endeavour constantly to update their own knowledge and skills about their subject so they can continue to mentor their mentees; without this desire to develop, they will no longer be good candidates to be mentors.

My reflections from my meeting with David are that confidence is key for anyone who wants to be successful in life. For outsiders, they may have got that confidence from their parents or carers. However, if that is not the case, the confidence to break barriers can come from other places including other family members, a local faith community, or a good school. The journey of building confidence never ends. It is vital to keep finding ways to grow, including seeking governance roles, not waiting till you reach a level where you can be the chair of J Sainsbury's. Start with your local school.

Aside from governance, other forms of public life can be equally as rewarding, including volunteering regularly. I was responsible for the government's relationship with civil society during my time in Downing Street. There are some amazing charities of all sizes and missions that would welcome volunteers. At the height of the coronavirus pandemic, we not only saw the power of civil society - which reached parts of the country that local and national government could not. They were also agile enough to be the first responders, and often gave us vital information to support the decision-making process. The Covid-19 vaccine rollout simply would not have been a success if it wasn't for volunteers working through the Red Cross, St John's Ambulance, and many others. We saw tens of thousands of Britons hold their hands up to offer to help as volunteers during this time. I believe that willingness is still there. The challenge is how to utilise it.

Having said that, it is not by accident that the most elite professions continue to be dominated by people from privileged backgrounds. The confidence that they have is usually on another level, partly as a result of exposure to confident role models from birth, and seldom because their abilities are particularly exceptional. For outsiders to succeed they must be unapologetic about occupying spaces. They must put themselves on cast lists for meetings, hold the pen, apply for that job. Let's recognise that the perceived superiority of others is simply that – intentionally crafted perceptions. Like a long queue for a popular nightclub, the perception of being elite is probably the main thing that drives their value. We must never forget that, for everyone, in economic productivity terms, nations need us all, insiders and outsiders, to be the best we can be. We need to grow the pie so that more people have a bigger piece.

Chapter 13

Neurodiversity

It's January 2023. A few months earlier, I had announced that I would be putting myself forward to be the Conservative candidate for the next London mayoral elections. Taking such a step less than two years after resigning from Number 10 Downing Street felt like quite a move, but of course there is a wider plan and clear (at least for me and my team) rationale. I think that London is ready for someone new to lead it, but for the Conservatives to win they will need to find a candidate who can appeal to people who presently might be less likely to vote for them. Someone who can broaden audiences. An outsider perhaps. If I am unsuccessful, this is still a great platform to have a conversation about the future of politics and policy. We need to build more houses, create opportunities for future generations, and find a more holistic response to tackling crime – including cybercrime, which is a growing challenge.

For me to contest for the candidacy I had to return to being on the list of approved candidates. Doing this has now become a more challenging task than it was previously, due to there being some disquiet around the quality of some of the people who have ended up as parliamentarians. There are more vigorous background checks now, and more stages in the assessment process. The final part of the assessment required me to travel up to Leeds at short notice for a full day of activities. I arrive a bit flustered as the day begins. During the first e-tray exercise (usually a test of a candidate's ability to deal with a real work scenario) I realise to my shock that I am unable to read the information on the screens in front of me. The words look blurry and are moving around. This slowed me down and I ended up not quite finishing the first task, which has an impact on my ability to deal with the second task and so my morning doesn't go as well as I would have liked.

By the afternoon I had settled down and the rest of the day runs relatively smoothly. As I head home, at the back of my mind I keep asking myself why I didn't declare in advance that I have dyslexia and dyspraxia. I was given ample opportunity to do this at various stages of the assessment process but chose not to. Had I declared this in advance I probably would have been given reasonable adjustments; maybe an extra five minutes during the morning exercises, which would have helped me to settle myself and to complete the tasks at hand.

I guess I chose not to declare primarily because I have learnt to live with dyslexia and dyspraxia and usually as long as I have time to settle my mind it is very easy for me to read and write on a computer. When I respond to things through writing on paper, I have to make sure that I use simple words. I did not feel there was a need for me to have any adjustments or to be viewed as different to other candidates during the process of getting on the candidates list. Though some parliamentarians, notably Matt Hancock, have been quite vocal about declaring their dyslexia, the difference is that they are already elected.

The scoring system for becoming an approved candidate is relatively opaque, and the selection process for seats once you are an approved candidate even more so – not just for the Conservatives but for every mainstream party. It makes people less comfortable declaring things that may count against them. Of course, politics needs more people from different backgrounds and different experiences to add value where decisions are being made.

After a few days of reflection, I decide that the right thing would be for me to declare these conditions, albeit after the event. I write to Conservative Campaign Headquarters letting them know. This leads me to reflect on how we understand the impact of neurodiversity or being neurodivergent. Writing this book has given me the chance to take a deep dive into some of the research, so let's start with a definition:

According to Harvard neurologist Nicole Baumer, neurodiversity is understood as 'the idea that people experience and interact with the world around them in many different ways. There is no one "right" way of thinking, learning, and behaving, and differences should not be viewed as deficits'. There has not yet been much research into quantifiable benefits of neurodiversity in the workplace, though preliminary results are compelling. Researchers have discovered that the proportion of individuals who exhibit neurodiverse traits working in science, technology, engineering and maths (STEM) is much larger than in other industries, suggesting that those with abilities such as attention to detail and hyperfocus are a beneficial, if partially untapped, talent pool for certain disciplines. The competitive advantage of neurodiversity builds on the well-documented business case for diversity in organisations.

Hewlett Packard Enterprise (HPE) have engaged in a programme designed to place more neurodiverse individuals in software testing roles at Australia's Department of Human Services (DHS), while also ensuring that workplaces accommodate individuals' support needs. Preliminary results found that neurodiverse testing teams are 30 per cent more productive than others.

In the 1990s people began to see that people with autism, dyslexia and other neurological conditions weren't ill. Instead, they began to be seen as 'neurodivergent'. These conditions were no longer diseases to be cured or problems to be overcome, they were simply a natural variation in the human genome that didn't make a person better or worse; it just meant they thought and learned differently. Simon Baron-Cohen, the British clinical psychologist and professor of developmental psychopathology at the University of Cambridge, thinks that children with autism do more than just act out bizarre obsessive-compulsive behaviours; they're also driven to figure out how complex things work.

Given that neurodiversity in history has only relatively recently received any attention, attributing diagnoses to historical figures can only be a speculative exercise based on biographical reports. But there are interesting examples of people who would be treated differently now. One notable figure is Paul Dirac, a physicist born in Bristol, who was outstanding in his field and widely regarded to be of the same calibre as Albert Einstein. Dirac formulated the eponymous equation describing the quantum behaviour of electrons. He additionally solved decades-long quandaries in physics by creating Fermi–Dirac statistics, as well as discovering the concept of antimatter in

1928. He was known to send a postcard home every week, and, following his successes, his postcard is reported to have read 'not much to report'. He was described as 'the strangest man' by Danish physicist Niels Bohr, and was said to exhibit behaviour that is often associated with autism or Asperger's syndrome, such as extreme reticence, long silences, monosyllabic responses, unemotional responses to significant events, and repetitious statements. Given both his brilliance in the field of physics and his social behaviour, Graham Farmelo – the author of Dirac's biography – made the argument that Dirac was autistic and stated that his behavioural traits were crucial to his success. Farmelo spoke to Simon Baron-Cohen about the possibility, and they concluded that Dirac exhibited additional qualities that could lead us to assume he was autistic. Baron-Cohen states that men with autism often have foreign wives, 'perhaps because the women were more tolerant of unusual behaviour in foreign men than in men from their own culture'. Dirac was married to a Hungarian woman for fifty years. In addition, 'people with autism are often extremely loyal', and Farmelo wrote that Dirac demonstrated great loyalty to his friends – physicists Pyotr Kapitsa and Werner Heisenberg.

In their book *The Mind of the Mathematician*, Michael Fitzgerald and Ioan James suggest that other scientists in history may have had Asperger's syndrome. Marie Curie, chemist and physicist, exhibited many of the traits that comprise diagnostic criteria for autism and related conditions. Curie 'did not greatly care what impression she created', was reported to be 'difficult to engage in conversations, and to be liable to naively misinterpret what she believed to be other people's reactions to her'. Her determination to isolate radium and her obsessive detailing of domestic expenditure reportedly showed signs of hyper fixation and hyperfocus. Curie is also quoted as saying, 'I feel everything very violently [. . .] with a physical violence', which bears a resemblance to the association of autism and overwhelming emotions.

Andy Warhol is another figure in history to whom traits associated with autism have been attributed. Born in 1928 in Pennsylvania, Warhol was an artist, film director and producer. He reportedly did not engage in socialisation easily, used the least possible words in speech, had difficulty recognising friends, and exhibited hyper fixation on topics such as the uniformity of consumer goods. Interviews with Warhol are famously monosyllabic and tended to mimic popular vocabulary used by teenagers. Some people, though, have been critical of the attribution of Warhol's behaviour to autism, citing contextual factors as being responsible. Mark Francis, the former curator of the Warhol Museum in Pittsburgh, has argued that the behaviour Warhol exhibited was designed to enhance a sense of mystery behind his art, and that he had never 'come across any medical evidence' to support the idea that Warhol was autistic.

Although none of this is conclusive, surely the important point is that it does demonstrate that there is value in supporting individuals who do not adhere to strict societal rules of what is deemed 'normal' behaviour.

Autism and Outsiderness

The literature examining the link between socioeconomic status and autism is conflicting. Studies in the United States have shown a negative association with socioeconomic status; this may be due to the relationship between wealth and access to healthcare, which may preclude some disadvantaged children from obtaining a diagnosis. Studies from other countries have reported no association, and sometimes that there is in fact a positive correlation between socioeconomic status and the prevalence of autism. One study by Brian Kelly, Stefan Williams and Sylvie Collins assessed this relationship. The study examined NHS records pertaining to the Born in Bradford birth cohort, consisting of 12,450 women who gave birth to 13,857 children between 2007 and 2011. The study found that the education status of the child's mother, rather than income status or neighbourhood material deprivation, was most strongly associated with the likelihood of a child having a recorded diagnosis of autism. The children of mothers with higher education status (having A level qualifications or higher) were twice as likely to have a diagnosis of autism recorded. The results support the position that there is clear potential in the UK for inequality in autism diagnoses; service provision is limited and potentially difficult to access, and carers need awareness of the potential for their child to be autistic, must engage with the healthcare system, have access to information, and navigate service provision pathways, all while advocating and demanding access to diagnostic service provisions.

It is unknown what causes autism or if it even has a cause, and, while it is suspected that both genetic and environmental factors are antecedent to the development of autism, evidence and research in the field is insufficient to establish exact causality. There is some evidence to support the notion that autism runs in families, with multiple genes likely being responsible rather than a single genetic indicator. Multiple factors have been demonstrated to increase the likeliness of autism in children, including advanced parental age, fragile X syndrome, Rett syndrome, natal factors (including extreme prematurity, low birth weight, and multiple pregnancies such as twins), and pregnancies spaced less than one year apart. Conversely, prenatal vitamins containing folic acid have been found to reduce the likelihood.

Simon Baron-Cohen also states that 'autism and Asperger's syndrome often (perhaps invariably) involve areas of strength – such as remarkable attention to detail, the ability to focus on a small topic for long periods, and to see repeating patterns – and these human qualities are not in need of treatment.' Neurodiversity is valuable, both in the personal and individual sense, and can also bring benefit in the professional sphere.

I'm not the only person to believe that that the inclusion of neurodiversity in the wider conversation on diversity is crucial to forming and building truly inclusive teams, as well as encompassing a broader range of considerations when hiring people. For example, the Australian Defence Department is developing a neurodiversity programme in cybersecurity. When assessing candidates for roles, the department has discovered levels of ability that far outweigh previous expectations of individual capacity for pattern finding within complex data.

Despite these benefits, unemployment among autistic people remains incommensurably high. I know of a candidate with two masters degrees, both with honours, and demonstrable ability in mathematics and software development, who had been unemployed for two years prior because he'd struggled with inaccessible hiring processes. Data supplied by the Office for National Statistics (ONS) in 2020 suggests that the unemployment rate among adults with autism in the UK is 78 per cent. Anka Wittenberg, a senior executive at global software company SAP, argues that if blanket processes are applied in the hiring process, the company will 'miss people with autism'. The social behaviours of neurodivergent people often oppose common notions of what makes a good employee – 'solid communication skills, being a team player, emotional intelligence, persuasiveness, salesperson-type personalities, the ability to network, the ability to conform to standard practices without special accommodations, and so on'. That is not to say that neurodiverse people cannot perform in these conventional ways, but in doing so they may also have to engage in masking – performing normative behaviours while hiding their true selves – which can lead to burnout and disengagement.

Interviewing, which is almost universal in recruitment, can preclude neurodiverse people from obtaining employment that reflects their ability. Traits that are often associated with neurodiverse candidates, such as not making the expected level of eye contact, going off on conversational tangents, or being overly honest about their weaknesses, obviously tend to lead to lower scores in interviews. Specialisterne, a social innovation company, created a process called 'hangouts', comfortable gatherings usually lasting half a day, whereby neurodiverse candidates can demonstrate their abilities in casual interactions with managerial staff. Following this process, some candidates are selected for two to six weeks of further assessment and training, involving activities that are gradually scaled to become more like the typical workday. These efforts are typically government- or not-for-profit funded and trainees are usually paid.

For people with extreme cases of neurodiversity it's clear that they need specialist support for them to be able to live as rich a life as possible. But for those who have moderate or harder-to-identify forms of neurological difference, there is a question around how they deal with it. Some people live their whole lives undeclared or without letting anybody know why or how they function slightly differently. Their attempt to function 'normally' means that they are living their lives as outsiders without them and/or other people necessarily knowing why. My own initial diagnosis of being on the autism spectrum is obviously a material factor in my behaviours. Why I am always questioning things. My firm reaction to an injustice and my tunnel vision at times. My seeming lack of ability to show excitement where I am expected to do so. My strong sense of smell which often looks compulsive when at home or in an office. Though I have been able to find ways to perform in public settings, my natural inclination to retreat is also something that I have had to manage because of the roles that I have occupied. I had gone through the whole education system with no one – me included – knowing why I struggled with certain things.

I can't actually remember why or how I was referred for an assessment. I just remember showing up and being asked to do various exercises, including looking at various things through different lenses. A bit like an eye test, only with more variables. When I received the results, I don't think I was surprised, but I was frustrated. Too many things about my childhood now made more sense. I rejected the opportunity to go to Imperial College because I felt I would struggle. Had I known why I felt this at the time perhaps I would have made a different decision and would have been given the support required for me to flourish. There was a reason why reading was a challenge, but maths was a breeze during my teenage years. I should have been given reasonable adjustments during exams. Teachers should have known I was different. Not worse . . . just different. We need to make sure that fewer children have the experience that I did. Struggling unnecessarily.

Neurodivergent people have unique value. It is good that this difference is increasingly not being viewed as a problem to be overcome, but a strength to be utilised. There was speculation that a certain high-profile member of the Number 10 team was also neurodivergent. Though it would explain a lot, as with the historical figures in this chapter, I suspect it will remain a subject of speculation without any definitive confirmation. That's a shame. I think society can respond to people better if they understand how and why they are different. It certainly would have been useful for me when dealing with the e-tray exercise in Leeds.

Chapter 14

Downing Street Reflections
– An Outsider Inside

Number 10 Downing Street, often referred to internally as the House, is a strange place to work because it's small but big at the same time. You have 150 to 200 members of staff, the majority of whom are civil servants, or officials as we call them. The extensive list of teams includes the custodians, press team, policy unit and private office, who are usually with the prime minister day to day. Less than a third of the staff members are special advisors, who are political appointees.

When I first started, my main goal was to stop getting lost within this rabbit warren of a building. I was unfortunately too busy to complete a full tour, which did not help. My next challenge was to make sure I could keep up with the various policy areas that I would feed into. This meant taking notes after an informal conversation, using a lot of Google to read up on things that were new to me, or reading books that I knew had a significant influence over how some colleagues were thinking about certain subjects. For example, I read a lot of American author and economist Thomas Sowell during this time because I wanted to understand the head of the policy unit, Munira Mirza.

Recruiting into Downing Street

People often ask me how one becomes a special advisor. In the summer of 2019 I messaged an associate, Cleo Watson, to see if Boris Johnson would be retaining a member of Theresa May's team. She responded by asking if someone had reached out to me yet. I asked her what about. I don't think she answered directly but at that point I had the feeling I would be asked to come in as a special advisor. The following day I did receive a call, and the rest as they say is history. Like all special advisors at the time, I was a direct appointment by the prime minister. It is not a job you apply for, and you are not given a job description. As a consequence, the pool of talent that advisors are drawn from is very narrow. The right people need to know you and be able to vouch for you. I first joined the Conservative Party as a nineteen-year-old involved in student politics, so by the time I entered Downing Street I had been in and around the political ecosystem for over a decade, but not enough to be a fully fledged insider. I never worked for a think tank, for example. However, I had run for the Croydon North seat in the 2017 general election and was an elected district councillor. I had also served on an advisory board for Theresa May.

Eventually, I wrote my own job description and would regularly update people on the work that I was doing, sending weekly emails to a wide cast list off my own bat. I felt I had more to prove. There were efforts to reform how special advisors were recruited, but nothing really changed. One such effort was when former senior special advisor Dominic Cummings decided that he wanted to put out a call for 'weirdos and misfits'. I was on holiday in Bali when a particular misfit, who was reported to have been an advocate of eugenics, was hired — I'm told as a contractor. That was the first time I was preparing to quit my role in Downing Street. The prime minister was unaware of this new hire, and thankfully he left before I returned. As the only black advisor in Downing Street during that period you can imagine it was quite unsettling for me . . . Certainly spoilt my holiday.

I honestly don't know how you can successfully reform the recruitment process for special advisors. It's a job that doesn't just rely on professional competence. You also need to have sound political judgement, which inevitably means that you will have already been in and around politics before taking the role. Being able to anticipate what will happen in advance — in effect being one step ahead — is a skill in itself. Knowing which stakeholder needs to be managed before an announcement often means you can put out a fire before it engulfs everyone and everything. Knowing how a potential policy will be received by different sections of the public and parliamentarians allows you to make a decision knowing the potential risks. You also need to decide on which battles you want to fight, as choosing too many can result in being isolated. Politics isn't as easy as it looks, especially in a functioning democracy where citizens rightfully have a voice and a choice. In theory a prime minister has four to five years to convince people to give them the opportunity to continue to govern, but in reality that time is shorter, especially if you make a catastrophically wrong calculation along the way.

Responsibility and Power

There are a few things you realise very quickly when you start work in Downing Street. Firstly, the sheer amount of power that is concentrated in the building is quite something. Nothing happens in government without Number 10 signing it off. From policy decisions to press releases, and even where a minister visits or speeches they give, every decision from each department must go through Number 10. The key teams within the building have sight of everything, and so every day your inbox is full of items that need to be signed off either by or on behalf of the prime minister before they can proceed. If it is not clear that a special advisor has confirmed that they are 'content' for something to proceed, then it does not happen. There are judgements made every day about what will end up in a prime minister's red box and what is left to their political team to decide. This effectively means that special advisors make most of the day-to-day decisions, including signing off press releases, looking through ministerial statements, and giving a steer on public appointments, only sighting the prime minister when it is felt that they should be aware of something. That is a difficult principle to explain when things go wrong.

Dan Rosenfield, who I mentioned earlier, is a perfect example of when not having a political background is problematic. He was appointed chief of staff following the sacking of Dominic Cummings and the exit of Edward Lister. On paper we all believed that he would be up to the task. He had what seemed to be good experience that would add value to the House during a period of great economic uncertainty, having previously been a private secretary in the Treasury during the Labour administration. What became apparent very quickly was that he could not offer the political judgement that would allow the prime minister to navigate certain terrain. Boris's biggest mistake was appointing a chief of staff with limited political experience. It's a very different skill set to being a senior civil servant. In Nikki da Costa, who was head of legislative affairs at Number 10, Munira Mirza, who was head of the Policy Unit, and Simone Finn, who was deputy chief of staff, you had three women more than capable of performing the role and with the experience and respect of their peers. For some reason a man with no political experience was deemed more suitable. It is not enough to have the skill, you must also get how politics works if you are to be a successful special advisor. If you do not, you must be able to learn quickly. It is also important to note that though Rosenfield was a political outsider, he was very much a civil service insider, which further complicated his relationship with those he needed to influence.

I am not so sure being so dependent on fewer than forty individuals to run the country on behalf of an elected prime minister is a good thing. John Whittingdale, the Member of Parliament for Maldon, once told me that under Margaret Thatcher there was only one special advisor – him. But times have changed, and politicians are more exposed by social media and rolling news services. I think part of the reason why things are this way is because the standard of ministers in government is not always consistent. Ministers come from different walks of life, often taking on briefs where they do not have expertise, and at times are not very critical thinkers, as their priority is often to stay in their jobs. Special advisors, on the other hand, particularly those based in Downing Street, are usually recruited because they have specialised in a specific policy area or have a unique skill, albeit through the ideological lens of the person who recruits them. This means they can give strong steers on policy directions and are more focused on delivery because they do not have to spend time doing more front-facing activities. This is another reason why your typical Downing Street special advisor does not spend too much time worrying about how well dressed they are when they turn up for work.

Some special advisors, particularly the younger ones, have loftier ambitions. A few hope to be prime minister one day, of course, and have been working towards fulfilling that ambition in their own way. However, there is a more collegiate attitude towards interdependent policy matters in the building than you would get if decisions were decentralised between departments who are very competitive and not very open with each other. Getting departments to work together was at times like pulling teeth.

Vision and Direction of Travel

People were critical of Downing Street's operation during my time there, saying that it was not working well for the prime minister. I would argue that the issue was not just the operation, but the overall direction that was set by the leadership. Though there have been over thirteen years of a Conservative-led government it has not been one consistent project. It has been different leaders with different plans, and limited continuity of strategy or people. Some of this is because of unfortunate events like the war in Ukraine and the coronavirus pandemic, but events outside of our control cannot do all the heavy lifting if we are honest. The usual period of renewal, where you have been in opposition and able to test ideas and collaborate as a group to create a plan for government, hasn't happened during the most recent changes in prime ministers. Not having a credible opposition during this time has been a contributing factor. Theresa May became prime minister straight from being Home Secretary and following a surprise defeat for David Cameron in the EU referendum. The same thing happened with Boris Johnson after Theresa May failed to secure a Brexit deal, and then Liz Truss following Boris Johnson's premature demise. Of course, you could argue that May, Johnson and Truss should all have been a little more prepared for the job that they had spent most of their lives trying to get. The current prime minister, Rishi Sunak, has chosen to focus on demonstrating his ability to deliver. As the general election gets closer he will begin to articulate his vision and pitch for a full mandate. Some think this is a risky strategy, but his saving grace is that after thirteen years in opposition, Labour still has no clear and compelling vision. Things haven't improved much in this area under the current leader of the opposition, Keir Starmer. He has had twelve slogans in three years. People are increasingly unaware of what Starmer actually stands for, which is not how he started.

Theresa May and the early parts of Boris Johnson's premiership were consumed by Brexit. But that was not the reason for the vacuum in terms of vision for the country. What happens when you have powerful political advisors and a leader with no clear vision is that those advisors take it upon themselves to execute their own ideas. Credit for the political realignment must be shared with Nick Timothy, Theresa May's former chief of staff. When Boris Johnson first entered Downing Street the likes of Dominic Cummings were able to focus the machinery of government on his priorities, which included civil service reform, an integrated review of Britain's defence capabilities, and investment in research and development. For other political advisors, they had cultural battles that they had been fighting outside and, now that they had power, they wanted to go further.

Regardless of your opinion on the merits of any of these things, the reality is that these agenda items were not set by the prime minister at the time. They were not the things that he came into power to do. Boris Johnson was someone full of positive infectious energy, always supportive during my inter-actions with him. However, there was never an occasion where special advisors as a political team or the whole House were given any real sense of direction by Boris Johnson. The only speeches I recall were to thank us for our hard work, or to ask if Downing Street should get a dog, but none to set out a direction of travel. Johnson has since admitted himself that he should have been closer to his team and offer more direction whilst in Downing Street. Perhaps this is a bit of an unfair analysis of the situation; after all Boris Johnson is the one who 'got Brexit done'. His commitment to 'levelling up' left-behind regions of the United Kingdom has been unwavering, and he took on the challenge of leading on tackling climate change despite many sceptics within his own party.

Many members of the political class, both actual and aspir-ing Members of Parliament, have a lesser sense of public service than is ideal. Politics for some is simply something to do. A club to join. A way to become or to remain an insider.

Being a special advisor was a seven-day-a-week job. When I woke up, I would be straight to my emails and checking mobiles for messages. I went to bed every night doing the same thing. There was always some drama. Somebody in government always did something stupid, or there was always a journalist who had found out something had happened or was about to happen and wanted a government response. Of course, we didn't always respond to journalist requests for comment, or sometimes we gave a set line. The role was all-consuming, which meant that I saw less of my family than I would have liked. During the height of the pandemic, I was going into the office every day. This was particularly difficult as my wife was pregnant at the time. I made sure to be extra careful and did not attend any social gatherings in the building. It was important to me that I led by example because of the privileged position that I was in. This meant that on the Christmas of 2020 I did not see my sister and niece, who had flown in from New York just days before the prime minister announced that we should not mix households during the Christmas period. That was hard.

Getting things done in government was a challenge. I found that there were a lot of experienced civil servants who had developed ways of stifling the political team if they did not agree with a direction of travel. If you wanted something done, they had ways of delaying you, knowing that you wouldn't follow up or that you might not even be in the role long enough to follow through. I wasn't arrogant enough to believe I would be there very long, so decided that I would be very comfortable being seen as a bit of a handful. I would set clear deadlines for things to be done, and sometimes even did things myself that would panic officials into action. The last thing an official in a department would want was for a Number 10 advisor to actually do work and not just give orders from our ivory tower. But I did not come from a think tank. I was not a policy wonk. I have always worked for the things that I wanted, and officials quickly realised that they could not just respond to me the way they did with others. This attitude towards my work is why I ended up playing a key role in vaccine deployment and why I got on so well with Nadhim Zahawi, the vaccines minister at the time. We both liked to get things done and not pontificate.

My direct nature was not always viewed as a bad thing. When there were policy areas that other special advisors were not interested in, the unsexy items, I would often be approached by departmental teams that needed the cover from a special advisor to help them push an agenda forward. One such example was an action plan for the Gypsy, Roma, Traveller population. Theresa May had promised an ambitious action plan for improving outcomes for this part of the population. It was to be far-ranging, covering education, employment, housing and more. Andrew Selous, the Member of Parliament for South West Bedfordshire, was particularly exercised about the subject as his constituency has the highest number of Traveller encampments in the land. He was an old mentor of mine in my early years in politics and had spoken to me about the subject at length. The team responsible for it at the Department for Communities and Local Government asked to meet with me to discuss it. Over a dozen of them showed up at Number 10, which I thought was a bit over the top to meet with one special advisor. After the meeting I agreed that it should be a priority and not abandoned, which gave them the impetus to restart the work that had begun under Theresa May. I am pretty sure the minister responsible wasn't too pleased about this. The work seemed to pause upon my exit.

Staff Culture

Downing Street is a place where you rely very much on your ability to use soft power. To make a difference through having a conversation or by convening the right stakeholders. I knew that if someone received an email from my Number 10 address it would be taken seriously. The convening power of government is one of the most underrated pieces of armour. It was very often enough to shift the dial.

One of the things you notice working in Downing Street – certainly I did under Boris Johnson – was the high staff turnover. It was like a revolving door, which spoke to the dysfunctional nature of the building. During the 2019 general election we all had to resign from our roles, as is normal, with the expectation that we would all return if we won. I'll never forget receiving a message to turn up at Downing Street at 5 a.m. the following day, only to arrive and to be told that some of my colleagues were not sent the same message – meaning that they had just put their heart and soul into helping to write the manifesto that returned the largest Conservative majority for a generation only to be told a few hours later that they had lost their job. Brutal. Politics.

There were close to no avenues for personal development when I first arrived, besides the Friday evening SpAd school, which was both brief in nature and briefed to the media shortly after. Again, to be fair, people were trying to change this, but the turnover of staff meant that most plans never materialised in meaningful ways. All the entrepreneurial activities and leadership roles I had been involved in prior to my time at Number 10 had meant I was able to perform the role in a proactive way, learning quickly and building my own domain from day one.

It is strange, but you kind of normalise the fact that you work in Downing Street. There isn't really time to be awestruck by ministers or your environment. I never took a picture outside that famous black door in my whole time working there. I had helped quite a few people take photos, but it was never something I thought to do. I would sometimes receive messages from friends or family saying, 'I just saw you walking into Number 10.' Sometimes I received messages from people who did not know that I was working there and were surprised to see me walking behind a journalist reporting live from Number 10. For me it was just going to work, being focused on making every day productive.

Without a doubt the most special people in the building were the officials who had worked there for many years. This included the custodians and the events team. They had great stories to tell and made the place feel like a home, even in those most challenging of moments. I remember one custodian telling me the story about when Nelson Mandela had visited, and another when Barack Obama entered with an unrivalled aura. There aren't many moments in modern British history that they did not have front row seats for.

Another question I am asked regularly is if I miss working in Downing Street. The honest answer is no. I hope I have many more years in public life doing other things. It was a great privilege, but I'm more interested in what comes next.

Chapter 15

Why Did I Leave?

I can now see that though the events that led to my resignation were contributing factors, I resigned from my role as special advisor to the former prime minister because of a battle within me. I was never going to be like the people that had gone ahead of me because I did not share their story. I did not go to a fee-paying school, to Oxford or Cambridge, or mix in the same social circles. Neither was I someone who grew up in inner-city London where people from minority ethnic backgrounds are highly concentrated. I grew up in the suburbs but also grew up in poverty. It was not that I did not want to be myself, authentic to who I was, it was just that there were not many other people like me around the places that I was entering as an outsider. That was the challenge that I was faced with. Being the first or one of few was not a source of comfort. It was lonely. There was no blueprint. These feelings were stored up inside as I dealt with the pressures of the role of special advisor, the challenges society was facing during a pandemic, and the personal cares of this world that we all face from time to time. One such personal care occurred just a few weeks into me starting my role as special advisor. My wife and I had a miscarriage. It was one of the hardest experiences I have ever had because I did not know how to respond. How to grieve. What I did know was that I had to be there for Barbara as she was going through the physical and mental trauma. But I did not know how to process the experience as the man in the situation, who had also lost a child. A year later, our wonderful daughter was born in the autumn of 2020. Having a baby at home (along with the accompanying sleep deprivation) whilst being involved in the national deployment of vaccines across the country also brought additional strain during the period that led to my resignation. I never spoke to anyone about this. I suppose when you have bottled up all these different things a breakdown of some form is inevitable.

The events that led to my resignation were maybe the straws the broke the camel's back. Eventually the pressure became unbearable, and the release was to remove myself from the situation. It has taken me over a year to realise all of this. The question now is what do I do with what I have learned?

Lessons Learned

Firstly, I need to speak up. To find my voice and talk to someone if I am not coping. In an interview with Tony Blair in *The Times* newspaper he was asked if he had things that he should probably speak to a psychiatrist about. This is a man whose decisions literally led to the deaths of over 150,000 people in Iraq and a greater number in Afghanistan. Even the strongest of sane human beings would struggle to sleep at night as a consequence of this. His response was that he probably needed to but did not see the use. A jaw-dropping (if extreme) example of what happens when someone doesn't want to seem sensitive or, to use a phrase Blair has since used with great disdain, 'woke'.

I can't help but contrast this with David Cameron, who often spoke movingly about his son Ivan, who was disabled and sadly passed away in 2009 – the year before Cameron became prime minister. It is good to talk. To confront the things that may otherwise haunt us. If not for ourselves, then for others who as a consequence we can help. People have been very honest and open with me throughout the process of writing this book. More than I have ever been with anyone. Some were more guarded than others. The ones who were less guarded also felt freer as human beings. I now need to become better at speaking to avoid an unnecessary future breakdown.

The second thing I have learned is that it is important to have spaces for people on similar journeys to have conversations so they know that though they may feel alone, they are not. At universities we have student clubs and societies designed to make sure when you arrive on a campus you can find people with mutual interests, beliefs and/or backgrounds. I think that's important as an adult as well. Having said this, outsiders should not just stay in groups and places where they have colleagues with the same interests or are around people with similar backgrounds; this could lead to internalising things during moments of conflict, and it is not how society grows. This may sound contradictory, but the nuance is around being proactive in creating a mixture of environments and a mixture of people that you interact with regularly. I think the word I'm looking for here is diversity.

I have joined forces with Festus Akinbusoye and Wilfred Emmanuel-Jones to set up the 2022 Group – a new home for black Conservatives who share similar backgrounds. We of course will also continue separately to engage with people of any background with similar policy interests. It doesn't have to be one or the other.

I think the final big lesson I have learned from this journey is that we must find a way to integrate groups while appreciating that we are a nation of people with many different backgrounds and histories. These histories come with their own trauma, often passed down through generations. It is simply not possible to fully harmonise a nation in a lifetime. Even within the most monolithic of environments you will find there are differences. We must have shared values that we can sign up to, while recognising that there are many people who for various reasons may see themselves as outsiders.

Epilogue

Writing this book has been a journey of personal discovery for me. I wanted to better understand why I chose to leave Number 10. I now feel that it was because as an outsider I was at times unable to navigate a new environment. Despite the confidence I had before taking on the role, there was another level of confidence that I had not tapped into before. A type of confidence that often comes as a result of being born into more privileged surroundings, attending a different type of school, and normalising a level of achievement that tends to raise personal expectations. I could have managed certain situations better, but taking on too many things led to burnout and eventual breakdown. That is ultimately my responsibility and no one else's, but it would have been good if someone was available to help me along the way.

Inviting Outsiders In

Outsiders have a unique value that they bring if they can seize the opportunity to flourish. They have the ability to build bridges between opposing groups if they have the trust of those groups or can see things through fresh eyes. They stand out because of their differences, which can be used tactically as a strength. Increased economic productivity comes if everyone, including outsiders, can realise their full potential. Outsiders have the keys to future prosperity because of workforce needs and the potential ability to connect with emerging markets. They can challenge long-held orthodoxy and broaden audiences in sectors that desperately need to find ways to stay relevant. Outsiders hold the keys to Britain's future. With Brexit, globalisation and the rise of emerging markets; the case for people who think differently and disruptively has never been stronger. Outsiders should get a bigger stake of rural Britain, through more opportunities to own or use land.

For outsiders to be able to use their superpower it is important for them to first accept their difference as a strength and not something to be hidden. They need to be confident in who they are and what they can bring to any environment. Having an established network of people to help them along the way is vital for success. Outsiders should be allowed to fail and bounce back the same way that others who are more fortunate have been able to do, and there should be inclusive environments to allow people to thrive and feel secure.

We know that the United States is engulfed in a culture war, but Britain has not yet reached a point of no return. We simply cannot afford to get to that place because it will be very difficult to reverse any damage to our social fabric as a result. That does not mean that divisions do not already exist; they certainly do, along the lines of race, class, geography, education and more. Those divisions must not be left unchallenged. We need to find ways to encourage people from different backgrounds to mix in a meaningful and sustainable way.

Parents play a vital role in the outcomes of their children, both socially and economically. A parent's occupation is still a key signifier for a child's outcomes. More needs to be done for people from under-represented backgrounds to be able to access better opportunities and to develop stronger skills. The confidence that comes from a child's early years is vital and we need the right investment to ensure that more young people are able to have this.

I know that leaders who are keen to know how they can build environments that enable outsiders to flourish will read this book and ask what they can do. Every organisation has its own culture and so there is no one-size-fits-all approach. It depends on the nature of the people you employ, where you are based geographically, the size of the business and many other factors. But broadly speaking, employees should be encouraged to build both vertical and horizontal relationships throughout an organisation. There should be regular communication, and the leader should embody the values that they wish to be upheld. Cultures can be expressed or implied, but in an ideal world they would be both. When someone walks into your office, they should be able to not only see what you stand for because it's written on the wall, but also feel it by observing how people behave.

Mentoring has an important role to play, despite sometimes feeling tokenistic. Using external expert providers is a useful way to overcome the stigma attached to internal schemes that target specific groups.

To build an inclusive business environment we need to open up opportunities. When I met with Wilfred Emmanuel-Jones he reflected on opportunities for under-represented founders and said, 'There are a lot of entrepreneurs out there. What they lacked was the opportunity. Because I could have quite easily ended up in prison with all the disadvantages. And it's about how does one tap into that creativity, that ability to think outside the box and give you that focus and a direction, and also the opportunity to get the finance? So they could take great ideas and make something about it. That's a real problem. I still own my business 100 per cent. Part of the reason why I still do is because I couldn't get funding in the first place because the thought of a black farmer was just too radical for funders. As it turned out, it was bloody good because I'm still in control of my business, but what we need is more diverse people at the top. It could then help to sort of construct programmes, initiatives to bring in people from backgrounds like mine.'

As Wilfred says, it should be everyone's responsibility to provide opportunities, not just the government's. That is why in 2020 I asked the British Business Bank to convene a group of experts to see how we can have a multifaceted approach to opening access to capital. This important work was submitted to the Commission on Race and Ethnic Disparities and passed on to the Chancellor's team. It found that there were simple things that could help to open up opportunities. For example, all venture capital firms could offer 'open office hours' for founders and for aspirant investors. This is simply having a few hours a month where people could pitch to them live and receive feedback where necessary. Venture capital firms and angel investors could also offer local networking events for entrepreneurs from under-represented backgrounds in ways and areas where these opportunities are not typically available. Similarly, institutional investors could offer an equivalent forum to 'open office hours' so that investors from under-represented backgrounds can meet with them and form relationships.

The UK investment management industry could agree a joint approach to better supporting entrepreneurs and businesses. They could consider how they could influence corporations to make use of their importance in areas such as supply chains, partnerships, local economies, trainee programmes, progression, and caring/family support. The group could also consider how the impact of these actions can be measured to ensure that progress by corporates is tracked and assessed. Market-wide institutions (such as NESTA and the British Business Bank) could be commissioned to develop, test and scale new types of investment and lending models for small businesses and high-growth businesses as well as social enterprises. These models could be built from the ground up around the needs and circumstances more common to entrepreneurs from non-traditional backgrounds. There continues to be a worrying gender disparity around business lending. These are some of the things that can be done to open up more opportunities, but it requires the government to play its part, while also using its convening power to inspire more action from investors.

As we have seen, there are different types of outsiders. You can be a social or demographic, psychological or tactical outsider. You can even be all three at the same time. That feeling of being the only or one of few is not always a good one, but hopefully this book has come some way towards demonstrating the power of the outsider. It is a superpower that if used correctly can help to change our world for the better.

Acknowledgements

Firstly, my wife Barbara, who has been quite the proof-reader. Thank you for your 'constructive' challenge during this writing process. It was genuinely welcomed (even though it didn't always sound like it) and a reminder about how lucky I am to have such a wise partner.

I want to acknowledge my Christian faith. It is an important part of my identity and has been the foundation for my world view. Loving our neighbour is a commandment with no prerequisite and the greatest among us will be the servant.

I may have written a book about outsiders, but frankly it probably would not have been as interesting if I had not worked in Downing Street. So, thank you to Boris Johnson, Cleo Watson, Jonathan Hellewell and Danny Kruger, who were responsible for me joining the team as special advisor. I am not quite sure if they are pleased with the part that they played considering how things ended, but alas we are where we are.

My team, particularly Conor McCrory, who has been the lead researcher for my project. Your work really opened my eyes to things I had yet to consider on this journey of discovery. I have had the privilege of engaging with some of the best policy minds in the country. Without a doubt, you have the talent to make it to the very top.

The individuals that allowed me to interview them for this book. Festus Akinbusoye, Wilfred Emmanuel-Jones, Samir Puri. Also, Eleanor Southwood, Baroness Sayeeda Warsi, Doctor Shubulade Smith, Kadiatu and Stuart Kanneh-Mason, Beveley Smith, and David Tyler. Conducting interviews was not the initial plan, but it has all worked out perfectly.

My siblings Victoria, Philip, and Rebekah. My other siblings that didn't feature in the book but of course have been vital in my story – Elizabeth and Christianna. My parents for bringing me into this world.

A special thanks to my editor Rupert Lancaster and assistant editors Zakirah Alam and Ciara Mongey. Thanks also to my agent Adrian Sington for being so supportive throughout this journey.

The various people that I have spoken to who have given me things to consider as I explored the concept of outsiders. The list is countless.

Finally, I want to thank you for taking time to read this book. I'd love to know what you think.

References by Theme

Imposter Syndrome

Albright, A. et al. (2021). 'After the Burning: The Economic Effects of the 1921 Tulsa Race Massacre'. Available at: https://www.nber.org/papers/w28985 (Accessed November 8 2021)

Baer, M. Frese, M. (2003) 'Innovation is not enough: climates for initiative and psychological safety, process innovations, and firm performance', *Journal of Organizational Behaviour,* 24(1), pp45-68.

Becker, H. S. (1997). Outsiders: Studies in the Sociology of Deviance. New York: Free Press.

Bourdieu, P. (1977). *Outline of a Theory of Practice.* Cambridge: Cambridge University Press.

Bourdieu, P. (1984). *Distinction: A Social Critique of the Judgement of Taste.* Cambridge, MA: Harvard University Press.

Caprino, K. (2020) *'Impostor Syndrome Prevalence In Professional Women And How To Overcome It'.* Available at: https://www.forbes.com/sites/kathycaprino/2020/10/22/impostor-syndrome-prevalence-in-professional-women-face-and-how-to-overcome-it/ (Accessed November 8 2021)

Boyle. M. (2021). *'I'm a fourth-generation black British man. Yet still I'm made to feel I don't belong'.* The Guardian. 31 October. Available at: https://www.theguardian.com/commentisfree/2021/oct/31/black-british-1800s-before-windrush (Accessed: November 3 2021)

Bravata, D.M et al. (2020) 'Prevalence, Predictors, and Treatment of Impostor Syndrome: a Systematic Review', *Journal of General Internal Medicine,* 35(4), pp1252-1275.

Bukodi, E. Goldthorpe, J.H. (2019) *Social Mobility and Education in Britain: Research, Politics, and Policy.* Cambridge:Cambridge University Press.

Cambridge Dictionary (no date) *OUTSIDER.* Available at: https://dictionary.cambridge.org/dictionary/english/outsider (Accessed:October 29 2021)

Clance, P.R. Imes, S.A. 'The imposter phenomenon in high achieving women: Dynamics and therapeutic intervention'. *Psychotherapy: Theory, Research & Practice.* 15(3), pp241–247.

Clance, P.R. Dingman, D. Reviere, S.L. Stober, D.R. (1995) 'Impostor Phenomenon in an Interpersonal/Social Context: Origins and Treatment'. *Women & Therapy,* 16(4), pp79-96.

Cochrane Mental Disorders Group (2019) *'Hundreds of thousands of young people feel isolated, lonely and uncertain about who to turn to when experiencing mental health problems – major new report'.* Available at: https://www.mentalhealth.org.uk/news/

hundreds-thousands-young-people-feel-isolated-lonely-and-uncertain (Accessed November 8 2021)

de Beauvoir, S. (2010) *The Second Sex*. New York: Random House Inc

Derrida, J. (1998) *Monolingualism of the Other*. Stanford: Stanford University Press.

Economic Times (2017) *What Makes These The World's Most Powerful Passports*. Available at: https://economictimes.indiatimes.com/magazines/panache/what-makes-these-the-worlds-most-powerful-passports/one-passport-to-rule-them-all/slide-show/61484055.cms (Accessed: November 5 2021)

Escamilla, D. Leder, P. White, L. (1992). *Essays From the Edge Citizenship and the Outsider in Literature and History*. Available at: https://files.eric.ed.gov/fulltext/ED392668.pdf (Accessed: November 1 2021)

Edmondson, A. (1999).'Psychological Safety and Learning Behavior in Work Teams', *Administrative Science Quarterly*, 44(2), pp350-383

Elias, N. and Scotson, J.L. (1994) *The Established and the Outsider*. London: Sage Publications.

Forbes (2011) 'Corporate Culture: Whose Job Is It?'. Available at: https://www.forbes.com/sites/johnkotter/2011/02/17/corporate-culture-whose-job-is-it/ (Accessed: November 5 2021)

Geraghty, T. (2020) 'Measuring Psychological Safety'. Available at: https://www.psych-safety.co.uk/measure-psychological-safety/ (Accessed November 8 2021)

Hazen, T.L. (2010) 'Identifying the Duty Prohibiting Outsider Trading on Material Nonpublic Information', *Hastings Law Journal*, 61(4), pp 881-916

Hegel, G.W.F. (1977) *Phenomenology of Spirit*. Oxford: Oxford University Press.

Jahan, S. Mahmud, A. (2015). 'What Is Capitalism? Free markets may not be perfect but they are probably the best way to organize an economy'. *Finance and Development.*, 52(2), pp44-45

Kahn, W.A. (1990) 'Psychological Conditions of Personal Engagement and Disengagement at Work'. *Academy of Management Journal*. 33(4), pp692-724.

King, A. (2002) 'The Outsider as Political Leader: The Case of Margaret Thatcher', *British Journal of Political Science*, 32(3), pp 435-454

Lacan, J. Grigg, R. (contributor) (2008) *The Other Side of Psychoanalysis: The Seminar of Jacques Lacan Book XVII*

Laurison, D. Friedman, S. (2019) '*The class ceiling: Social mobility and why it pays to be privileged*'. Available at: https://ukdataservice.ac.uk/case-study/the-class-ceiling-social-mobility-and-why-it-pays-to-be-privileged/ (Accessed: November 5 2021)

Lean in (2018). '*What being an "Only" at work is like*'. Available at: https://leanin.org/women-in-the-workplace-report-2018/sexual-harassment-in-the-workplace#! (Accessed November 4 2021)

McGregor, L. Doshi, N. (2015) '*How Company Culture Shapes Employee Motivation*'. Available at: https://classdat.appstate.edu/COB/MGT/VillanPD/OB%20Fall%202021/Unit%203%20-%20Cohesion/Org%20Culture%20Articles/How%20Company%20Culture%20Shapes%20Employee%20Motivation.pdf (Accessed: November 5 2021)

Naples, N. (2003) 'The Outsider Phenomenon', in Hesse-Biber S. N. and Yaiser, M. L (eds.) *Feminist Perspectives on Social Research*. Oxford: OUP USA.

Nance-Nash, S. (2020) *Why imposter syndrome hits women and women of colour harder*. Available at: https://www.bbc.com/worklife/article/20200724-why-imposter-syndrome-hits-women-and-women-of-colour-harder (Accessed: November 4 2021)

Nembhard, I.M. Edmondson, A. (2006). 'Making it safe: The effects of leader inclusiveness and professional status on psychological safety and improvement efforts in health care teams', *Journal of Organizational Behaviour*, 27(1), pp941-966.

Nurse, N. (2021) '*4 Tips for When You're the Only Person of Color in Your Office*', Available at: https://www.themuse.com/advice/only-person-of-color-in-office (Accessed November 8 2021)

Oliker, D.M. (2021) *On Being the Outsider.* Available at: https://www.psychologytoday.com/gb/blog/the-long-reach-childhood/201211/being-the-outsider (Accessed: October 29 2021)

Ryan, R.M. Deci, E.L. (2000) ;*Self-Determination Theory and the Facilitation of Intrinsic Motivation, Social Development, and Well-Being'.* Available at: Self-Determination Theory and the Facilitation of Intrinsic Motivation, Social Development, and Well-Being (Accessed: 1 November 2021)

Said, E. (1978) *Orientalism.* New York: Random House Inc.

Sakulku, J. Alexander, J. (2011). 'The Impostor Phenomenon', *International Journal of Behavioural Science,* 6(1), pp75-97.

Sneader, K. Yee, L. (2019) '*One is the Loneliest Number'.* Available at: https://www.mckinsey.com/featured-insights/gender-equality/one-is-the-loneliest-number (Accessed November 8 2021)

Sorokin, P.A. (1959). *Social and Cultural Mobility.* Illinois: The Free Press.

Staszak, J. (2008) '*Other/otherness'.* Available at: https://www.unige.ch/sciences-societe/geo/files/3214/4464/7634/OtherOtherness.pdf (Accessed: 1 November 2021).

Tulshyan, R. Burey, J. (2021) *Stop Telling Women They Have Imposter Syndrome.* Available at: https://hbr.org/2021/02/stop-telling-women-they-have-imposter-syndrome (Accessed November 4 2021)

Varrella, S. (2021). '*How often do you feel lonely?'.* Available at: https://www.statista.com/statistics/1222815/loneliness-among-adults-by-country/ (Accessed November 8 2021)'

Warnock, D.M (2016). 'Paradise Lost? Patterns and Precarity in Working-Class Academic Narratives', *Journal of Working Class Studies, 1(1), pp28-44*

Waterfield, B. Beagan, B. Mohamed, T. (2019). '"You Always Remain Slightly an Outsider": Workplace Experiences of Academics from Working-Class or Impoverished Backgrounds', *Canadian Review of Sociology,* 56(3), pp368-388

Williams, P. (2021) '*The Rising Importance Of Psychological Safety In Life And Work'.* Available at: https://www.forbes.com/sites/forbescoachescouncil/2021/03/17/the-rising-importance-of-psychological-safety-in-life-and-work/ (Accessed November 8 2021)

Wright, R. (2003) *The Outsider.* New York: Harper Perennial.

Yohn, D.L. (2021). '*Company Culture Is Everyone's Responsibility'.* Available at: https://hbr.org/2021/02/company-culture-is-everyones-responsibility (Accessed November 5 2021)

Zanchetta, M. Junker, S. Wolf, A.M. Traut-Mattausch, E. (2020) '"Overcoming the Fear That Haunts Your Success" – The Effectiveness of Interventions for Reducing the Impostor Phenomenon. *Frontiers in Psychology.* 11:405. doi: 10.3389/fpsyg.2020.00405

Zarya, V. (2017) '*Why There Are No Black Women Running Fortune 500 Companies',* Available at: https://fortune.com/2017/01/16/black-women-fortune-500/ (Accessed November 8 2021)

The Outsider Phenomenon

Academia (No Date) '*Lisa Mckenzie'.* Available at: https://lse.academia.edu/LisaMckenzie (Accessed November 19 2021)

Andersson, J. (2021). '*Mohther and son, 7, forced to move into caravan 120 miles away from family home so he can attend school',* The I. Available at: https://inews.co.uk/news/mother-caravan-120-miles-away-from-home-disabled-boy-attend-school-1134954 (Accessed November 23 2021)

BBC (2018) '*David Blunkett says he tried 'too hard' to prove himself*'. Available at: https://www.bbc.co.uk/news/uk-politics-parliaments-42733612 (Accessed November 22 2021)

Becker, H. S. (1997). Outsiders: Studies in the Sociology of Deviance. New York: Free Press.

Bloom, D. (2016) '*Fed-up Tory Paul Maynard invites Labour MP to "step outside" in grumpy Commons argument*', The Mirror, Available at: https://www.mirror.co.uk/news/uk-news/fed-up-tory-paul-maynard-8143450 (Accessed November 23 2021)

Booth, R. (2017) '*New intake brings number of disabled MPs in Commons to five*', The Guardian. Available at: https://www.theguardian.com/society/2017/jun/11/new-intake-brings-number-of-disabled-mps-in-commons-to-five (Accessed November 23 2021)

Bourdieu, P. (1977). *Outline of a Theory of Practice.* Cambridge: Cambridge University Press.

Bourdieu, P. (1984). *Distinction: A Social Critique of the Judgement of Taste.* Cambridge, MA: Harvard University Press.

Clance, P.R. Imes, S.A. 'The imposter phenomenon in high achieving women: Dynamics and therapeutic intervention'. *Psychotherapy: Theory, Research & Practice.* 15(3), pp241–247

Daley, K. (2018) '*Natives Race and Class in the Ruins of Empire*'. London: Two Roads.

Davis, D. (2021) '*Why Black and Latinx women are more likely to struggle with impostor syndrome—and how to overcome it*', Available at: https://www.cnbc.com/2021/08/04/why-black-and-latinx-women-struggle-more-with-impostor-syndrome.html (Accessed November 24 2021)

Dunning, J (2010) '*Paul Maynard MP: life with cerebral palsy and epilepsy*'. Available at: https://www.communitycare.co.uk/2010/07/01/paul-maynard-mp-life-with-cerebral-palsy-and-epilepsy/ (Accessed November 22 2021)

Ellsworth, D. Mendy, A. Sullivan G. (2020) '*How the LGBTQ+ community fares in the workplace*', Mckinsey & Company. Available at: https://www.mckinsey.com/featured-insights/diversity-and-inclusion/how-the-lgbtq-plus-community-fares-in-the-workplace (Accessed November 23 2021)

Hall, R (2021) '*Women of color spend more than $8 billion on bleaching creams worldwide every year*', The Conversation. Available at: https://theconversation.com/women-of-color-spend-more-than-8-billion-on-bleaching-creams-worldwide-every-year-153178 (Accessed November 29 2021)

Hamilton, P. (2020) '*Imposter Syndrome and the Consequences of Ableism*'. Available at: https://taboumagazine.com/online-features/imposter-syndrome-and-the-conse-quences-of-ableism (Accessed November 24 2021)

Huitt, R.K. (1961) 'The outsider in the senate: an alternative role', *The American Political Science Review,* 55(3), pp 566–575

JRank (No Date) '*John Barnes Biography*', Available at: https://biography.jrank.org/pages/2784/Barnes-John.html (Accessed November 19 2021)

King, A. (2002) 'The Outsider as Political Leader: The Case of Margaret Thatcher', *British Journal of Political Science,* 32(3), pp 435-454

Lean in (2018). '*What being an "Only" at work is like*'. Available at: https://leanin.org/women-in-the-workplace-report-2018/sexual-harassment-in-the-workplace#! (Accessed November 23 2021)

Maynard, P. (2018) '*Helping every child with cerebral palsy to achieve their full potential*', The House. Available at: https://www.politicshome.com/thehouse/article/help-ing-every-child-with-cerebral-palsy-to-achieve-their-full-potential (Accessed November 23 2021)

Mckenzie, L. Dabrowski, V. (2015) ''*Getting By: Estates, Class and Culture in*

REFERENCES BY THEME

Austerity Britain': An Interview with Dr. Lisa McKenzie'. The Culture Society. Available at: https://www.theoryculturesociety.org/blog/interviews-lisa-mckenzie-getting-by-estates-class-and-culture-in-austerity-britain (Accessed November 19 2021)

Mckenzie, L. (2015) *'Lisa Mckenzie: who would be a working-class woman in academia?'.* Available at: https://www.timeshighereducation.com/lisa-mckenzie-who-would-be-working-class-woman-academia (Accessed November 19 2021)

Mckenzie, L. (2018) *'End working class prejudice rather than focusing on social mobility'.* Available at: https://news.sky.com/story/end-working-class-prejudice-rather-than-focusing-on-social-mobility-11504251 (Accessed November 19 2021)

Mcleod, S.A (2008) *'Asch Experiment',* Available at:https://www.cbsd.org/cms/lib/PA01916442/Centricity/Domain/2773/commonlit_asch-experiment_student.pdf (Accessed November 19 2021)

Mcleod, S.A. (2014) *'Lev Vygotsky'.* Available at: https://1filedownload.com/wp-content/uploads/2019/12/Simplypsychology.Org-Vygotsky.pdf (Accessed November 29 2021)

McLoughlin, R. (2021) *'Change minds over disability, urges former Home Secretary'.* Available at: https://jerseyeveningpost.com/news/2021/10/24/change-minds-over-disability-urges-former-home-secretary/ (Accessed November 22 2021)

McRae, D. (2021) *'John Barnes on racism and society: 'There are invisible banana skins',* The Guardian. Available at: https://www.theguardian.com/football/2021/oct/11/john-barnes-interview-on-racism-and-society-there-are-invisible-banana-skins (Accessed November 19 2021)

Mishra, N. (2015) 'India and Colorism: The Finer Nuances', *Perspectives on Colorism,* 14(4), pp725-750.

Mullholland, H. (2011) *'Charity voices anger after MPs 'mocked Tory with disability',* The Guardian. Available at: https://www.theguardian.com/politics/2011/feb/08/charity-anger-mps-paul-maynard-disability (Accessed November 23 2021)

Norwood, K.J. (2015) '"If You Is White, You's Alright" Stories About Colorism in ories About Colorism in America', *Global Perspectives on Colorism,* 14(4), pp585-607

Obama, M. in Adams, O. (2020) *'Michelle Obama shares tips for tackling imposter syndrome at work',* Available at: https://www.marieclaire.co.uk/news/celebrity-news/michelle-obama-imposter-syndrome-689340 (Accessed November 24 2021)

Obama, M. in Welch, A. (2018). *'What is impostor syndrome? Michelle Obama says she has it, and "it doesn't go away".* Available at: https://www.cbsnews.com/news/what-is-impostor-syndrome-michelle-obama-says-she-has-it/ (Accessed November 24 2021)

Palmer, S. (2020) *'Black employees hold just 1.5 per cent of senior roles, research reveals',* People Management. Available at: https://www.peoplemanagement.co.uk/news/articles/black-employees-hold-just-1-5-per-cent-of-senior-roles#gref (Accessed November 23 2021)

Pring, J. (2019) *'Anger over appointment of 'disability hate tweet' MP as mental health minister',* Disability News Service. Available at: https://www.disabilitynewsservice.com/anger-over-appointment-of-disability-hate-tweet-mp-as-mental-health-minister/ (Accessed November 23 2021)

Rakoska, B. (2016) *'Disability and Tokenism: Why No One Can Speak On Behalf of Everyone'.* Available at: https://rootedinrights.org/disability-and-tokenism-why-no-one-can-speak-on-behalf-of-everyone/ (Accessed November 22 2021)

Roediger, D.R. (No Date). *'Historical Foundations of Race'.* Available at: https://nmaahc.si.edu/learn/talking-about-race/topics/historical-foundations-race

Sharma, S., Rai, E., Sharma, P. et al (2009) 'The Indian origin of paternal haplogroup

R1a1* substantiates the autochthonous origin of Brahmins and the caste system', *Journal of Human Genetics'*, 54(1), pp47-55.

Shotter, J. (1993) 'BAKHTIN AND VYGOTSKY: INTERNALIZATION AS A BOUNDARY PHENOMENON', *New Ideas in Psychology'*. 11(3), pp379-390.

Simons, S.S. (2021) 'ER Goddess It's Not Imposter Syndrome—It's Gender Bias', *Emergency Medicine News*. 43(5), pp1-34

Tarvainen, M. (2019) *'Ableism and the Life Stories of People with Disabilities'*. Available at: https://www.sjdr.se/articles/10.16993/sjdr.632/ (Accessed November 22 2021)

Tharoor, S. (2017) *'Inglorious Empire What the British did to India'*, Glasgow: Bell & Bain Ltd.

Tulshyan, R. Burey, J. (2021) *Stop Telling Women They Have Imposter Syndrome*. Available at: https://hbr.org/2021/02/stop-telling-women-they-have-imposter-syndrome (Accessed November 4 2021)

Villegas, S. (2021) *'Race And Imposter Syndrome: Acknowledging And Addressing Discrimination In The Workplace'*, Forbes. Available at: https://www.forbes.com/sites/forbesbusinesscouncil/2021/03/30/race-and-imposter-syndrome-acknowledging-and-addressing-discrimination-in-the-workplace/ (Accessed November 24 2021)

Villines, Z. Sullivan, D. (2021). *'What is ableism, and what is its impact?'*. Available at: https://www.medicalnewstoday.com/articles/ableism?c=565494408431 (Accessed November 22 2021)

Vsauce (2017) *'Conformity - Mindfield (ep 2)'*, Mindfield, [youtube video], Available at: https://www.youtube.com/watch?v=fbyIYXEu-nQ (Accessed November 19 2021)

Waterfield, B. Beagan, B. Mohamed, T. (2019). '"You Always Remain Slightly an Outsider": Workplace Experiences of Academics from Working-Class or Impoverished Backgrounds', *Canadian Review of Sociology*, 56(3), pp368-388

Wong, K. (2018) *'Dealing With Impostor Syndrome When You're Treated as an Impostor'*, The New York Times. Available at:https://www.nytimes.com/2018/06/12/smarter-living/dealing-with-impostor-syndrome-when-youre-treated-as-an-impostor.html (Accessed November 23 2021)

Zimmer, L. (1988) 'Tokenism and Women in the Workplace: The Limits of Gender-Neutral Theory', *Social Problems*, 35(1). pp64-77

The British Empire

Britannica, The Editors of Encyclopaedia, 2023. 'British Empire'. Available at: https://www.britannica.com/place/British-Empire (Accessed 03/04/2023)

Britannica, The Editors of Encyclopaedia, 2022. 'Commonwealth'. Available at: https://www.britannica.com/topic/Commonwealth-association-of-states/Structure-and-activity (Accessed, 30/03/2023).

Buccholz, K, 2020. 'The Countries Most Active in the Trans-Atlantic Slave Trade'. *Statista*. Available at: https://www.statista.com/chart/22057/countries-most-active-trans-atlantic-slave-trade/ (Accessed 03/04/2023)

Daley, K., 2018. *Natives Race and Class in the Ruins of Empire*. Two Roads: Great Britain.

Thecommonwealth.org, 2023. 'Member Countries'. Available at: https://thecommonwealth.org/our-member-countries (Accessed 30/03/2023).

Commonwealthofnations.org, 2020. 'History of the Commonwealth'. Available at: https://www.commonwealthofnations.org/commonwealth/history/ (Accessed 30/03/2023)

Imperial War Museum, N.D. 'The End of the British Empire After The Second World War'. Available at: https://www.iwm.org.uk/history/the-end-of-the-british-empire-after-the-second-world-war (Accessed 03/04/2023).

Laidlaw, Z, 2015. 'Empire and after'. *British Library* Available at: https://www.bl.uk/magna-carta/articles/empire-and-after#:~:text=Britain's%20empire%20was%20 the%20most,colonial%20descendants%20invoked%20Magna%20Carta.   (Accessed 03/04/2023)

Lowcountry Digital History Initiative, N/D. 'The Trans-Atlantic Slave Trade'. Available at: https://ldhi.library.cofc.edu/exhibits/show/africanpassageslowcountry-adapt/introductionatlanticworld/trans_atlantic_slave_trade#:~:text=In%20the%20 fifteenth%20century%2C%20Portugal,a%20small%20number%20to%20Europe. (Accessed 03/04/2023)

Marshal, P. 1964. THE FIRST AND SECOND BRITISH EMPIRES: A QUESTION OF DEMARCATION. History. Vol49, No 165. Pp 13-23.

Culture Wars

Anthony, A. (2021) *'Everything you wanted to know about the culture wars – but were afraid to ask'*, The Guardian. Available at: https://www.theguardian.com/world/2021/jun/13/everything-you-wanted-to-know-about-the-culture-wars-but-were-afraid-to-ask (Accessed: November 8 2021)

Bloom, D. (2021) *'Boris Johnson is pursuing 'culture wars' to keep Brexit voters on side, top pollster says'*, The Mirror. Available at: https://www.mirror.co.uk/news/politics/boris-johnson-pursuing-culture-wars-24371803 (Accessed November 8 2021)

Duffy, B. et al. (2021). *'Culture wars in the UK: how the public understand the debate.* Available at: https://www.ipsos.com/sites/default/files/ct/news/documents/2021-05/culture-wars-in-the-UK-how-the-public-understand-the-debate. pdf (Accessed November 8 2021)

Ebisch, B. (2019) *'Why sensationalized news stories are damaging to society'*, Available at: https://www.thewilkesbeacon.com/opinion/2019/04/16/why-sensationalized-news-stories-are-damaging-to-society/ (Accessed November 30 2021)

Encyclopaedia Britannica (2011) *'Sensationalism philosophy and psychology'*, Available at: https://www.britannica.com/topic/sensationalism (Accessed November 30 2021)

Frye, W. B. (2005) *'A qualitative analysis of sensationalism in media'*. Available at: https://researchrepository.wvu.edu/cgi/viewcontent.cgi?article=4222&context=etd (Accessed November 30 2021)

GovUK (2019) *'Elitism in Britain, 2019'*, Available at:https://www.gov.uk/government/news/elitism-in-britain-2019 (Accessed November 30 2021)

Glaze, B. (2021) *'Culture wars battle is 'fabricated' by politicians, says report'*, The Mirror. Available at: https://www.mirror.co.uk/news/politics/culture-wars-battle-fabricated-politicians-24509258 (Accessed November 8 2021)

Hunter, J.D. (1991) *Culture Wars: the Struggle to Define America*.New York: Basic Books.

Maddox, D. (2020) *'Boris leads war on woke-ism: PM in fightback against attempts to rewrite British history'*, The Daily Express. Available at: https://www.express.co.uk/news/uk/1349026/Boris-johnson-news-culture-war-british-history-left-wing-woke-culture (Accessed November 9 2021)

Maidment, R. et al. (2021) *'Cancel culture comrades! A third of Labour supporters support silencing people whose views they disagree with and more than half think the UK is institutionally racist'*, The Daily Mail. Available at: https://www.dailymail.co.uk/news/article-9756573/Pollster-says-culture-war-main-UK-political-battleground.html (Accessed November 8 2021)

Mathers, M. (2021) *"Fabricated' culture wars pit working-class communities against each other, report says'*, The Independent. Available at:https://www.independent.co.uk/news/uk/politics/uk-culture-wars-fabian-society-b1882562.html

McNeill, K. Harding, R. (2021) *'Counter Culture: How to Resist the Culture Wars and Build 21st Century Solidarity.* Available at: https://fabians.org.uk/wp-content/uploads/2021/07/FABJ9000-Fabian-Ideas-pamphlet-210628-WEB.pdf (Accessed November 30 2021)

The Oxford Royale Academy. (No Date). *'Black and White and Read All Over: A Guide to British Newspapers'*. Available at: https://www.oxford-royale.com/articles/a-guide-to-british-newspapers/ (Accessed: November 8 2021)

Smith, M. (2017) *'Complaints that the British press has a right-wing bias have long been made by left-wingers – but is this a state of affairs the public recognises?'*. YouGov, Available at: https://yougov.co.uk/topics/politics/articles-reports/2017/03/07/how-left-or-right-wing-are-uks-newspapers (Accessed: November 8 2021)

Taber, G. as cited in Drake, D. (2013) *'Extra, Extra! Sensationalism in Journalism'*, Available at: https://globalyouth.wharton.upenn.edu/articles/college-careers-jobs/extra-extra-sensationalism-in-journalism/ (Accessed November 30 2021)

Tryl, L. (2021). *'We can end the culture wars by following the example of gay rights'*, The Independent. Available at: https://www.independent.co.uk/voices/culture-wars-gay-rights-leadership-woke-b1893654.html (Accessed November 8 2021)

Tingle, R. (2021) *''Race matters... but CLASS is the biggest barrier': Equality campaigner Trevor Phillips warns 'shoehorning' America's culture wars into British life is a 'desperate mistake''*, The Daily Mail. Available at:https://www.dailymail.co.uk/news/article-9683733/Trevor-Phillips-warns-against-shoehorning-Americas-culture-wars-British-life.html (Accessed November 8 2021)

Varga, J. (2021) *'Brits have little time for political correctness or 'culture wars' according to new survey'*, The Daily Express. Available at: https://www.express.co.uk/news/uk/1454359/culture-wars-ipsos-kings-college-london-survey-attitudes-to-woke-behaviour-ont

Vetteh, P.H Kleemans, M. (2017) *'Proving the Obvious? What Sensationalism Contributes to the Time Spent on News Video'*, Available at: https://journals.sagepub.com/doi/full/10.1177/1931243117739947 (Accessed November 30 2021)

Walker, P. (2021) *'Politicians and media told to stop fabricating culture wars'*, The Guardian. Available at: https://www.theguardian.com/society/2021/jul/12/politicians-and-media-told-to-stop-fabricating-culture-wars (Accessed November 8 2021)

Wooding, D. (2021) *'CLASS WARFARE Activists are roping school pupils into vicious 'culture wars', senior MP warns'*, The Sun. Available at: https://www.thesun.co.uk/news/14541168/activists-roping-kids-into-culture-battles-schools/ (Accessed November 9 2021)

Wootton, D. (2020) *'It's rich for Labour to accuse the Tories of a culture war after they've belittled BAME women'*, The Sun. Available at: https://www.thesun.co.uk/news/11877905/labour-accuse-tories-culture-war-bame-women/ (Accessed November 9)

YouGov, (2020). *'YouGov / Matt Chorley Survey Results.* Available at: https://docs.cdn.yougov.com/pc3w47othg/Internal_PoliticalTerms_201216.pdf (Accessed November 9 2021)

YouGov, (2021a) *'YouGov - Defining Woke.* Available at: https://docs.cdn.yougov.com/xu2oj6jxzz/YouGov%20-%20What%20is%20woke.pdf (Accessed November 9 2021)

YouGov, (2021b) *'YouGov Survey Results.* Available at: https://docs.cdn.yougov.com/8otmtu3old/RedWallConstituencies_Website_v2.pdf (Accessed November 9 2021)

Identity Politics

Akala (2018). *'Natives, Race and Class in the Ruins of Empire'*. London: Two Roads.

Ambrosino, B. (2017). *'The invention of 'heterosexuality''*. Available at: https://www.bbc.com/future/article/20170315-the-invention-of-heterosexuality (Accessed November 15 2021).

Black Past (1977) *'THE COMBAHEE RIVER COLLECTIVE STATEMENT'*. Available at: https://www.blackpast.org/african-american-history/combahee-river-collective-statement-1977/ (Accessed November 15 2021)

REFERENCES BY THEME

Cinelli, M. Et al (2021). *'The echo chamber effect on social media'*.Available at: https://www.pnas.org/content/pnas/118/9/e2023301118.full.pdf (Accessed November 15 2021)

Cohen, G. L. Sherman, D. K. (2014). 'The Psychology of Change: Self-Affirmation and Social Psychological Intervention'. *Annual Review of Psychology,* 65(1), pp333-371.

Encyclopaedia Britannica, (2019). *'Social class'.* Available at: https://www.britannica.com/topic/social-class (Accessed November 15 2021)

Friedkin, N.E. (1984) 'Structural Cohesion and Equivalence, Explanations of Social Homogeneity', *Sociological Methods & Research,* 12(3), pp235-261.

Duffy, B. et al. (2021). *'Culture wars in the UK: how the public understand the debate.* Available at: https://www.ipsos.com/sites/default/files/ct/news/documents/2021-05/culture-wars-in-the-UK-how-the-public-understand-the-debate.pdf (Accessed November 8 2021)

Feld, S. L. (1982) 'Social Structural Determinants of Similarity Among Associates', *American Sociological Review,* 47(6), pp797-801.

Ignatieff, M. (2018) *'Is identity politics ruining democracy?.* Available at: https://www.ft.com/content/09c2c1e4-ad05-11e8-8253-48106866cd8a (Accessed November 15 2021)

Laqueur, T. (1992) 'Making Sex: Body and Gender from the Greeks to Freud'. Cambridge, MA: Harvard University Press.

Roediger, D.R. (No Date). *'Historical Foundations of Race'.*Available at: https://nmaahc.si.edu/learn/talking-about-race/topics/historical-foundations-race (Accessed November 15 2021)

Vinogradoff, P. (1913). 'Foundations of Society (Origins of Feudalism)'. *Cambridge Medieval History.* 2(1), pp630-654.

Wason, P.C. Johnson-Laird, P.N. (1972). *Psychology of Reasoning, Structure and Content.* Cambridge MA: Harvard University Press.

Disability Rights

Baar, M (2017) *'Disability Goes Global: The Repercussions of the International Year of Disabled Persons (1981) for Global Health',* London School of Hygiene & Tropical Medicine. Available at: https://www.lshtm.ac.uk/newsevents/events/disability-goes-global-repercussions-international-year-disabled-persons-1981#:~:text=1981%20was%20designated%20by%20the,Persons%20(1982%2D1993). (Accessed September 16 2022)

Barnes, C (1992) *'Disabled People In Britain and Discrimination. A Case for ati-discrimination Legislation'.* C. Hurst & Co: Bloomsbury.

Close, M. (2020) *'Disabled People's Movement - History Timeline',* Disability Equality NW. Available at: http://disability-equality.org.uk/history/ (Accessed September 16 2022)

The Disability discrimination act 1995: The campaign for civil rights. (2015) Youtube video, added by Scope. Available at: https://www.youtube.com/watch?v=dwP1xuZZFuY (Accessed September 16 2022)

Disability Now (2010) *'Direct action! Life on the streets'.* Available at: https://disabilitynow.wordpress.com/2010/11/07/direct-action-life-on-the-streets/ (Accessed September 16 2022)

Greater Manchester Coalition of Disabled People (2010) *'A Brief History of Disabled People's Self-Organisation'.* Available at:https://historicengland.org.uk/content/docs/research/brief-history-disabled-peoples-self-organisation-pdf/ (Accessed September 16 2022)

Inclusion London (2020) *'Timeline of the Disabled People's Rights Movement in the UK'.*

Available at: http://disability-equality.org.uk/history/ (Accessed September 16 2022)

Lewis, P (2020) '*Disability Discrimination Act: 1995 and now*', House of Lords Library. Available at: https://lordslibrary.parliament.uk/disability-discrimination-act-1995-and-now/ (Accessed September 16 2022)

Oliver, M. (1990) '*The Individual and Social Models of Disability*'. Available at: https://disability-studies.leeds.ac.uk/wp-content/uploads/sites/40/library/Oliver-in-soc-dis.pdf (Accessed September 16 2022)

RNIB (No Date) '*Marching into history*'. Available at: https://www.rnib.org.uk/campaigning/marching-history (Accessed September 16 2022)

United Nations: Department of Economic and Social Affairs (No Date) '*The International Year of Disabled Persons 1981*). Available at: https://www.un.org/development/desa/disabilities/the-international-year-of-disabled-persons-1981.html (Accessed September 16 2022)

Neurodiversity

Autistic Science Person (No Date) '*Why ABA Therapy is Harmful to Autistic People*', Available: https://autisticscienceperson.com/why-aba-therapy-is-harmful-to-autistic-people/ (Accessed January 11 2022)

Austin, R.D. Pisano, G.P. (2017) '*Neurodiversity as a Competitive Advantage*', Available at: https://hbr.org/2017/05/neurodiversity-as-a-competitive-advantage (Accessed January 12 2022)

Autistic Self Advocacy Network (2022) '*Our history*', Available at: https://autisticadvocacy.org/about-asan/our-history/ (Accessed January 5 2022)

Autistic Self Advocacy Network (2022 B) '*About Autism*', Available at: https://autisticadvocacy.org/about-asan/about-autism/ (Accessed January 11 2022)

Autistic Self Advocacy Network (2011) '*Autistic Access Needs; Notes on Accessibility*', Available at: https://autisticadvocacy.org/wp-content/uploads/2016/06/Autistic-Access-Needs-Notes-on-Accessibility.pdf (Accessed January 11 2022)

Autism Mythbusters (No date) '*The Truth About ABA*', Available at: https://autism-mythbusters.com/parents/therapy/the-truth-about-aba/ (Accessed January 11 2022)

Bailin, A. (2019) '*Clearing up Some Misconceptions About Neurodiversity*', Scientific American, Available at: https://blogs.scientificamerican.com/observations/clearing-up-some-misconceptions-about-neurodiversity/ (Accessed January 11 2022)

Baron-Cohen, S. (2009) '*Does autism need a cure?*', DOI: https://doi.org/10.1016/S0140-6736(09)60891-6

Baumer, N. & Frueh, J. (2021) '*What is neurodiversity?*', Available at: https://www.health.harvard.edu/blog/what-is-neurodiversity-202111232645 (Accessed January 5 2022)

Brett, D. et al. (2016) '*Factors Affecting Age at ASD Diagnosis in UK: No Evidence that Diagnosis Age has Decreased Between 2004 and 2014*', Available at: https://www.ncbi.nlm.nih.gov/pmc/articles/PMC4860193/ (Accessed January 6 2022)

British Medical Association (2019) '*Failing a generation: delays in waiting times from referral to diagnostic assessment for autism spectrum disorder*', Available at: https://www.bma.org.uk/media/2056/autism-briefing.pdf (Accessed January 10 2022)

British Medical Association (2020) '*Autism spectrum disorder*', Available at: https://www.bma.org.uk/what-we-do/population-health/improving-the-health-of-specific-groups/autism-spectrum-disorder (Accessed January 6 2022)

Bowers, R. (2019) '*The Importance of Diversity of Thought*', Training Industry, Available at: https://trainingindustry.com/magazine/may-jun-2019/the-importance-of-diversity-of-thought/ (Accessed January 11 2022)

REFERENCES BY THEME

Cambridge University (2020) '*Dr Temple Grandin explains why we need "different kinds of minds"*', Available at: https://www.jesus.cam.ac.uk/articles/dr-temple-grandin-explains-why-we-need-different-kinds-minds (Accessed January 12 2022)

Citizens Advice (2022) '*Duty to make reasonable adjustments for disabled people*', Available at: https://www.citizensadvice.org.uk/law-and-courts/discrimination/what-are-the-different-types-of-discrimination/duty-to-make-reasonable-adjustments-for-disabled-people/ (Accessed January 12 2022)

Close, F. (2009) 'Paul Dirac: a physicist of few words', *Nature*, 459(1), pp326-327

College of Physicians of Philadelphia (2022) '*The History of Vaccines*', Available at: https://www.historyofvaccines.org/index.php/content/articles/do-vaccines-cause-autism (Accessed January 4 2022)

Chauhan, C. et al. (2020) 'The safety of health care for ethnic minority patients: a systematic review', DOI: https://doi.org/10.1186/s12939-020-01223-2

Child Autism UK (No date) '*Testing for autism*', Available at: https://www.childautism.org.uk/about-autism/testing-for-autism/ (Accessed January 6 2022)

Child Autism UK (No date B) '*Funding for Early Intervention*', Available at: https://www.childautism.org.uk/funding-for-early-intervention/ (Accessed January 10 2022)

Cumming, E. (2014) '*Dan Aykroyd: My Harley-Davidson is a form of psychiatric therapy. You get on that and you don't need a shrink*", The Guardian, Available at: https://www.theguardian.com/lifeandstyle/2014/nov/22/dan-aykroyd-this-much-i-know (Accessed January 12 2022)

Czech, H. (2018) 'Hans Asperger, National Socialism, and "race hygiene" in Nazi-era Vienna, *Molecular Autism*, 9(1), pp1-43

Dattaro, L. & Jeffrey-Wilensky, J. (2021) '*Massive U.K. study finds racial and ethnic disparities in autism diagnoses*', Spectrum News. Available at: https://www.spectrumnews.org/news/massive-u-k-study-finds-racial-ethnic-disparities-in-autism-diagnoses/ (Accessed January 10 2022)

Davidson, S. (2018) '*Does ABA harm autistic people?*', Autistic UK CIC, Available at: https://autisticuk.org/does-aba-harm-autistic-people/ (Accessed January 11 2022)

DeBenedette, V & Underwood, A. (2021) '*CDC: 1 in 44 American Children are Diagnosed With Autism*', Verywell, Available at: https://www.verywellhealth.com/cdc-autism-children-5212627 (Accessed January 13 2022)

Devita-Raeburn, E (2016) '*The controversy over autism's most common therapy*', Spectrum News. Available at: https://www.spectrumnews.org/features/deep-dive/controversy-autisms-common-therapy/ (Accessed January 4 2022)

Devlin, H. (2018) '*Thousands of autistic girls and women 'going undiagnosed' due to gender bias*', The Guardian, Available at: https://www.theguardian.com/society/2018/sep/14/thousands-of-autistic-girls-and-women-going-undiagnosed-due-to-gender-bias (Accessed January 10 2022)

Dillenburger, K. Jordan, J.A. McKerr, L. (2016) 'School's out forever: Postsecondary education trajectories for students with autism', *Australian Psychologist*, 51(4), pp215-304

Elizabeth Blackwell Institute for Health Research (2020) '*Autism at university - being an autistic student*', Bristol University, Available at: https://www.bristol.ac.uk/blackwell/news/2020/autism-at-university--being-an-autistic-student.html (Accessed January 6 2022)

Falck-Ytter, T. & Lodén, S. (2020) '*The perils of suggesting famous historical figures had autism*', Available at: https://www.spectrumnews.org/opinion/viewpoint/the-perils-of-suggesting-famous-historical-figures-had-autism/ (Accessed January 12 2022)

Furdyk, B. (2021) '*Elon Musk says He's The First 'SNL' Host With Asperger's, But Twitter*

Remembers Dan Aykroyd', ET Canada, Available at: https://etcanada.com/news/778328/elon-musk-says-hes-the-first-snl-host-with-aspergers-but-twitter-remembers-dan-aykroyd/ (Accessed January 12 2022)

Gov UK (No date) *'Children with special educational needs and disabilities (SEND)'*, Available at: https://www.gov.uk/children-with-special-educational-needs/extra-SEN-help (Accessed January 6 2022)

Gupta, A. (2021) *'Why You Need Neurodiverse Talent'*, Gartner, Available at: https://www.gartner.com/en/articles/why-you-need-neurodiverse-talent (Accessed January 11 2022)

Hauser, M (2010) *'Temple Grandin'*, TIME, Available at: http://content.time.com/time/specials/packages/article/0,28804,1984685_1984949_1985222,00.html (Accessed January 12 2022)

Hekler, E. (2019) *'Lived experience and scientific consensus'*, Available at: http://opening-pathways.org/lived-experience-consensus (Accessed January 6 2022)

Herman, E. (2019) *'BERNARD RIMLAND, INFANTILE AUTISM: THE SYNDROME AND ITS IMPLICATIONS FOR A NEURAL THEORY OF BEHAVIOR, 1964'*, The Autism History Project. Available at: https://blogs.uoregon.edu/autismhistoryproject/archive/bernard-rimland-infantile-autism-the-syndrome-and-its-implications-for-a-neural-theory-of-behavior-1964/ (Accessed January 4 2022)

Hey, L. (2021) *'Autism in the UK: prevalence, assessment and the impact of the Covid-19 pandemic'*, Hogrefe, Available at: https://www.hogrefe.com/uk/article/autism-in-the-uk-prevalence-assessment-and-the-impact-of-the-covid-19-pandemic (Accessed January 6 2021)

IMDB (No date) *'Dan Aykroyd'*, Available at: https://m.imdb.com/name/nm0000101/filmotype/actor?ref_=m_nmfm_2 (Accessed January 12 2022)

In the Loop About Neurodiversity (2019) *'Good Autism Advocacy Organizations Vs. Bad Autism "Charities"'*, Available at: https://intheloopaboutneurodiversity.wordpress.com/2019/11/28/good-autistic-advocacy-organizations-vs-bad-autism-charities/ (Accessed January 11 2022)

James, I. (2003) 'Singular Scientists', *Journal of the Royal Society of Medicine*, 96(1), pp36-39

King, B. & King, V. (No Date) *'An Open Letter to Families Considering Intensive Behavioural Therapy for Their Child With Autism'*, Available at: http://www.astraeasweb.net/politics/aba.html (Accessed January 11 2022)

Krzeminska, A. Austin, R.D. Bruyère, S.M. & Hedley, D. (2019) *'The advantages and challenges of neurodiversity employment in organizations'*, Available at: https://www.researchgate.net/profile/Darren-Hedley-2/publication/335655301_The_advantages_and_challenges_of_neurodiversity_employment_in_organizations/links/5d8b4083299bf10cff0b7bf5/The-advantages-and-challenges-of-neurodiversity-employment-in-organizations.pdf (Accessed January 12 2022)

Legislation Gov UK (2010) *'Equality Act 2010'*, Available at: https://www.legislation.gov.uk/ukpga/2010/15/contents (Accessed January 12 2022)

Maidment, A. (2020) *'Covid could be leaving thousands with undiagnosed autism as uncertainty makes life harder for those on the spectrum'*, Manchester Evening News, Available at: https://www.manchestereveningnews.co.uk/news/greater-manchester-news/covid-could-leaving-thousands-undiagnosed-19304165 (Accessed January 10 2022)

McCready, J. & Kaikini, S. (No Date) *'ABA & Autism in the UK'*, ABAA4ALL, Available at: https://www.abaa4all.com/aba-in-the-uk (Accessed January 6 2022)

McGuinness, S. as cited in Autism UK (2021) *'History of Autism'*, Available at: https://autismuk.com/home-page/history-of-autism/ (Accessed January 4 2022)

Mckinsey & Company (2020) *'Diversity wins: how inclusion matters'*, Available at: https://

www.mckinsey.com/featured-insights/diversity-and-inclusion/diversity-wins-how-inclusion-matters (Accessed January 12 2022)

Michigan State University (No date) '*Anthony Ianni*', Available at: https://raind.msu.edu/people/anthony-ianni (Accessed January 12 2022)

Miller, K.K. (2015) '*The Autism Paradox*', AMA Journal of Ethics, Available at: https://journalofethics.ama-assn.org/article/autism-paradox/2015-04 (Accessed January 11 2022)

The Minnesota Governor's Council on Developmental Disabilities (2022) '*Itard and the Wild Boy of Aveyron*', Available at: https://mn.gov/mnddc/parallels/three/4.html (Accessed January 4 2022)

National Autistic Society (No date A) '*What is autism?*'. Available at: https://www.autism.org.uk/advice-and-guidance/what-is-autism (Accessed January 4 2022)

National Autistic Society (No date B) '*How to talk and write about autism*', Available at: https://www.autism.org.uk/what-we-do/help-and-support/how-to-talk-about-autism (Accessed January 4 2022)

National Autistic Society (No date C) '*The causes of autism*', Available at: https://www.autism.org.uk/advice-and-guidance/what-is-autism/the-causes-of-autism (Accessed January 4 2022)

National Autistic Society (No date D) '*The diagnostic assessment*', Available at: https://www.autism.org.uk/advice-and-guidance/topics/diagnosis/diagnostic-assessment/parents-and-carers (Accessed January 6 2022)

National Autistic Society (No date E) '*Autism and BAME people*', Available at: https://www.autism.org.uk/advice-and-guidance/what-is-autism/autism-and-bame-people (Accessed January 10 2022)

National Health Service (2019) '*What is autism?*', Available at: https://www.nhs.uk/conditions/autism/what-is-autism/ (Accessed January 6 2022)

National Health Service (2019B) '*Where to get support if you're autistic*', Available at: https://www.nhs.uk/conditions/autism/support/ (Accessed January 6 2022)

NCBI (2004) '*Understanding Racial and Ethnic Differences in Health in Late Life: A Research Agenda*', Available at: https://www.ncbi.nlm.nih.gov/books/NBK24693/ (Accessed January 10 2022)

Office for National Statistics (2020) '*Outcomes for disabled people in the UKL 2020*', Available at: https://www.ons.gov.uk/peoplepopulationandcommunity/healthandsocialcare/disability/articles/outcomesfordisabledpeopleintheuk/2020 (Accessed January 12 2022)

Omer, S.B. (2020) '*The discredited doctor hailed by the anti-vaccine movement*', Available at: https://www.nature.com/articles/d41586-020-02989-9 (Accessed January 10 2022)

Randerson, J. (2009) '*A prenatal test for autism would deprive the world of future geniuses*', The Guardian, Available at: https://www.theguardian.com/science/blog/2009/jan/07/autism-test-genius-dirac (Accessed January 12 2022)

Remington, A.M. Swettenham, J.G. & Lavie, N. (2012) 'Lightening the Load: Perceptual Load Impairs Visual Detection in Typical Adults but Not in Autism', *Journal of Abnormal Psychology*, DOI: http://dx.doi.org/10.1037/a0027670

Roman-Urrestarazu, A. et al. (2021) 'Association of Race/Ethnicity and Social Disadvantage With Autism Prevalence in 7 Million School Children in England', DOI:http://jamanetwork.com/article.aspx?doi=10.1001/jamapediatrics.2021.0054

Rose, D. (2015) '*when disabled people took to the streets to change the law*', British Broadcasting Corporation. Available at: https://www.bbc.co.uk/news/disability-34732084 (Accessed January 4 2022)

Ruzich et al. (2015) '*Sex and STEM Occupation Predict Autism-Spectrum Quotient (AQ) Scores in Half a Million People*', DOI: https://doi.org/10.1371/journal.pone.0141229

Saner, E. (2007) '*Soul Survivor*', The Guardian, Available at: https://www.theguardian.com/film/2007/sep/19/1 (Accessed January 12 2022)

Sasson, N.J. et al. (2017) '*Neurotypical Peers are Less Willing to Interact with Those with Autism based on Thin Slice Judgments*', *Scientific Reports*, Available at: https://www.nature.com/articles/srep40700#citeas (Accessed January 10 2022)

Templegrandin.com (No date) '*Temple has been honored with a sculpture housed within the JBS Global Food Innovation Center on the Colorado State University Campus*', Available at: http://www.templegrandin.com/ (Accessed January 12 2022)

Tenorio, R. (2021) ''*Why didn't you tell me?: Anthony Ianni's journey through sports with autism*', The Guardian, Available at: https://www.theguardian.com/sport/2021/nov/24/why-didnt-you-tell-me-anthony-iannis-journey-through-sports-with-autism (Accessed January 12 2022)

Undercover Autie (No date) '*Why Do We Refuse to Give Autistic People A Voice?*', Available at: https://www.undercoverautie.com/blog/2017/12/29/why-society-refuses-to-give-autistic-people-a-voice (Accessed January 10 2022)

United Kingdom Government (2009) '*Autism Act 2009*', Available at: https://www.legislation.gov.uk/ukpga/2009/15/introduction (Accessed January 5 2022)

United Nations (1948) '*Universal Declaration of Human Rights*', Available at: https://www.un.org/en/about-us/universal-declaration-of-human-rights (Accessed January 12 2022)

Wiggins, L.D. et al. (2020) Disparities in Documented Diagnoses of Autism Spectrum Disorder Based on Demographic, Individual, and Service Factors, *Autism Research*,13(3), pp464-473

Wilson, M (2012) '*A brief history of autism*', SEN Magazine. Available at: https://senmagazine.co.uk/content/specific-needs/1350/a-brief-history-of-autism-the-big-ideas-that-have-shaped-our-understanding-of-autism/ (Accessed January 4 2022)